THE WARNER LOUGHLIN TECHNIQUE

AN ACTING REVOLUTION

THE WARNER LOUGHLIN TECHNIQUE

AN ACTING REVOLUTION

Warner Loughlin

HOWLAND | TILLEY PRESS

HOWLAND | TILLEY PRESS
Los Angeles, California
New York, New York
The Warner Loughlin Technique: An Acting Revolution

Cover design: Glen M. Edelstein
Interior design: Glen M. Edelstein

Printed in the United States of America
18 19 20 21 22 9 8 7 6 5 4 3 2 1

Library of Congress Cataloging-in-Publication Data is available

978-0-9995270-0-9 (Trade paperback)
978-0-9995270-2-3 (eBook)

To
Ben and Margaret
Kyle and Tony

"The only real voyage consists not of seeking new landscapes, but in having new eyes; in seeing the universe through the eyes of another, one hundred others – in seeing the hundred universes that each of them sees."

~ Marcel Proust

CONTENTS

THE WARNER LOUGHLIN TECHNIQUE

AN ACTING REVOLUTION

"There are those whose lives affect all others around them. Quietly touching one heart. Who in turn, touches another, reaching out to ends further than they would ever know."
~William Bradfield

MYTH OF THE TORTURED ACTOR

Where is it written that in order to be a gifted actor, you must be filled with rage or pain or strife? Who says you must be brooding and difficult; that as an actor you must view the world differently than everyone else? I can tell you that ideas like these have been written or implied in far too many acting books. This misconception is taught and even *encouraged* in a great percentage of acting classes around the world.

How many classes have you taken in which the primary goal of the teacher was to make you cry? Chances are it was also suggested that if you couldn't achieve hysterics, you were somehow not quite as talented as the next actor. I can tell you that it's more than possible for me to walk out onto the street right now, grab a passing stranger, spend a few minutes with him and make him cry. Does that make him an actor? I think not. I would hope not!

How many teachers have *insisted* that you must have been wronged by your parents, siblings, best friends, or lovers? How many have asked you to expose yourself emotionally and physically - with an inane exercise that sacrificed your privacy - for all your classmates to see? How many of them initially made you feel like you could conquer the world, only later to make you feel undeserving, idiotic and talentless! Ego is the great killer of creativity. If your teacher's ego is bigger than the state of Texas ... good Lord, leave. Your class should be about YOU, not the teacher. You must learn to be a self-sufficient actor able to create characters in your own right. Characters that are beautifully unique to you and only you.

This technique teaches you to effortlessly access and actually experience the specific and unique emotions of the character. With it, you'll find the joy and freedom to be the character in the moment, and you'll discover the limitless possibilities in creating a character as only *you* can.

You will let go of the need to nail an emotion; rid yourself of superficially executing beats and actions; drop the reliance on "super objectives," "objectives" and "intentions" and forget the constant checking of your work to see if you are hitting moments in the way that you want to. All of this puts you "in your head." I call it "third-eyeing" a performance, meaning you're actually trying to watch your own work as you do it. And you'll find it makes you completely self-conscious. You'll think about how a line is going to sound when you say it, or what you look like doing an action. When you do these things, you are not acting. You are simply watching yourself. You should be joyously free when you're acting, not judging whether or not you are believable in the moment.

The whole idea is to *walk* as the character walks; to *talk* as the character talks; to *think*, *breathe* and *react* as he or she reacts. So much so that there will be moments when you're utterly surprised by how you feel and stunned that an emotion popped up that you weren't expecting. What a kick that is!

You can apply this technique to any character in the dramatic realm, be it TV, film or stage. TV comedy, and to a degree, film comedy, is a different, albeit beautiful, beast. Some of the principles here can certainly be applied to comedy. But to truly master the art of comedy, I would encourage you to refer to the Warner Loughlin Technique for Comedy.

The technique in this book will allow you to have a uniquely powerful presence when you're on camera and an exuberant, full life when you are not. *Go. Be. Brilliant.*

"Twenty years from now you will be more disappointed by the things you didn't do than by the ones you did do. So throw off the bowlines. Sail away from the safe harbor. Catch the trade winds in your sails.
Explore. Dream. Discover."
~ Mark Twain

THE PATH YOU CHOOSE IS THE JOURNEY YOU TAKE

Along with countless other actors, I was taught that the only true way to experience authentic dramatic sizzle in my characters is through recalling personal angst or tragedy from my past. "Substitution" is the acting term used for this. To briefly explain, the actor substitutes a personal past memory and emotion for the character's emotion in the scene. Every theater actor I knew in my younger years used this method. I bought it. It made sense. At that time. Sure, I could get to those ugly, painful memories. But only sometimes on some nights. Mostly I just didn't want to feel that tragedy all over again. But alas, it was for art, and nothing was going to stop me from acting. Not even if it killed me. And it was ... slowly.

I most certainly recommend dealing with your own personal demons, your own pain, under the appropriate circumstances, because healing those hurts will free you to be a better actor. But don't use the set as a place to do it. It's a bit selfish, and it can produce a creative stop. (When the pain of the past is so prevalent, we may choose to feel nothing instead. We literally choose to stop feeling. Because to feel something would open the floodgates of emotion and diminish our sense of control.) I know that some actors claim that reliving a past tragedy is like therapy. For some it might be, and for others it's definitely not. Either way it's not as cathartic as some people might think. Acting isn't therapy. It's an art form.

When you use a substitution, you'll definitely feel something on occasion. But you'll also find it will be fleeting and unreliable. Not the sort of words you want to use in connection with your craft or your career. With a substitution, you're essentially revisiting an experience that you have already lived. Then, on the second take, you're revisiting the re-visitation. In much the same way that a recording of a recording of a recording starts to sound less and less like the original, in using a particular event from my past over and over again, I found it wouldn't affect me with the same power as it did the first time. Which is really terrifying when you absolutely *have* to do an emotional scene on camera. What happens with that repetition is that you desensitize yourself to the pain. Your mind tells you to avoid it. That's human nature. It's our survival mechanism kicking in.

Overall, you can count on one of two things happening when you repeatedly relive a tragedy in your life: either you relive it so much that you don't feel it anymore (so how is that good for your work?), or you incite more of it. Intentionally bringing forth a memory with the express goal of feeling pain *is asking that pain to be present again in your life*. How is that good for your life or your career? There actually was a point when I was desperately looking for pain in my life, hoping for pain, so that I could use it in my work. I learned the hard way that when you ask for it, you certainly get it.

As children, we only touch a hot stove once! We learn that it's painful and avoid it at all costs. But actors who use a substitution "touch that hot stove" over and over again. Think about what that requires. You touched it and it burned. Now in choosing to touch it again, there will be a bit of anticipation, hesitation and resistance, don't you think? But you do it anyway, and yes, it still hurts, but somehow, it's less painful now, because you knew what was coming. When you're in the middle of a scene, the last thing you want is anticipation, hesitation and resistance to an emotion, which eventually leads you to beating yourself up for not being able to "get there." As actors, we're often quite good at beating ourselves up. Maybe it's time to stop that.

Stay true to human nature. Sane human beings don't go around seeking pain and torment! Why should actors? If your mission as an actor is to create authentic human behavior, why in the world would you seek to work against natural human instincts?

Most colleges and acting studios have for generations been teaching techniques that deal with some form of substituting your own life experiences. Were they all wrong, you ask? I wouldn't say they were all wrong. I am saying that what they came up with was the best they could do at the time. Most of these techniques were based upon a convoluted form of Stanislavski - a reinterpretation of his system. Most people would agree that Stanislavski was a bit of a genius when it came to acting in the theater. That's my point. Only theater existed when his technique was conceived. It was all they knew. So it suited the theater, the medium in which they worked. While the mediums have changed drastically with the advent of TV and film, the teaching of the craft has been slow to catch up. Most schools or studios, even here in LA, still teach only these methods that were invented specifically for theatre. The technique you are about to master, while designed to create beautifully nuanced, magical and unique characters in television and film, still works magnificently on stage, where you will experience the joy of new discovery throughout the run of the play.

But working in TV and film requires something very different from theater. No longer are you experiencing emotions once per night as you do in a play. On set you must repeat an emotion, take after take. No longer are you performing a piece with a structured beginning, middle and end. For the most part, every scene is shot out of sequence. It's kind of like jumping rope backwards under water while chewing gum. Discombobulating at best.

My early training was all about theater. Substitution was the only technique that I had been taught. There was one event that I would eventually draw upon several times when I needed the devastation to be present in my character. It happened in college.

I had fallen in love with a wonderful man. Jimmy was a year older and had just graduated that May but would be staying in Chapel Hill for most of the summer. Eventually the day came when Jimmy had to leave and begin what looked to be a very promising career. But first he was traveling to California to visit a dear friend for a week or so.

He packed up his little beat-up orange Volkswagen. At well over six feet, he looked hilarious in that car. We cried and hugged. It was sad, but he was also excited for what the future would hold. We promised to write or talk every day. Pre cell phone days, that was difficult. As Jimmy was a man of his word, sure enough, I received a letter almost daily.

Late one morning, having fallen asleep on the couch while cramming for an exam, I was roused from my exhaustion and half-sleep by crying and whispers. I opened my eyes to find my friends all around me. In the wee hours of the morning, Jimmy had been senselessly struck in a head-on collision by a drunk driver on the Pacific Coast Highway in Malibu, California. He was dead.

It took years for that wound to heal and even longer before I could consider drawing upon it for my work. But my training had taught me that this was the sort of experience that would be ideal to use for a substitution. Whenever I needed to bring up tears, rage, or debilitating grief, I would recall the moment I heard of Jimmy's death. Sometimes, yes, I would cry. But mostly, *I just didn't want to go there!* We aren't meant, as human beings, to keep re-experiencing tragedies; we're meant to heal from them. But again, this was for art. This was for my craft that I so dearly loved.

So here I was in LA. It was my first TV job, and I had a 6:00 AM make-up call. I was determined to be brilliant. I was going to the "Jimmy place" no matter how painful it might be. I was happy that the emotional, "learning-my-husband-had-been-killed" scene was to be shot in the morning. It would be good to get that part of the day over with. (Read: *utter dread!*) In the make-up chair, I tried my best to dredge up painful memories of Jimmy's loss. By the time we were ready to shoot, I was *there*, back in the gnarling pain I'd spent so much time trying to heal, full of emotion, ready to explode. The master shot was, well, masterful. The second time we shot the master, the emotion lessened a little, but it was still powerful. (Note also, at that time, I was so inexperienced that I didn't realize that a master shot is usually very wide and not where you want to let the depth of all your emotions explode; you want to save a little of that emotion for your coverage, or close-ups.) My coverage was second, so I was still able to dribble up a bit of emotion when camera rolled. I was thrilled.

We broke for lunch, and I felt like a success. What a relief! I had managed to access that horrible grief. Okay, not on every take, but at least I had mostly gotten there. There were plenty of auditions in which the emotion eluded me no matter how hard I tried to vomit up the pain. This was a clear WIN! So I thought ...

The next shot after lunch was the "happiest-day-of-my-life-thrilled-to-be-with-my-love" scene. Take one ... take two ... take three ... The director yelled cut. He had an odd look on his face as he walked up to me. Uh-oh. He took me aside (very embarrassing) and said, "Do you realize you are carrying the tragedy of the scene we shot this morning into the happy scene we're doing now?"

I was stumped. "Nooooo." I had not realized it.

"It's like you have a little black rain cloud over your head. You're supposed to be *haaaapppy in this scene*! Get it?!"

I tried to make adjustments to please the director, but no matter what I did, I could *not* shake a part of that sadness. The grief of losing Jimmy was too present. It was still there, it was absolutely real, and it was *mine*. I learned that day that dropping in and out of my own experiences is a far more difficult thing than dropping in and out of the life of a character.

I don't think the director was ever quite happy with the scene. I certainly wasn't. The crying in the first scene looked a little forced; there was something missing in it. I could actually tell that I was someplace else. In order to use a substitution, you *must* be someplace else: your own life. A substitution requires the impossible – being in two places at the same time. You must momentarily drop out of the character and into your own past. The falseness of it is readable on screen. You can't think a character thought and a personal thought at the same time. Seeing that performance in context, it felt selfish. It felt – forgive the term – very masturbatory. It was uncomfortable to watch.

But how else could you possibly bring up an organic and true emotion in the moment if you didn't use a substitution? How do you play, say, a victim of abuse if you have never been abused in your real life? Even with an understanding of how that character feels, how do you play it without using some sort of false substitution?

Being a good actor means being able to access the emotion when you need it. But the *way* in which you access it and the ability to control it are vitally important to your being a stable, competent, professional actor and a healthy human being. Each of us has a finite set of life experiences. When we draw solely upon our personal experiences, we are drawing from a limited or *finite* well. When we tap into our imaginations, on the other hand, we can draw from an *infinite*, abundant and free flowing well.

So if old schools of thought ask you to REENACT or RECREATE the character using your limited and finite set of experiences, I am asking you to CREATE the character using the infinite well of imagination. Therein lies the difference. You are CREATING! Let's go conquer it!

"And the day came when the risk to remain tight in a bud was more painful than the risk it took to blossom."
~ Anais Nin

THE JOURNEY BEGINS...

This process asks you to go full circle in your brain - a whole brain approach that gets you to use more of what you've got. You're going to go from the more analytical left side, the side of the brain that specializes in logic, facts and linear thinking, over to the right side, which deals with creativity and imagination and is the side of the brain that is most engaged when we are acting. You don't have to know the scientific particulars of how each side of the brain functions to do this - you already visit both sides of the brain every day in one way or another. Some actors, just like non-actors, are more comfortable staying on one side or the other. This technique is about being willing and able to use both - and doing it intentionally.

To begin the process of breaking down the character, I like to start on the left. It satisfies the logical thinker and helps define a clear beginning path to discovery.

It's important to keep in mind that in this initial analytical work, we are seeking to discover the character and the world in which he lives. We are not trying to determine how the scene is to be played. Later, we'll place our beautifully fleshed out, fully developed character into the particular circumstances of the scene at hand.

For better or worse, over the course of your career, you'll come across countless scripts that you don't particularly like. Try not to judge right away, and whatever you do, don't let your feelings about the material distract you from the work you have to do. If you can reserve judgment until you've stepped inside the character's shoes, you will feel differently about the script as a whole. For the purposes of explanation, we'll take a look at the Jonathan character in the scene that follows shortly.

Many times, when you pick up sides for an audition, or you're reading a screenplay for a film you're about to do, it's likely that your first reaction will be something along the lines of, "Ooh, I know how she feels, I know how he feels. I know that feeling. I can relate to that. It should sound like this. It should feel like that." *That's what I want you to avoid. For now.* In these beginning steps, squash for a moment the need to relate to the character's feelings.

Sounds crazy, right? Think of it this way: you are capable of relating to every human emotion. But *you* are not the character. Yet. Connecting with material can be great. But at this stage, it's far too early to make assumptions based on your own thoughts and feelings, when we don't yet know how the *character* feels. We haven't investigated the life enough to know who this character is. You may know how *you* would feel, but we haven't investigated his life enough to know how *he* feels.

Without investigation into Jonathan's life, if it looks to you as though Jonathan is upset in the scene, you'll *play* upset rather than *being* upset. Playing *at* something is not nearly as rewarding, and you'll play it from the only reference point you have right now: yourself.

To me, understanding and being able to experience someone else's emotions is a huge part of the joy of acting. And you will do this when we have completed the analytical work and moved over to the more creative right side of the brain. In the final step of character discovery that we call Emotion with Detail, you will actually viscerally experience the emotionally pertinent, relevant events and moments of Jonathan's life.

To discover a character's deepest wounds, to uncover the source of those wounds, and then to actually experience what that feels like is one of the richest rewards of this beautiful craft. Let's begin that journey of discovery now.

"It's not what you look at that matters, it's what you see."
~ HENRY DAVID THOREAU

THE GIVENS

Our first step in this left brain, analytical stage of breaking down the character is all about digging into the text and extracting all that you can from what's on the page. I like to call it the "Givens."

The Givens are just that – only what's given in the scene. For now, I want you to be a detective. Read the scene objectively, as if you're going to tell someone else what this scene is about. Look for the broad strokes, the factual information. This is not about emotions or impressions but about *evidence* in the text that requires *no interpretation.* What do we learn for certain about this character, his history, his relationship to the other character in the scene?

Suppose you read a line explaining that your character graduated from Harvard. The Given would be that the character is a Harvard graduate, not that he's a genius. One is fact, while the other is interpretation. Make sense? In other words, we're looking for pure facts without assumptions. Knowing that a character walked three miles in the rain doesn't tell you that he/she loves the rain.

Avoid your character's point of view here. Maintain an objective distance. You're looking for clues regarding the character, circumstances, relationships, etc. For example, does it say that this character is married, unmarried, living in the city, living in the country, has a child or doesn't?

There are parts of this process that you'll write down and parts that you won't. You'll put your pen away when it's time for your imagination to fly. But right now, in the analytical stage, it's best to write down your thoughts. First, let's read the scene below objectively like a detective looking for *just the facts without assumptions*: the who, what, when, where. Things you could prove in a court of law. Avoid the 'why' for now. That comes later.

INT. GRANDDAD'S GARAGE - MORGANVILLE (POP.1,135)- LATE AFTERNOON

Garage turned sanctuary. Dust dances in the rays of sun shining through the windows. An odd contrast to JENNIFER, dressed in this year's Chanel suit. Her eyes are swollen, red, her makeup smudged.

We hear the DISTANT MURMUR OF HUSHED VOICES, CLATTERING DISHES from the main house, making the garage feel silent.

Jennifer cautiously sits on the worn leather recliner, Grandpa's chair. A momentary smile at the duct tape on the worn arms. She hugs her knees to her chest, in a reverie.

The room is a shrine:
- football posters taped to the wall.
- a rattling white refrigerator.
- the tiny, salvaged TV with tin foil wadded atop its antenna.
- the American flag on the wall, now faded and dusty.
- Jennifer's childhood fishing rod proudly displayed next to Grandpa's clunky one.

The wooden door behind Jennifer scrapes open and jars her back to reality.

JONATHAN stands in silence.

(O.S)
JONATHAN
Hey there.

A brief smile crosses her face. She turns to him.

JONATHAN
You look...beautiful.
I mean–you look–

Awkward silence.

JONATHAN
Sorry. Don't quite know what to say.

JENNIFER
It's okay. Nobody ever does, really.

Jonathan fidgets, tugs at his too-short suit sleeves, clearly uncomfortable.

JONATHAN
I thought you might be out here. Didn't mean to disturb you. Just wanted you to know I came.

Jennifer smiles. Their eyes lock for a very fleeting moment. Silence. As he turns to go:

JENNIFER
(quickly)
For what it's worth, you look great too. And tell me that's not the same suit you wore to Winter Formal.

Jonathan laughs, breaking the tension.

JONATHAN
Yeah.

He fidgets again.

JONATHAN
I'm pretty sure if you look real close you can still see the "Boone's Farm" you spilled on the lapel.

JENNIFER
Hey! Only cuz you pulled me onto the dance floor—

JONATHAN
—only cuz it was *our* song...
...and...

JENNIFER
(softly, sadly)
Yeah.

More awkward silence.

JONATHAN

Anyway. Just wanted to come
by to tell you how sorry I
am - how - you know - how sorry...

Jonathan hangs his head, looking like he might
burst into tears.

Jennifer looks away, shifts in the chair.

JENNIFER

Jonathan. I know he was like a
grandpa to you too...

JONATHAN

No, he was more like a
father to me. The only decent
man who ever cared.

JENNIFER

I know. And this is your loss
too. I know he loved you
very much—

JONATHAN

Yeah.

JENNIFER

And really, I think the only
reason he thought that you and
I shouldn't—

JONATHAN

—Yeah can we just not talk
about this now?

JENNIFER

Sure....I'm sorry.

Silence. Heavy air.

He turns to leave again, stops.

JONATHAN

(reluctantly)

No Jen, *I'm* sorry. I'm
sorry I didn't fight for
you harder I'm sorry I let
you go to the city I'm sorry
that I... didn't get to make
you happy.

JENNIFER

You did make me happy, Jonathan.

He looks at her with pained eyes.

JONATHAN

(softly, relenting,
without venom)

Just not happy enough. I couldn't
have. He was right. He knew you
could only be truly happy if you got
out of this place.

JENNIFER

Jonathan...

JONATHAN

No. It's okay. I respected
that. I respected him.
I just forgot to respect
myself.

He leaves.

All alone, Jennifer's veneer cracks and she sobs uncontrollably.

Let's take a look at a list of Givens created by a fellow actor and compare them to your own:

GIVENS:

- This is a small town. Population 1,135.
- Jennifer's grandpa just died.
- Jennifer is in the garage, which was his sanctuary.
- Grandpa's sanctuary contains:
    - Football posters taped to the wall.
    - Rattling white refrigerator.
    - Tiny salvaged TV, tin foil on the antenna.
    - Faded and dusty American flag on the wall.
    - Jennifer's childhood fishing rod next to Grandpa's.
- Mourners have gathered in the main house.
- Jennifer wears this year's Chanel suit.
- Jonathan wears a too-small suit from a Winter Formal that they both attended.
- Jonathan and Jennifer had a song in high school.
- Jonathan says Grandpa was like a father to him.
- Jennifer left this town to go to the city.
- It was Grandpa's wish for Jennifer to go.
- Jonathan didn't fight to keep Jennifer from going to the city.
- Jonathan leaves and Jennifer cries.
- Jonathan is still in love with Jennifer.

Much of this is great. I would argue that Jonathan still being in love with Jennifer is ultimately an assumption no matter how obvious it may seem. But for that reason, I would leave it out of the Givens. I would also say that Jonathan *assumes* that it was Grandpa's wish for Jennifer to leave. Jennifer doesn't refute that, but this argument wouldn't hold up in a court of law, right? So, like a detective, let's stick to *just the facts*. We're looking for broad and general strokes here. With each step of the process, you'll get more and more specific.

You might also make a note of the questions or first gut instincts you have; facts may not always be immediately clear. So I might make a quick side note: *Grandpa didn't want Jonathan and Jennifer to be together?

All of these things seem obvious, and writing them down may seem like an exercise in futility right now. But there are times that once I'm deep into the imaginative work, I will have forgotten one thing or another – sometimes it's a crucial thing and sometimes ... not so much. Let's start digging into the character now.

THE GIVENS: A QUICK REVIEW

- **From an objective distance, write down only that which is explicit in the scene – just the facts. Who? What? When? Where?**
- **Avoid the "Why?" for now. That comes later.**
- **Make no assumptions based on these facts, even if you have immediate associations.**
- **Make note of any unusual or particular facts or circumstances in the scene. (i.e. She's in a Chanel suit, etc.)**
- **Leave all emotion out for now.**

"Life is like a grindstone, and whether it grinds a man down or polishes him up depends on the stuff he's made of."
~ Josh Billings

HOWS OF BEHAVIOR

We've nailed down the facts, and it's time to dig deeper. As I said before, each step of this process will get more and more specific. The next part of the analytical stage, still in our left brain here, deals with what a character *does* in the scene and *how* he does it rather than how he *feels*. I call these details the HOWS of BEHAVIOR.

Believe me, you're gonna fight yourself trying not to immediately intuit how the character is feeling. But if you try to figure that out now, you will just be making assumptions. It is possible, don't you think, for a person to feel one way and then behave another way?

This initially feels odd. I know. Wouldn't how a character *feels* be more important than how the character *behaves*? That would be no, not *more* important, at least in this stage of the process. We're still on the left, analytical side of the brain in this step rather than the right, more emotional side of the brain. The behavior gives us the insight, the clues, that will eventually lead us to the most specific, nuanced emotion rather than the broad, general emotion. So slow down - let go of the need to conquer the scene at this point, and let's focus on conquering Jonathan.

Master the character first, and then put the character in the circumstances of the scene.

Now you might say that Jonathan is behaving like a guy who's upset that he lost his girlfriend and also the man who treated him like a grandson. The tendency would be to "play" upset, right? I agree he probably is upset. But to simply play that emotion, in a broad general sense of the word, would be to give a generic performance, much along the lines of a cold read. A cold read will never be as engaging and intriguing as a nuanced and emotionally rich character.

If you were to do the scene right now without investigation into Jonathan's life, the only choice you have is to play it from your own personal perspective, using your own life and feelings as a reference point. Inevitably, there will be a circumstance within the scene when your *personal* reactions to a line will be different than Jonathan's. And it will trip you up. What if, for instance, *you* would have walked out of the garage at the moment that all that emotion began to well up? But you can't, because the scene says you can't. Or what if the *real you* would never, ever apologize and tell a woman you had no respect for yourself? It will feel false to you. If it feels inherently false to you, it will feel the same to an audience.

When you "play at" something in a broad and general way, you miss all the nuance, all the emotions specific to this character alone. You'll give the safe read. Instead, we want to look at a character and create him from whole cloth.

Think about how we experience emotion in real life:

A specific **event** happens...
we interpret that event...
which causes us to have an **emotion...**
which leads to specific **behaviors.**

EVENT – EMOTION – BEHAVIOR

Jonathan's *behavior* is the manifestation of his *emotion*, which is caused by *his interpretation of events*. If we start by noting Jonathan's behavior, we can work backwards to understand not only his emotions but the underlying events that may have caused those emotions – the source, so to speak. Understanding the source, or the springboard, that caused these emotions is half the battle in conquering the character. Ultimately the true joy is in feeling those emotions as he feels them - and you'll get to do just that in the latter steps of this process. To get there, let's stick with observing pure behavior right now and becoming even better at it.

In addition, it's important to look at what the character's behavior is in response *to.* For example, let's say three guys are standing on the street corner. A bully walks up to Guy #1 and punches him. Guy #1 draws back and cowers. The same jerk walks over to Guy #2 and punches him. This fellow stands firm, gives the bully a good hard look and walks away. The bully walks up to Guy #3 and slugs him. Guy #3, without hesitation, swings, connects and knocks the bully out flat. These are three different kinds of behavior - three different responses to the same stimulus. Each of these responses is indicative of a different kind of person, each with his own combination of life experiences, distinct life perspectives and interpretations, and different viewpoints.

The same behavior displayed by two different people could indicate two different emotions. Imagine seeing two people sitting side by side with their eyes closed and their hands folded and raised in a prayer-like position. One could be anxiously pleading, and the other could be calmly practicing the art of letting go. It's hard to know, just by looking, what is going on underneath the behavior, which is why we have to be determined to get under the surface. After all, each human being has different life experiences (events) just in a single morning much less in a lifetime. Because of different interpretations based on everything they've already been through, those events will generate different feelings (emotions) and create different patterns of responding (behavior) in their lives accordingly.

It can also be that a person behaves one way and feels another. You may have deep, deep feelings for a person but may not be willing to show them. You could meet the Queen of England and be gracious, calm and collected, yet be terrified underneath. How you feel and how you behave are sometimes two entirely different things. But behavior is *always* the truest indicator we have of where to start.

In the beginning, behavior and feelings can be hard to separate. Sometimes, in fact, they can be absolutely contrary. The best example

I can think of is the bitchy girl from high school. Remember her? She controlled all the girls around her. She acted as if she knew all; as if she were the authority on what was in and what was out. She demanded attention. She exuded confidence. She demanded to have friends around her, but the friendships that she had were conditional.

I'd be willing to bet that even though she looked like she had everything together at school, there was something underneath it all that you didn't know, something negative in her life underlying that entitled behavior. Maybe she didn't get enough attention from a parent. Maybe she had suffered some type of tragedy that you never knew about. But for whatever reason, she felt compelled to come to school and *behave* in a way that seemed completely rotten from the outside. If she had troubles of some sort at home or in her personal life, she likely needed to find attention and validation and a sense of control somewhere. When she came to school, she was with her peers, so she behaved in the way that she did and got the attention and validation that she needed and craved. Her behavior served her well.

I asked an actress once, "Remember the bitch in high school?" She said, "Yeah, that was me." We laughed. Then I hesitantly (and probably rudely enough) asked her, "Did you have any trouble at home?" She burst into tears and confessed that her stepfather had abused her.

That's a good example of the fact that how someone behaves does not necessarily parallel how they feel. The high school "mean girl" may act powerful, but she doesn't necessarily feel that way. As my mother said on a regular basis, "Actions speak louder than words." How a person (and yes, a character) behaves says much more about them than what they actually express in words. **Behavior is the** ***manifestation*** **of how you feel.**

Though your feelings will always affect your behavior, behavior and feelings are two different things. Just as similar feelings can produce different behaviors in different people, different feelings can produce the same behavior. That's why we need to go deeper.

In this step of the Hows, we're looking for patterns of behavior. Do you ever do something and say to yourself, "WHY do I KEEP doing that?!" As human beings, we keep repeating and repeating behavior. Both good and bad! If you look closely at someone's life, you can start to see a pattern of behavior. You'll get so many clues that you didn't see before. The actor must know much more than the character knows. The actor knows why the character is behaving in a certain way, even though the character is often unaware. So the character keeps repeating the patterns. Just like in real life. He gives us a glimpse of his soul.

In adult life, we either seek to repeat that which we've known since childhood, or we seek to repeat that which we could not fix in childhood. It's repeat or repair in a sense.

We repeat patterns over and over again like a worn-out vinyl record that we're tired of hearing but can't quite stop listening to. We repeat these patterns in an attempt to repair something in childhood. Or we repeat them simply because that's what we've known and observed throughout our childhood; what we've learned from our parents, siblings or friends.

It's the same idea you hear people discuss when they talk about abused children sometimes growing up to be abusers. A child who is abused may struggle to learn new patterns. He or she may not know another way to love or connect with others. Abusive behavior may feel more natural than not, because it's all he or she knows. Sure, this is a dramatic example, but it demonstrates the same psychological principle by which we all learn to behave. We're creatures not only of habit, but also of patterns. Said another way, patterns are habits we can't seem to break. Coming to see our patterns and their sources can be the key that unlocks our understanding of who we are. It's what allows us to break free. It's what lets the light in.

I guess I'm perfectly willing to embarrass myself, because I'll give you an example from my own life. For years, I would choose to be in relationships with men that, should we say ... just didn't work out. I'm being really kind here. Finally, my dad said, "Are we seeing a pattern here?" I adamantly said, "No! This guy's a director, that one's an actor, the other is a mortgage broker for goodness' sake! They're all so different!"

Later, I thought about what he'd said. He was the smartest human being I've ever known, and he knew me pretty well. It occurred to me to use this technique – this process – to look at my own life. What did I discover? A pattern so obvious I couldn't believe I hadn't seen it before. I needed to find where the pattern had started. I needed to find its source.

In the beginning, I couldn't see why I couldn't make a relationship work. I had such a good relationship with my father. My quest to discover more opened my eyes. When I was about three and a half or four, my dad became gravely ill. He had encephalitis, which is an acute inflammation of the brain. Mostly, in those days you died from that. When you're four years old, nobody comes up to you and says, "Hey, your dad might die." But even at four, you get the general sense that everything is not okay. Daddy's not there, Mother's upset, and I'm having feelings about it. It's easy to forget that a child is a human being capable of picking up on the behaviors of other people. The behavior of others around me led me to figure out, "Something is really, really wrong!"

We were living overseas at the time because of my father's work, and my sister and I were put back on a plane to the States by ourselves. I was picked up by an aunt I had never met, taken to a house I had never seen in a town I had never been to. My world was shaken.

My dad eventually recovered, and we were all reunited. I should have been all good, right? But look at the seeds that experience planted in me.

My dad was everything to me. I was the boy he never had. I was daddy's little girl. He taught me how to hunt, to fish, to survive in the woods. He taught me how to swim and how to ride a bike, how to sew, to cook, to drive. He fixed every breakfast I ever ate and made my lunch every day before school. He opened my eyes to classical music. He taught me how to waltz dancing on the tops of his feet. He could speak Spanish fluently and even knew a little French and some German. He would blame that on the fact that he could read and write Latin. He was a scientist – a geologist by trade. Complex math to him was as simple as breathing. To me, sharp objects driven under my fingernails would be preferable. That scientific mind of his never ceased to amaze me. Nor did his ability to paint, draw and play piano by ear. He was wonderful. By all accounts I should've been one of the lucky ones who stroll off into the sunset perfect romance. So why in God's good name would I have picked the men I did?

I *interpreted this event* of my dad's illness as a life or death situation. He was everything in my world. My safety. As a child, I could not heal him. I could not make his encephalitis go away. So in my adulthood, I picked men - good men - who were somehow hurt or broken, because I wanted to heal them. *This was the pattern.* I was seeking to repair. Look at what I do as a profession! I'm a teacher. I didn't start out as a teacher; I started out as an actress. But if you look at what I truly love to do ... I love to look at a scene and make it better. I love to take actors and make them stronger. I'm still, to this day, repeating a pattern, but now I do it in a healthier way than by picking men who are somewhat broken.

My pattern was established in childhood. Seeing it opened a window inside me. So when we look at the Hows of Behavior in a character and the patterns of behavior that we see, they open a window into the psyche, into the unique makeup and experiences of that character.

We establish patterns at an early age and repeat them over and over again. Sometimes we're trying to repair - to change the outcome next time around. Other times, we repeat the patterns in order to prove to ourselves that something we believe to be true about us is actually true. Something along the lines of, "I'm not very good, so I'm not going to put much work into this ____. Then the inevitable happens. "See? I wasn't good at ______! I knew it!" You established a pattern then repeated it in order to tell yourself that your beliefs - the stories in your head about yourself - are true.

The patterns of behavior in a character are extremely character indicative. They give a glimpse into what might have happened in his/her life. So pay close attention to any instance of a character repeating a behavior over and over again when he is faced with certain stimuli. Does he seem to behave brusquely? In the face of what? Does he seem to behave aggressively? In the face of what? Does he seem to deny? Change the subject? Attack? In the face of what?

Notice I say, "seems to behave." This is another way to stay flexible, to allow yourself to learn more and more about the character as you go along. If a character says, "I'm sorry," you're pretty safe in writing down "apologizes," but not every behavior is so cut and dried. You might want to write down something like "seems to apologize without really meaning it," if the circumstances of the scene suggest it. *Either way, don't feel that you're married to any of the observations you make at this point.* You can always change your mind when you get more information.

The best way I can define a How of Behavior is this: **it's the most specific verb, verb + adjective, or verb + adverb combination that you can come up with to describe the character's behavior in a particular moment.** I say specific, because the more detail you can cram into these one or two little words, the more results you'll get later on. If I told you a man "walked" into a room, you'd get a little bit of information, but if I told you he "sauntered" or "tottered" or "stepped cautiously," you'd get a lot more.

Go line by line in the scene, determining what Jonathan's specific behavior is for each line that he speaks and for every non-verbal action that is narrated in the script. Note what the behavior is in response to (the stimulus). You'll want to pay particular attention to exactly what the writer gives you. You may have heard some people suggest that you "just mark out everything except the dialog." Well, I suppose you could. But then you'd be missing oh-so-much that the writer painstakingly tried to offer you. Each parenthetical, each pause, each dot-dot-dot is a way for the writer to convey to you what he or she is envisioning. So if it's on the page, pay attention to it! (Note this is not true of some directions written in a play. These directions are often the stage manager's notes on the actor's first performance of a play that is later published.)

Again, remind yourself that it's the "Hows of *Behavior*" not the "Hows of *Feeling*" that you are going for. You don't know *how the character feels* until you know exactly *who the character is.* If you're playing Jonathan, until you know Jennifer – why you loved her, why you love her still, and why her grandpa was like a father figure to you – you will not care the way Jonathan does. *You cannot know what you've lost until you know what you've had.*

Take a separate piece of paper, your character journal if you want, and write the Hows down, like a list. You'll want to take care not to write the behaviors down in the actual script, because when you do you'll have a tendency to play *at* that behavior. Looking at the particular Hows of Behavior on the scripted page will reinforce an association in your brain. Keep in mind that you are breaking down the character right now. Not the scene.

Now I know that coming up with so called "appropriate" verbs can be a little tricky in the beginning. So here's a little help – a few suggestions compiled by an amazing actress and phenomenal teacher at the Studio, Hillary Tuck.

VERBS FOR THE HOWS/SEEMS TO'S

The idea here was to put the verbs in loose, vacillating categories that give you a jumping off point. Some verbs could be in several categories. Some will be in the wrong category for what that word means to you. So move them around, make it your own and add whatever you like.

PRAISE/SUPPORT/GIVING/PULLING CLOSE TO

boost	acclaim	alleviate	calm	acknowledge
amaze	coach	admire	approve	coddle
adulate	assist	comfort	advocate	assure
commiserate		affirm	baby	commune
aid	back	compliment	befriend	believe
bend	bestow	bolster	council	pledge
delight	praise	educate	rally	encourage
protect	latter	reassure	galvanize	rely
henpeck	honor	hover	nurture	reward
sacrifice	validate	seal the deal	save	steady
step up	open up to	stand up for	train	translate
trust	sympathize	uplift		

RETRACT/ACQUIESCE/GIVE IN/PULLING AWAY

accept	approach	abdicate	avoid	abort
bury	abstain	censure	accept	choke
cloak	accommodate	concede	adapt	allow

appease	anesthetize	conciliate	concur	pacify
placate	concur	recede	relent	conserve
repress	cow down to	retreat	escape	fade
falter	hide	mollify	settle a debt	
soothe	close off	tolerate	tread lightly	withdraw

REDIRECT/RECOVER/BOUNCE BACK

adjust	bear	calculate	anticipate	clarify
appeal	compose	avert	recoup	evade
evaluate	dance around	develop a plan	maintain	realize
sidestep	skirt the issue			

AGGRESSION/PUSH FORWARD

abolish	assert	blame	challenge	charge
accuse	attack	blast	chasten	acerbate
bad mouth	block	chastise	admonish	badger
bombard	chide	aggravate	banish	bar
bother	amplify	browbeat	collar	annihilate
beat	brutalize	commandeer	annoy	begrudge
bully	antagonize	belittle	compete	argue
berate	ascertain	besiege	assail	betray
assault	bite	retaliate	debate	condemn
dig at	force	plow ahead	defame	condescend
disapprove	handle	pressure	defend	confront
discard	harass	quash	deflate	contradict
dismiss	humiliate	degrade	control	disregard
ignore	demean	corner	disturb	judge
corrupt	demoralize	drive them away	lash out	denigrate
educate	pester	nab	rib	deny
cripple	enflame	needle	deprive	criticize
erupt	obliterate	cross examine	explode	patronize
devalue	crucify	fan the flames		

persecute	invalidate	undermine	thwart	shame
curtail	gouge	prove himself	rebel	rebuff
reject	reprimand	ridicule	vex	get a rise out of
warn	shun	wheedle	spoil	sever ties
scoff	taunt	terrorize	threaten	squash
torment	pull no punches		steal thunder	
make a mountain out of a molehill				

LOVE

adore	charm	allure	chase	arouse
cherish	attract	beckon	beguile	court
flirt	paw at	dazzle	humor	pounce
desire	hypnotize	drink them in	idolize	enchant
intoxicate	seduce	woo	smother	worship
snuggle	spellbind	tempt	titillate	vow

MANIPULATE

cheat	cloak	coax	bribe	bully
butter up	bait	bamboozle	bargain	barter
bedevil	bluff	beguile	bewitch	brainwash
compel	coerce	con	conceal	confuse
cover	deceive	delude	fake	haggle
massage	dupe	feed their fear	hoodwink	mislead
enchant	finagle	ingratiate	mold	ensnare
flatter	lure	persuade	scare	schmooze
ensnare	twist	stir the pot	trifle	spin
stack the odds				

COUNSEL

advise	caution	enlighten	forewarn	mentor
mediate	tutor	urge	warn	teach
preach				

PAUSE/TAKE IN

absorb	analyze	appraise	compute	compose
assess	consider	grapple	perceive	ponder
scrutinize	sit on it	track	wade	weigh

ABSOLUTION/ALLOW/FORGIVE

absolve	acquit	reconcile	condone	pardon
repent	exonerate	permit	grant	rationalize
sanction	unburden	undo	unify	rectify
repair	remedy	resolve	restore	

ASK

beseech	pitch	convince	plead	crawl
propose	fish	proposition	offer up	sell

PAIN/SORROW

console	pity	mourn	zone out	agonize
bawl				

SURPRISE

astonish	astound	baffle	bedazzle	befuddle
scare	pull the rug out from underneath you			
send you for a loop				

Remember these are just suggestions. If you have trouble coming up with a behavior for a certain line, then by all means skip that one and come back to it. Sometimes I like to make a note of the elusive behavior like this: "Hmmm...????" Sometimes I just don't know! What's important is to not get tripped up on this step! Do not spend an inordinate amount of time trying to come up with the perfect explanation of behavior. Be far more concerned with spotting a pattern in the behavior rather than naming it.

It is important to look at Jennifer's behavior to a degree, but we want to discern her behavior only because we want to see what Jonathan is *responding to.* We write all this down so that we can begin to see Jonathan's patterns of behavior emerge.

Believe it or not, you can take one scene, one event, in a character's life and start to determine who they might be. You may not precisely intuit the exact backstory of the character as the writer imagines it, but you will be very close to the mark in determining the *emotional* life. The emotional resonance will be extremely close – and that's what counts.

What if you have the whole screenplay? Then, good! You will have many, many more clues as to the behavior of this character. You do not have to take every single scene the character appears in to determine the Hows of Behavior. It's interesting to choose several scenes to explore, especially those that are particularly emotional or meaningful. Or scenes in which the character interacts with different people. For example, he/she might behave differently around a love interest as opposed to a parent. Just choose several key scenes. You'll find that the Hows are similar from scene to scene. You'll be shocked at how consistent the behavior will be.

In the beginning of this process, it's difficult to look at a behavior in an unemotional way. But you can discipline yourself: if you start to write down a feeling, say, "No, no, no, wait a minute, I'm looking at behavior."

The more you do this, I'm telling you, the more you'll get used to it and the easier it will be. You'll start looking at behavior in a slightly different way. We really aren't used to looking at behavior and placing a label on it. We are used to picking up clues from people: from their physical bearing, their body language, and tone of voice. Because it's happening to us in the moment. As clinical psychologist Dr. Peter Desberg describes it, research shows that when subjects were shown pictures of people's eyes, it was enough to identify the emotion they were going through close to 90% of the time. Our minds aren't trained to consciously analyze behavior and to name it, because we already process the important information, subconsciously and automatically, when it comes from other people. It's a little foreign to us in the beginning to examine it so methodically, but keep at it; it's worth it.

Now let's look at the actual "Hows of Behavior" from our scene, from the first moment we see Jonathan.

```
Jonathan stands in silence.
```

You might say, "He doesn't do anything. He's just standing there!" Exactly. Standing there saying nothing is a *behavior*. There is great presence in silence, and there is always a reason for it. Silence speaks. Silence can mask much thought or feeling.

Initially, our minds go to the thought that Jonathan might be afraid to speak to Jennifer. But that is an emotion, and we are avoiding discerning the emotions right now. What's he afraid of? I have no idea. We don't know him well enough yet to know why, or if he's afraid, or of whom or what.

So, for this first line:

```
                    (O.S)
                  JONATHAN
     Hey there.
```

... keeping the stimulus in mind, I would write something along the lines of:

HOWS OF BEHAVIOR:

Stimulus	Behavior
When he sees Jennifer in the sanctuary→	he seems to hesitate to speak to her and then does so briefly.

```
A brief smile crosses her face.  She turns to him.
```

She smiles. But he doesn't see it. She's not facing him at the moment. Then she turns to him, and he says:

```
                    JONATHAN
      You look...beautiful.
      I mean—you look—
```

Notice the ellipsis, the "...". I like to call an ellipsis a "hanger-on." The character hesitates, or hangs onto, a thought. Maybe he was going to say something then changed his mind. Maybe he doesn't know what to say.

So, for the line, "`You look...beautiful`" I would write for the Hows:

Stimulus	Behavior
When she turns to face him→	he seems to blurt out a compliment.

For the line, "`I mean—you look—`", he seems to be doing the same thing. He's hesitant to tell her she looks beautiful. Take that a step further. It's almost as if he tries to *clarify* what he meant to say and then cuts himself off. Then he tries to *clarify his thoughts again.* Then cuts himself off again. So I might write something like:

Stimulus	Behavior
When she faces him (when he's in her presence?)→	he seems to have trouble clarifying his thoughts, or expressing himself.

I added (in her presence?), because I had a little gut reaction that it might be Jennifer's presence that causes Jonathan trouble in clarifying his thoughts, and I wanted to make note of it. It could very well be that he doesn't know what to say, because he's upset over Grandpa. If that's your choice, your gut reaction, you should make note of it. Just know that whatever observations you make at this point *can't be right or wrong.* They're all part of your exploration of Jonathan. Because all of us are different, we will each see something slightly different when observing behaviors. This is the reason that, ultimately, your performance will be different from anybody else's.

Back to the script now ...

```
Awkward silence.
```

Okay, then there's that awkward silence. Our first reaction might be that Jonathan is embarrassed. But that's an emotion, right? So just rephrase that, and put it into behavioral terms. How about:

Stimulus	Behavior
When in this circumstance→	he seems to be confused as to how to behave, or what to say.

```
                    JONATHAN
       Sorry.  Don't quite know
       what to say.
```

Here he seems to apologize. And then he comes out with the truth. He admits that he doesn't know what to say. So we add that to the list.

Stimulus	Behavior
When he doesn't know what to say→	he seems to apologize.
When he doesn't know what to say→	he seems to admit he doesn't know what to say.

Notice we didn't just write, "apologizes to her." We wrote, "When he doesn't know what to say, he seems to apologize for it." This is important, because we included more information. We made it more specific by adding the circumstances behind this particular apology.

Finally, Jennifer speaks!

```
                    JENNIFER
      It's okay.  Nobody ever
      does, really.
```

Even though we're not concentrating on Jennifer right now, it's safe to say she's letting him off the hook.

And Jonathan's response to that?

```
Jonathan fidgets, tugs at his too-short suit
sleeves, clearly uncomfortable.
```

He fidgets! What comes to mind is that he might be embarrassed by his suit. Feels uncomfortable? Feels like he should go? Note that fidgeting is sometimes a physical response to an unexpressed emotion or feeling. It's a displacement of sorts. You're feeling anxious or stressed, and all that energy is expressed through the physical behavior of fidgeting. But we're not discerning emotions right now, so let's turn all that into behavior.

Jennifer verbally lets him off the hook, and he still acts as though he's uncomfortable being there. So we could say:

He's confused as to how to act in this circumstance?

But we said that already. Even though we have already said that, it's okay. It's actually good. Write it again! *Always write down behaviors that repeat themselves.* It helps us to identify a potential repetitive pattern of behavior.

Stimulus	Behavior
When she lets him off the hook→	he seems to be confused as to how to behave or what to say and displaces his emotion by fidgeting.

The next bit of dialogue is:

```
                JONATHAN
I thought you might be out
here.  Didn't mean to disturb
you.  Just wanted you to know
I came.
```

He wants her to know he came by to pay his respects. That's definitely there. But if you think about it, that's a little bit broad and vague. Ask what the "face value" behavior is. The behavior, without any emotion involved, might be something like: "He confesses that he was looking for her." Now you may not feel as though he's confessing anything at this moment. If so, it's okay. That's merely my interpretation of the behavior. Yours may be entirely different. Again, that's another reason that your performance will be unique. But for now, let's say:

Stimulus	Behavior
When in an uncomfortable position→	he seems to confess that he was looking for her.

Then, "Didn't mean to disturb you" seems a bit like an apology. "Just wanted you to know I came" seems like another way to tell her that he cares.

These are all gut reactions. What if they're wrong? There is no wrong! Always listen to your gut. It's your interpretation here. As long as you're observing a behavior at this stage and not assigning an emotion, you'll be fine.

Stimulus	Behavior
When in an uncomfortable position,→	he seems to apologize and assume he's disturbed her.

Stimulus	Behavior
When in an uncomfortable position→	he seems to let her know he cares. (or assumes he disturbed her...)

Next comes ...

```
Jennifer smiles.  Their eyes lock for a very
fleeting moment.  Silence.  As he turns to go:
```

He locks eyes with her. Maybe he's caught up in her. Has to stare at her for a moment. Maybe he's connecting with her. What is that behavior in response to, in this moment? She smiled at him. So maybe you could write something like:

Stimulus	Behavior
When Jennifer gives him a sign of encouragement→	he seems to connect with her.

There's silence after that. What is that silence? I'm gonna say he's uncomfortable with the contact with her, because the next thing he does is turn to go.

Stimulus	Behavior
When connecting with Jennifer→	he seems to be uncomfortable with the intimacy.

Then Jennifer says:

```
                JENNIFER
               (quickly)
     For what it's worth, you
     look great too. And tell me
     that's not the same suit you
     wore to Winter Formal.
```

```
Jonathan laughs, breaking the tension.
```

She says it quickly, almost as a way to keep him in the room. It seems as though she's lightening the situation by making playful fun of his suit. She's teasing, I think. Now what if the actress playing Jennifer doesn't play it as if she's teasing? Well, Jonathan does laugh. The stage directions give us that. So even if she plays it in a non-teasing way, it's safe to say that he takes it that way. Remember too, we're looking for clues to build character, not clues as to how to 'play' Jonathan or the scene at this moment.

So, in this particular moment, how does Jonathan react? He laughs. And the tension is broken. So I would write:

Stimulus	Behavior
When Jennifer breaks the tension with teasing→	he seems to lighten up and allow her to draw him back into the room.

```
                    JONATHAN
        Yeah.

He fidgets again.
```

Almost like he didn't mean to give in to it?

Stimulus	Behavior
When he chooses to stay in the room→	he seems to be uncomfortable again - and fidgets.

Then, he teases her back, here:

```
                    JONATHAN
        I'm pretty sure if
        you look real close you
```

can still see the "Boone's
Farm" you spilled on the lapel.

Jennifer is playful right back with:

JENNIFER
Hey! Only cuz you pulled
me onto the dance floor–

Perhaps playfulness is a big part of their relationship? Or their past relationship?

I would write that down. But I'd make a side note of it, only because playfulness in their relationship is an assumption I'm making. I think it's a pretty reasonable assumption. That's not a bad thing at this point. Just hold off on hard set conclusions right now. It's enough to say:

Stimulus	Behavior
When Jennifer playfully teases→	he seems to tease back.

JONATHAN
–only cuz it was *our* song...
and...

He's explaining why he pulled her out to the dance floor. Then there's that ellipsis. Like he wanted to say more - about their relationship or about their song - but didn't. He doesn't finish saying what he's thinking.

Stimulus	Behavior
When Jennifer playfully teases→	he teases back and explains why he pulled her out to the dance floor.

Stimulus	Behavior
When he explains himself→	he seems to stop himself as if he is hesitant to talk more (about their past?)

Then Jennifer responds with sadness. And there's awkwardness again.

```
                JENNIFER
           (softly, sadly)
     Yeah.

More awkward silence.

                JONATHAN
     Anyway.  Just wanted to come
     by to tell you how sorry I
     am - how - you know - how sorry...
```

Then he tells her he just wanted to come by and express his sorrow. I wonder if part of the reason he came was to see her. I'm sure he's sad about Grandpa, too. Or I wonder if he felt that he should come pay his respects. Lots of unanswered things here – a good reason to begin with the Hows of Behavior and keep going deeper into the character's psyche.

Imagine if you were doing this scene cold. You would truly just be playing at "sad." You wouldn't know whether to play "sad about losing her" or "sad about losing Grandpa" or what. There's so much more here, as we're beginning to see, that we would have missed. (So, keep reminding yourself that at this stage that you are not breaking down the scene to determine how to play it. You are breaking down the character.)

For the above line I might record the How like this:

Stimulus	Behavior
When Jennifer expresses sadness→	he seems to not know what to say and eventually expresses his concern for her.

Jonathan hangs his head. Looks like he might burst into tears at any moment.

Hmm ... He's hanging his head. Perhaps he can't look at her because he's about to cry and is uncomfortable crying in front of her. Safe to say he's very emotional right now. For this, I'd probably write something like:

Stimulus	Behavior
When he expresses his concern→	he seems to become emotional and seeks to hide it from her.

Jennifer looks away, shifts in the chair.

JENNIFER

Jonathan. I know he was like a grandpa to you too...

JONATHAN

No, he was more like a father to me. The only decent man who ever cared.

It seems as if Jennifer reaches out to comfort him. He corrects her and says he felt more for Grandpa than she realizes. He doesn't seem to have any trouble expressing his feelings when it comes to Grandpa.

Stimulus	Behavior
When Jennifer presumes to understand his feelings for Grandpa→	he seems to correct her and freely express his feelings for Grandpa.

Now we're talking about the feelings of the character. Is that okay? Actually, the important parts that we wrote were, "*corrects* Jennifer when she presumes to understand his feelings for Grandpa" and "*freely expresses* his feelings for Grandpa." *Correcting* and *freely expressing* are not emotions, they're behaviors.

```
                JENNIFER
I know.  And this is your loss
too.  I know he loved you
very much—

                JONATHAN
Yeah.
```

Either he's hesitant to talk about how Grandpa felt about him, because it makes him sad, or maybe he's afraid he'll cry again. We don't know. We're not dealing with feelings yet. We don't know exactly what the emotion is. So to simply describe the "face value" behavior, it's safe to say:

Stimulus	Behavior
When Jennifer speaks about Grandpa's feelings for Jonathan→	he seems to cut her off and is unwilling to go further with the conversation.

```
                JENNIFER
And really, I think the only
reason he thought that you and
I shouldn't—
```

JONATHAN
—Yeah can we just not talk
about this now?

Okay. She must have hit some kind of nerve there! He cut her off then abruptly asks her not to talk about it right now. Although he does put it in the form of a question: "Can we just not talk about this right now?" (Interesting that he asks rather than demands.) Make note of what he absolutely doesn't want to talk about. My gut says that he doesn't want to talk about their relationship and the possible end of it.

Stimulus	Behavior
When Jennifer continues to speak of Grandpa's thoughts→	he seems to cut her off again and asks not to talk about the relationship between the two of them.

JENNIFER
Sure...I'm sorry.

Silence. Heavy air.
He turns to leave again, stops.

You might write:

Stimulus	Behavior
When Jennifer gives in to him and apologizes→	he seems to want to leave and then changes his mind.

JONATHAN
(reluctantly)
No Jen, *I'm* sorry. I'm
sorry I didn't fight for
you harder I'm sorry I let

```
you go to the city I'm sorry
that I... didn't get to make
you happy.
```

He spends all this time hesitating to talk to her about his feelings, and then he can't seem to help himself. He blurts it out. He blurts out that he made mistakes with her. There's a lot of "I'm sorry" in there. He seems to regret it. I don't think it's an apology to her so much as he's mad at himself? Now, *regret* and *mad* or *angry* are all emotions. While all those things may indeed be present, what is the "face value" behavior that is manifested? He blurts out (but maybe didn't want to) the *admission* that he made mistakes in their relationship.

Stimulus	Behavior
When he chooses to finally speak his mind→	he seems to reluctantly blurt out with repeated apologies and admit he wasn't enough to make her happy.

```
                    JENNIFER
        You did make me happy Jonathan.

He looks at her with pained eyes.

                    JONATHAN
              (softly, relenting,
                without venom)
        Just not happy enough. I couldn't
        have. He was right. He knew you
        could only be truly happy if you got
        out of this place.
```

Here he admits that he wasn't or isn't capable of making her happy, like he's not enough for her, and this town would never be enough for her. He's also giving a lot of credit to Grandpa, saying Grandpa was right. So, I would write:

Stimulus	Behavior
When Jennifer exclaims that he did make her happy→	he seems to refute this - adding that her leaving was the right thing to do; admitting Grandpa could 'see' that which he couldn't.

JENNIFER

Jonathan...

JONATHAN

No. It's okay. I respected that. I respected him. I just forgot to respect myself.

He leaves.
All alone, Jennifer's veneer cracks and she sobs uncontrollably.

With that I would say:

Stimulus	Behavior
When Jennifer speaks and then hesitates→	he seems to let her off the hook; express his respect for Grandpa; express the disrespect he has for himself.

Stimulus	Behavior
When he admits that he doesn't respect himself→	he leaves quickly.

So, look at that! You've got your Hows of Behavior! You've already done more work that a lot of actors would do. And this is only the beginning.

Remember, we're building the character at this point. We are not trying to discern how the scene is to be played. So look at your list now, and read it out loud to yourself. Reading out loud helps to reinforce the information in your mind. You'll start to see patterns emerging.

HOWS OF BEHAVIOR:

- *When he sees Jennifer in the sanctuary* → he seems to hesitate to speak with Jennifer, then does so briefly.
- *When she turns to face him* → he seems to blurt out a compliment.
- *When she faces him (when he's in her presence?)* → he seems to have trouble clarifying his thoughts or expressing himself.
- *When in this circumstance* → he seems confused as to how to behave or what to say.
- *When he doesn't know what to say* → he seems to apologize.
- *When he doesn't know what to say* → he seems to admit he doesn't know what to say.
- *When she lets him off the hook* → he seems confused as to how to behave or what to say and displaces his emotion by fidgeting.
- *When in an uncomfortable position* → he seems to confess that he was looking for her.
- *When in an uncomfortable position* → he seems to apologize and assume he's disturbed her.
- *When in an uncomfortable position* → he seems to let her know he cares.

- *When Jennifer gives him a sign of encouragement* → he seems to connect with her.
- *When connecting with Jennifer* → he seems uncomfortable with the intimacy.
- *When Jennifer breaks the tension with teasing* → he seems to lighten up and allow her to draw him back into the room.
- *When he chooses to stay in the room* → he seems uncomfortable again and fidgets.
- *When Jennifer playfully teases* → he seems to tease back.
- *When Jennifer playfully teases* → he teases back and explains why he pulled her out to the dance floor.
- *When he explains himself* → he seems to stop himself as if he is hesitant to talk more (about their past?).
- *When Jennifer expresses sadness* → he seems to not know what to say and eventually expresses his concern for her.
- *When he expresses his concern* → he seems to become emotional and seeks to hide it from her.
- *When Jennifer presumes to understand his feelings for Grandpa* → he seems to correct her and freely express his feelings for Grandpa.
- *When Jennifer speaks about Grandpa's feelings for Jonathan* → he seems to cut her off and is unwilling to go further with the conversation.
- *When Jennifer continues to speak of Grandpa's thoughts* → he seems to cut her off again and asks not to talk about the relationship between the two of them.
- *When Jennifer gives in to him and apologizes* → he seems to want to leave and then changes his mind.
- *When he chooses to finally speak his mind* → he seems to reluctantly blurt out with repeated apologies and admit he wasn't enough to make her happy.
- *When Jennifer exclaims that he did make her happy* → he seems to refute this, adding that her leaving was the right thing to do, admitting that Grandpa could 'see' that which he couldn't.

- *When Jennifer speaks and then hesitates* → he seems to let her off the hook, express his respect for Grandpa, express the disrespect he has for himself.
- *When he admits that he doesn't respect himself* → he leaves quickly.

What patterns or common themes do you see? There seems to be a hesitancy to express his feelings. He is frequently uncomfortable and manifests that physically (the fidgeting). He expresses much respect and admiration for Grandpa and seems to have much regret and disrespect for himself. Does he have low self-esteem? Keep these patterns (and this question) in mind throughout the rest of our exploration into Jonathan.

You might come up with slightly different observations, and that's fine. We are all unique individuals with differing perspectives. The beauty is that because of it, each actor will create their own exceptional and interesting performance.

A QUICK HOWS OF BEHAVIOR REMINDER:

- **We don't know how a character feels, because we haven't investigated his/her life on the first reading of a scene. But the writer has given us character-indicative behavior to work with.**
- **Take one scene, or several if given the entire screenplay; write down, line by line, how the character is behaving but NOT how the character is feeling.**
- **Make note of what stimulus the behavior is in response to (i.e. When her boyfriend talks about her ex...she seems to deflect with humor; when the conversation gets too intimate...he seems to change the subject; when asked about the past...he seems to be curt, etc.).**
- **Write every behavior down. Actions are also behaviors.**
- **Remember that silence is a choice, and the choice to be silent is a behavior too.**
- **When a behavior in the scene occurs more than once, make sure to write it down again. You are looking for *patterns* of**

behavior, and those patterns will be your most important discovery at this stage of the process.

- **Read the "Hows of Behavior" out loud, even if you're by yourself, to help reinforce the information in your brain.**
- **Complete ALL Hows of Behavior in the scene before moving on to the Whys in the Core Knowledge.**
- **You do NOT have to use every scene in the screenplay.**

Now, keeping in mind all the work we've done so far, give the scene another quick read. You have a little more depth of knowledge to draw from, and it will likely read slightly differently now.

INT. GRANDDAD'S GARAGE – MORGANVILLE (POP.1,135)- LATE AFTERNOON

Garage turned sanctuary. Dust dances in the rays of sun shining through the windows. An odd contrast to JENNIFER, dressed in this year's Chanel suit. Her eyes are swollen, red, her make-up smudged.

We hear the DISTANT MURMER OF HUSHED VOICES, CLATTERING DISHES from the main house, making the garage feel silent.

Jennifer cautiously sits on the worn leather recliner, Grandpa's chair. A momentary smile at the duct tape on the worn arms. She hugs her knees to her chest, in a reverie.

The room is a shrine:
- football posters taped to the wall.
- a rattling white refrigerator.
- the tiny, salvaged TV with tin foil wadded atop its antenna.

- the American flag on the wall, now faded and dusty.
Jennifer's childhood fishing rod proudly displayed next to Grandpa's clunky one.

The wooden door behind Jennifer scrapes open and jars her back to reality.

JONATHAN stands in silence.

(O.S)
JONATHAN
Hey there.

A brief smile crosses her face. She turns to him.

JONATHAN
You look...beautiful.
I mean—you look—

Awkward silence.

JONATHAN
Sorry. Don't quite know
what to say.

JENNIFER
It's okay. Nobody ever
does, really.

Jonathan fidgets, tugs at his too-short suit sleeves, clearly uncomfortable.

JONATHAN
I thought you might be out

here. Didn't mean to disturb
you. Just wanted you to know
I came.

Jennifer smiles. Their eyes lock for a very fleeting moment. Silence. As he turns to go:

JENNIFER
(quickly)
For what it's worth, you
look great too. And tell me
that's not the same suit you
wore to Winter Formal.

Jonathan laughs, breaking the tension.

JONATHAN
Yeah.

He fidgets again.

JONATHAN
I'm pretty sure if
you look real close you
can still see the "Boone's
Farm" you spilled on the lapel.

JENNIFER
Hey! Only cuz you pulled
me onto the dance floor—

JONATHAN

Only cuz it was *our* song...
and...

JENNIFER

(softly, sadly)

Yeah.

More awkward silence.

JONATHAN

Anyway. Just wanted to come
by to tell you how sorry I
am - how - you know - how sorry...

Jonathan hangs his head, looking like he might
burst into tears.

Jennifer looks away, shifts in the chair.

JENNIFER

Jonathan. I know he was like a
grandpa to you too...

JONATHAN

No, he was more like a
father to me. The only decent
man who ever cared.

JENNIFER

I know. And this is your loss
too. I know he loved you
very much—

JONATHAN

Yeah.

JENNIFER

And really, I think the only reason he thought that you and I shouldn't—

JONATHAN

—Yeah can we just not talk about this now?

JENNIFER

Sure....I'm sorry.

Silence. Heavy air.

He turns to leave again, stops.

JONATHAN

(reluctantly)

No Jen, *I'm* sorry. I'm sorry I didn't fight for you harder I'm sorry I let you go to the city I'm sorry that I... didn't get to make you happy.

JENNIFER

You did make me happy Jonathan.

He looks at her with pained eyes.

JONATHAN
(softly, relenting,
without venom)
Just not happy enough. I couldn't
have. He was right. He knew you could
only be truly happy if you got
out of this place.

JENNIFER
Jonathan...

JONATHAN
No. It's okay. I respected
that. I respected him.
I just forgot to respect
myself.

He leaves.

All alone, Jennifer's veneer cracks and she sobs uncontrollably.

Let's go further now. We'll come up with some Core Knowledge for Jonathan, and from that we'll see if we can discern Jonathan's Base Human Emotion.

"Your work is to discover your world and then with all your heart give yourself to it."
~ Buddha

THE WHYS THAT LEAD TO CORE KNOWLEDGE

Core Knowledge is the history of the character. It consists of the major events in the character's life. Why do I need to know his life events? For the same reason that you would not be the person you presently are without the life events, and your interpretation of those life events, that shaped you. We are looking to fill in the puzzle that is Jonathan. Remember: event and the interpretation of it - emotion - behavior. We've seen the resulting behavior when we explored the Hows of Behavior. Much of how a person behaves is, in fact, learned behavior - a learned response to events or circumstances in life. By examining the clues in the script and coupling them with the behaviors we've observed, we are able to make logical and intuitive decisions about the life events. These life events, in turn, will lead us to specific emotions unique to Jonathan.

In our own lives, we experience something (event), view it in a certain way (interpretation), feel a certain way about it (emotion) and behave accordingly. But when breaking down a character, all we have initially is the end result (behavior). In order to fully and deeply know this character, it's important to determine specific life events and how those events impacted him emotionally.

I like to stay a little bit loose with the history of the character if I can, and I never fully write it out. I make "jogger" notes, so to speak - little notes that will jog my memory and remind me of what I've created.

I know many of us were taught to write extensive backstories that go on, page after endless page. Many actors simply stop there. But I find that while that would, to an extent, give me certain *knowledge* of the character, it doesn't do much to make me *feel* the character. Mark Twain would say, "Knowledge without experience is just information." I couldn't agree more. So I will actually experience the emotions of the character in depth with *Emotion with Detail*, a later step in the process. And I'll use Core Knowledge as a platform to construct those Emotion with Detail moments.

Another reason not to write the backstory down in novel form is that, at this stage, you don't want to lock yourself into too many details just for the sake of being specific. I construct the Core Knowledge loosely for a number of reasons, but the greatest of them is that creating a hard and fast history for my character at this point might preclude me from making important emotional discoveries later during the Emotion with Detail phase.

I also want to be careful not to assign random and superfluous events to the character's life. For example, in your scene, you wouldn't want to decide that Jonathan was a high school football player just for the sake of making that choice. He may very well have been a football player, but if you make that choice in your Core Knowledge, you want to have made it for a strong reason. Or because it's explicit in the script. If the script made reference to Jonathan having a difficult time in his life because of a knee injury in high school that he still seems to be bitter about, you could very well create an event - or Core Knowledge point - surrounding it.

In that case you might invent, for instance, that playing football had been a lifelong dream of Jonathan's - he was seen as having pro potential - everyone in town knew his name - girls threw themselves at him ... and then his knee was crushed the week before the championship game - he lost his scholarship to college - went into deep depression and made some rather bad choices afterward, such as drinking to escape the pain. *Now* you have put an emotional reason behind the decision to make the Core Knowledge choice that he played football. *That is how you make a strong choice. Give it an emotional reason to exist* while making sure that it is both appropriate to the character and the story.

Unless the screenplay lays out for you the events that happened in the character's life, you will want to invent them. You can't truly know someone unless you know their 'life story,' so to speak. If there are specifics in the screenplay that mention a past event in the character's life, you would absolutely include that in your Core Knowledge. Always go with what the writer gives you. Every little detail that the writer includes will be somewhat character indicative. What is the writer telling us about Jonathan with the mention of his too-small suit? Is he too poor to afford a properly fitting suit, or does he simply not need one in his line of work?

Even what the writer chooses to give the character in terms of a profession is character indicative. A photographer views the world through a lens. It's possible he/she could be someone who chooses to look at life through a filter rather than experiencing it. A painter might be a character who chooses to express emotions through color and texture and image that he can't express otherwise. A writer might be a solitary figure, able to express on the page that which he cannot speak. Sometimes a character's name can speak volumes about character traits. Do you get two different impressions of a character named Charles Edward Worthington III and one named Bubba Johnson? Charles's name might indicate that he was born into a proud family that likes the world to know where they came from, and Bubba may or may not be someone's given name. It's often a nickname - it's hard to know. So perhaps he was born into a family that didn't care as much about lineage. This, of course, isn't always the case, but the point is, you don't want to ignore any detail the writer tells you - they're all important clues.

Though you may only have one scene to read for an audition, you always want to present a character that is deeply human and fully realized. How could you do that if you didn't invent and create him or her? We begin with what's on the page - always working with and never against it - and we build from there. It's absolutely essential to know your character's childhood; it takes a lifetime to form an adult human being. And you'll notice that there are certain ages in our lifetime that seem to be particularly difficult, emotional or meaningful in some way. For me, these milestones went something like this: first, third, sixth, eighth grade, high school - tenth, eleventh and twelfth grades; freshman year of college and graduation; and the shock of the real world. Everyone is different. Although I am not using my own life events, I do find that when I'm building a character, I have the tendency to note these particular ages in the character, because they were significant times in my own life. Your meaningful years might be quite different. So might the character's. But acknowledging our own helps us remember to find some acknowledgement for theirs.

In this part of the process, we are beginning to move further away from the more analytical left side of the brain and allowing our right side, the more creative part of the brain, to have a bit more input. In doing so, I'll explain two rather different ways to arrive at Core Knowledge. The first approach will appeal to more intuitive thinkers. The second will resonate more with those who are linear thinkers. You choose. There is no right or wrong. One will speak to you more than the other.

Any little gut reactions you have that don't quite fit in to a specific life event, time, date or place, I like to quickly make note of them in a separate section headed "Notes and Ideas." These are general and sometimes random thoughts or ideas that might occur to me throughout my character investigation. I can include or reject them later.

INTUITIVE CORE KNOWLEDGE

Looking at the scene with Jonathan and Jennifer, what does your intuition say? What are some hints in the script that will give you an idea of what his life has been like? What begs for a question? Once again, there is no right or wrong. You will be on track when you choose something based on an emotional reason to exist. You will be off track if you make a choice that is arbitrary and unnecessary. As you go through and make choices about who Jonathan is and where he came from, the key is to keep asking *why.* As long as you keep answering the *why*, you'll make emotionally justified, constructive decisions.

This is also a good time to glance back at your Givens. Just when you thought that "exercise in futility" wouldn't be of value, you'll find that it will help refresh your memory and further spark your imagination. Also note the patterns of behavior we saw earlier.

When I read the script, or sides in this case, one of the first things that pops out to me is that Jonathan mentions that Grandpa was the only man who was ever decent to him. Hmmm ...

Why? If Grandpa was the only decent man in Jonathan's eyes, it tells me a little bit about how Jonathan viewed his father. Without a lot of respect or maybe a great deal of fear? Why? What was going on with his father? Was he absent? Abusive? Overly demanding or unusually strict? My instinct might say that maybe Jonathan's father abused him in some way - maybe hit him or was emotionally abusive to him. Fearing him would make a great deal of sense to me given that we saw in Jonathan's patterns of behavior a repetition of hesitancy to speak freely about his emotions. We also noted a pattern of displacing his emotions with fidgeting. A fearful child may hesitate to speak up for fear of retribution from the parent.

Perhaps his father was an alcoholic and often raged out of control. That makes sense to me. Let's choose that for now. We can always change it later if we feel the need. So what would that tell me about Jonathan's early grade school years? It's possible he kept to himself a lot, because he didn't want anyone to know about his father. He would be hesitant to try things that other kids did, because if he failed, it would further reinforce his low self-esteem.

Jonathan and Grandpa had a very close relationship, and Jonathan had great respect for him. *Why?* How did that come to be? How did they meet? My imagination might lead me to surmise that maybe Grandpa lived in the same neighborhood. Being in a small town, it's likely that Grandpa might very well have known about Jonathan's father.

We have clues as to what kind of man Grandpa was. We see in his "sanctuary" that he had an old American flag on the wall, a rattling refrigerator, football posters taped to the wall, a salvaged TV with tin foil wadded atop the antenna, fishing rods. He repaired his armchair with duct tape. What kind of insight might all these clues give us about the kind of man Grandpa was? Maybe he was somewhat frugal – didn't like to throw things away as long as they still had some use. He might be patriotic – hence the American flag. Probably a man's man – from the football posters on the wall. He likely enjoyed the serenity of fishing and loved doing this with Jennifer (Jennifer's childhood rod and his clunky one propped next to it).

Take these two ideas of who Grandpa was and who Jonathan's father was and meld them together. If I ask myself, "How did Jonathan meet Grandpa?" I might come up with something like this:

Let's suppose that Jonathan's dad was on a drinking binge one summer day on a Saturday and that drinking made him more angry than usual. To escape the wrath of his father, Jonathan fled to his favorite hideout on the lake. Let's make it a clump of bushes near the shore. As he hides there, he spies an older man and a young girl about his age (Grandpa and Jennifer). He watches with rapt attention how the older man teaches this young girl how to hold her fishing rod, how to cast the line and reel it back in. It would likely point out to him how much was missing in his own life. Just then Grandpa notices Jonathan hiding in the bushes and calls for him to come out. Grandpa recognizes him as the boy down the street. Knowing about his home life predicament, Grandpa invites Jonathan to learn to fish as well. Think of how this would make Jonathan feel in this moment. Here's a man who is willing to take his time to patiently teach him something new – as opposed to his father, whose main pastimes are drinking, yelling and demanding. It would certainly serve to bond him to Grandpa and open up a path in which Jonathan would look to Grandpa for guidance and strength. See? We simply put two pieces of a puzzle together: who we assumed Grandpa to be and who we built Jonathan's father to be.

Since this is just a quick idea that popped into my head, and because I still want to allow myself some flexibility to explore it more emotionally in the Emotion with Detail phase, I might make the Core Knowledge note as simple as:

He first met Grandpa at the lake as he was escaping another of his dad's drinking binges.

I don't necessarily have to write out the epic explanation that led me to that thought. I'll reserve that specific elaborative scenario for the more in-depth and emotionally charged Emotion with Detail later on. Emotion with Detail – the last step in my character exploration – will allow me to live this event richly and vividly in my imagination. I'll do this, *because I need to feel it, not just know it.* We'll get there. For now, let's keep moving.

What do we think about Jonathan's socioeconomic status growing up? If this is a small town, I would say that Jonathan's family was of lower to middle-lower income. If his dad was a prolific drinker, then he very well might have job troubles and a difficult time making ends meet. This would also cause much tension in the household and further drive Jonathan to seek the company and guidance of Grandpa as a father figure.

So what is Jonathan's mother like? Does she stand by and watch when her husband goes on a drinking binge? Does she ignore it? Does she fight with his father? I would choose that Jonathan's mother was a bit meek, shy, and very fearful of Jonathan's father. Why choose that? Because of the behavior we see presently in Jonathan. As I said before, much behavior is in fact learned behavior. Whether we see it in a parent, a sibling or a close friend, we learn behaviors from others. As children, we observe how others behave and mentally note the outcome of their behavior. That's sometimes how we get what we want or need as children. We learn to behave in a specific way, because, either consciously or subconsciously, we are hoping for a specific desired outcome. In Jonathan's case, that might have meant survival.

What other clues do we pick up in the script? Jonathan's too-short suit stands out to me. Why would he wear this? My imagination would say that either he can't afford a nice suit, or maybe he doesn't need one. Let's look at the possibility that he doesn't need one in his line of work. Okay, what does he do for work? I get the sense that he might do something with his hands. Now I don't know why, but that feels right to me. Something else might feel right to you, and if so, then choose that.

We see that Grandpa probably liked to fix things rather than discard them. (Duct tape on the chair. Tin foil atop the antenna.) Maybe he instilled that in Jonathan as well. What kind of job would a guy in a small town have that has to do with working with his hands? Maybe a carpenter, or a mechanic. Let's choose mechanic.

Now letting my imagination fly... Present day, Jonathan works as a mechanic. Let's say he got a job in a gas station as soon as he was legally able to work. At sixteen. Maybe he had a proclivity for cars from working with Grandpa on his. Grandpa could have taught him how to fix and maintain it as a way of spending more time with him. Maybe this was a way for Jonathan to have a car at sixteen - he bought an old junker and fixed it up with Grandpa's help. Maybe the owner of the gas station was impressed enough to promote him to mechanic and then eventually to head mechanic.

See how one thing leads to another? What else, clue-wise, do you pick up in the script? How about the events surrounding Winter Formal? Well, we know that both Jonathan and Jennifer were at the dance. Were they there together, or alone, or even with someone else? To me it feels more like they were together - in a relationship. We get the sense that there was a lot of tension surrounding that event. Jonathan didn't seem to want to talk about it. So let's explore *why*.

What was their relationship like? We've established that they met at an early age that day at the lake. Let's say that they became close friends as time went on - given that Jonathan hung around Grandpa a lot. I could see them being almost like best friends for a length of time. Until high school maybe, where their friendship turned into something more romantic. Which makes me ask, what was Jennifer like?

Examine what we know. She left to go to the city. She's now wearing a Chanel suit. I get the sense that she hasn't been back to town lately. Whatever she does as a career now, I'm assuming it pays fairly well. I could see her as the kind of girl who made great grades in school - who accomplished much. Given who I think Grandpa was, I could see him making Jennifer toe the line and encouraging her to do the responsible thing in life. I could also see a scenario in which it's possible that Grandpa raised Jennifer. Maybe her parents died young and Grandpa took her in. There's a guarded quality to her – as if she's reluctant to expose her feelings. This could very well be a learned behavior. I could see making a case that Grandpa taught her to think before she speaks. For some reason, I get the sense that she was popular and well-liked in school. Let's say she was head cheerleader. (Now if we read the script in full and find out otherwise, we can easily change this.) I chose head cheerleader simply because this would be a nice juxtaposition to Jonathan's life. The guy who works in the gas station dates the popular girl. That also supports his feelings of low self-esteem – of feeling less than.

Something happened on that night at the Winter Formal. What was it? Jonathan seems as if he'd like to avoid thinking about it. What if Jennifer loses her virginity on that night? Or maybe they conceive a child on that night. Let's say that Jonathan wanted the child, but Jennifer had higher hopes and dreams for herself. Grandpa encouraged her to leave this town. That could certainly have led to a heartbreaking split and an uncomfortable change in the relationship with Grandpa. If all of these events occurred quickly, it would be interesting to play with the idea that Jonathan and Jennifer had no real closure to their relationship. Argh! Even more painful, right? Another reason for his hesitancy to speak with her in the beginning of the scene.

Would it be wrong to say that the uncomfortable event on Winter Formal night was a simple argument that escalated unnecessarily and caused a breakup? No, not wrong. But choices such as losing her virginity or conceiving a child are stronger, deeper and more meaningful. This is how you make strong choices. Give them enormous emotional resonance. The darker the material and characters are, the darker your choices can be. If you're playing a serial killer, the life events or Core Knowledge points can be chillingly dark, deeply psychological and perverse. Let the life events you choose be dictated by the material. For this particular scene, I think we've chosen well. Conceiving a child would have an enormous emotional impact on them both.

This event – the loss of Jennifer and a possible baby – would be a really powerful one to explore in emotional depth through an Emotion with Detail. You will experience this event as Jonathan experiences it. You'll step into his shoes and feel what he feels, rather than just having the knowledge that it occurred.

You see how everything you're doing, each puzzle piece you fit into place, is loading the character with emotional fuel? Look at how much more powerful the moment will be when Jonathan first sees Jennifer after such a long time. It will be charged with all kinds of emotions of loss. When she brings up the Winter Formal, it will be an additional reminder of what they could have had.

Is Jonathan in a relationship now? Let's say yes. And let's make it with a girl that they both knew in high school. Maybe this girl has a child from a previous relationship that Jonathan is now helping to raise. A choice like this may serve to make him feel torn or conflicted when he sees Jennifer again after such a long time. You could also make an argument that he is alone. This choice might serve to make him feel more of a hunger for Jennifer and what they used to have.

What about siblings? My gut says Jonathan is an only child. It feels like Grandpa was very important to him, like family to him. If he had brothers or sisters, he might have gone to them for emotional support. Only children have a different life experience than children who grow up in a household with siblings. Birth order counts for a lot: an older child will typically behave differently than a middle child or the baby of the family. There's also an argument that could be made that Jonathan is the youngest of, say, a household full of boys. What if the older brothers were very successful in some way, and Jonathan feels inadequate because of that? But for me, Jonathan being an only child feels right.

From here, let your imagination fly even further, and begin to make decisions as to what life events occurred – the basic outline of his history or Core Knowledge. Still, I'm doing it rather loosely. No need to write a novel. Unless the script – which we don't always have – says otherwise, choose events and situations that are supported by an emotional reason to exist. Choose that which resonates with you.

Here is a basic outline of our Core Knowledge arrived at from the *intuitive* gleaning of clues:

- He's an only child.
- He's from a small town and still lives there.
- His socioeconomic level was middle to lower income.
- His father was an alcoholic and physically and emotionally abusive to him.
- He first met Grandpa at the lake as he was escaping another of his dad's drinking binges.
- He found a father figure and mentor in Jennifer's grandpa.
- Jennifer and Jonathan were best friends as kids.
- They remained friends until they started dating freshman year in high school.
- His first job was at a gas station at sixteen.
- They conceived the night of the Winter Formal.
- Jonathan and Grandpa's relationship became strained.
- Grandpa suggested that Jennifer should leave this town.
- There was no closure to the relationship.
- He was promoted to mechanic and is now the head mechanic.
- He's now in a relationship with a girl that they both knew in high school. She may or may not have a child from a previous relationship.

The beauty of Core Knowledge is that you can always go back and revise or add anything you like, particularly anything that makes the character burn with more emotional fuel.

Always go with your gut and be confident in your ability to make these choices for the character you're building. Another actor might find a plausible way to construct a Core Knowledge in which Jonathan and Jennifer grew up differently. They might create a scenario in which Jonathan's family had money, in which any number of details were different, and these choices wouldn't be wrong either, as long as they have emotional significance and you can give each choice an *emotional reason to exist.* But your Jonathan, the Jonathan you'll play, is a character that only you could create; your instincts are the only ones that matter. Your choices must resonate within you.

(This "Intuitive Core Knowledge" approach may readily speak to you. Below is an alternative way to discern the life events, called "Linear Core Knowledge." I have explained it in an intentionally redundant way in order to point out that the same conclusions may be drawn in the Linear approach as in the Intuitive approach. The approach that is easiest for you, the one you'll ultimately use in building your characters, is completely up to you!)

LINEAR CORE KNOWLEDGE

All the decisions and events we've created so far in our imagination have been based on clues we found in the script. If you're an actor who adores the detail of it all and is a linear thinker by nature, I'll show you another way to approach your Core Knowledge - and here's one of the ways your Hows of Behavior will be helpful:

Take each one of the HOWS and begin to ask WHY. Why might a particular behavior occur? What overall, big-picture issues did the character deal with in the past? What do these clues tell you about the emotional issues that may be present in the character today? Keep narrowing it down to an event by asking "why."

I urge you to let go of having to determine a specific Core Knowledge point for every single How of Behavior. You'll get yourself in the weeds, so to speak. Give yourself permission to let your imagination fly, knowing that it is all fluid and there are no rights or wrongs.

It's very important to remember that you're *not* trying to figure out how each line is to be played right now. You're *not* trying to figure out what the subtext is or what Jonathan is feeling right now. You're *not* trying to figure out an action to be played on the line. **You are garnering clues into what his past was like.** You are searching for nuggets that lead you to discover what might have happened in the past. You are trying to discern the overwhelmingly pertinent and potentially emotional events that caused his life to take a turn - for the better or for the worse. Simply said, you are looking for something significant that might have had an impact on his life. Remember, any Core Knowledge points we discern from this can always change later.

Take the HOWS OF BEHAVIOR
ask, *WHY*
get big-picture clues, that lead to
CORE KNOWLEDGE

Take a look at some ideas below:

How of Behavior: When he sees Jennifer in the sanctuary → he seems to hesitate to speak and then does so briefly.

WHY?

Hasn't seen her for a while? He's cautious? Afraid of her reaction? Is he always hesitant around people?

Now letting my imagination fly and expanding on that:

It feels like he may not have seen her since she left town several years ago. Maybe their relationship didn't have closure, and he's unsure of her reaction to him. I'm going to say it's been five years - enough time for her to be successful. Chanel suits aren't cheap. Yes, she could have borrowed one, but I'm making the decision that it's hers.

So a CORE KNOWLEDGE point derived from this might be: **Hasn't seen her for 5 years. Relationship ended with no closure.**

WHY?

Why would it end with no closure? Maybe it ended abruptly. It sure feels like Grandpa had something to do with it or that he at least encouraged Jennifer to end the relationship and get out of the town. What if she was pregnant her senior year in high school, and Grandpa encouraged her to not keep the baby. Maybe Jonathan wanted to keep the child. There are many possibilities, but for now let's say:

A CORE KNOWLEDGE point might be: **Jennifer became pregnant senior year in high school - causing tension in the relationship.**

How of Behavior: When she turns to face him → he seems to blurt out a compliment.

WHY?

Possibly old feelings of some kind still exist?

I think this supports our above observations that the relationship may have ended without a lot of closure.

How of Behavior: When she faces him → he seems to have trouble clarifying his thoughts, or expressing himself (in her presence?).

WHY?

Doesn't know how she presently feels about him?

Expanding on that:

Again, it reinforces that there was no closure and that he hasn't spoken to her for a while. Maybe he hasn't spoken to her since she terminated the pregnancy. So is he in a relationship now? I would think so. The strong choice is to put him in a relationship that doesn't quite measure up to what he had with Jennifer - or at least what he remembers it to be. Let's give him a live-in girlfriend, a girl that Jennifer knew from high school who is now a single mom with a two-year-old - a child that might be a reminder of the child he never had with Jennifer. Paying most of the bills for the both of them would likely be a struggle. Seeing that Jennifer is doing well (in her Chanel suit) would increase his feelings of inadequacy.

So a CORE KNOWLEDGE point might be: **Jonathan is in a relationship with a girl they both knew in high school who is now a single mom with a two-year-old. Jonathan struggles to pay most of the bills.**

How of Behavior: When in this circumstance → he seems confused as to how to behave, or what to say.

WHY?

Fears a negative reaction from saying the wrong thing? Or doing the wrong thing?

Expanding on that:

What circumstances could make a child fearful of doing or saying the wrong thing? Perhaps an emotionally or physically abusive father? What if his father was an alcoholic and frequently raged out of control? This scenario could also set up a home that was likely financially unstable with his father having a tough time making ends meet. This would also account for Jonathan's attachment to Grandpa.

So some CORE KNOWLEDGE points might be: **Jonathan's father was an alcoholic, likely emotionally and physically abusive. Jonathan comes from a lower to lower-middle income household.**

How of Behavior: When he doesn't know what to say → he seems to apologize.

WHY?

Socially awkward? Feels less than others a good deal of the time?

Expanding on this:

I would imagine that, as a child with a difficult home life where alcoholism was prevalent, Jonathan probably had few friends. What would they think if he invited them over to his house? He probably wouldn't have been allowed to. Or if he did a time or two, I would imagine he would have been embarrassed by his dad's behavior and quickly learned not to put himself in that situation again. Looking for a strong choice here, I might place a Core Knowledge event in, say, the first grade. That's a difficult time for most children. And if something significant happened in first grade it might give us some insight into how other children treated him thereafter.

So a CORE KNOWLEDGE point might be: **Embarrassing event in first grade (possibly something with his father, in front of other children, that would cause him to withdraw).**

How of Behavior: When he doesn't know what to say → he seems to admit it.

WHY?

It's an honest thing to do. Especially since he seems to be somewhat unsure of how she feels about him. Was there always honesty between them?

It's beginning to feel more and more like they had a special bond. I would begin to ask, when did this bond start? And why? Maybe they met each other as kids - from roughly the same neighborhood. It's a small town. I can imagine Jonathan seeking to stay out of his house as much as possible. So let's say Jonathan (being somewhat of a loner) goes to a particular place on the lake when he needs to escape the abusive household. Let's further imagine that Grandpa and Jennifer were there fishing. (Taking note that we saw fishing rods in Grandpa's "sanctuary.")

Jonathan keeps referring to Grandpa as the only decent man he ever knew. Maybe Grandpa recognized him that day as the boy who lived down the street. In a small town, it's likely that Grandpa would have known about Jonathan's dad and his drinking problem. Sensing that he was going through a hard time, maybe Grandpa invited Jonathan to fish with them, and the bond between the three of them began. Let's make the timeframe for this the sixth grade. That's old enough in a small town to be out unsupervised. As far as a dating relationship goes, let's say that Jonathan and Jennifer started dating freshman year of high school.

So a CORE KNOWLEDGE point might be: **Sixth Grade: Father had an emotional outburst. Jonathan goes to his 'escape' place on the lake. Meets Grandpa and Jennifer. Grandpa teaches him how to fish. Friendship begins. Freshman year high school: Jonathan and Jennifer begin to date.**

How of Behavior: When she lets him off the hook → he seems confused as to how to behave and physically fidgets.

WHY?

Awkward? Unsure of himself? Wants to say something but can't quite do it?

Physical behaviors that occur repetitively can come from an emotional response to something. Fidgeting is a way of displacing the emotion and putting it into a physical response. While we could choose to find a correlating Core Knowledge event that marks the beginning of his fidgeting, I would rather *discover* when that behavior first occurred as I experience my Emotion with Details later on. You may find many unusual behaviors and quirks in a character when you begin to live out the emotionally pertinent moments through the process of Emotion with Detail.

This fidgeting or displacing of emotion also supports the idea, and our previous Core Knowledge point, that his father could have been abusive. In other words, when an emotion springs up in him that he doesn't want to express or fears expressing, it manifests in the physical expression of fidgeting.

How of Behavior: When in an uncomfortable position → he seems to confess that he was looking for her.

WHY?

To me, this reiterates that he cares for her - and possibly still does deeply.

This doesn't particularly bring up a new Core Knowledge point for me - but heck, if your imagination finds one, then good!

How of Behavior: When in an uncomfortable position → he seems to apologize and assume he's disturbed her.

WHY?

Is it out of respect for her? This could be respect for her inner character (disposition) or respect for what she's accomplished, etc. She's out of his league?

We've established that they probably haven't seen each other for around five years now. If we choose that Jennifer has been quite successful, a strong choice for Jonathan would be that he is not so successful. An even stronger choice, and more embarrassing for him, would be to say that he still works in the same place he did in high school. Which leads me to ask: okay, where did he work in high school in a small town with few jobs available? My imagination leapt to a gas station. Let's say he got the job in high school and has now worked his way up to head mechanic. This is a nice juxtaposition with Jennifer. She left town and became successful. He stayed and, although he did well by many standards, he is nowhere near Jennifer in economic status. At least in his mind, and that's the only place it counts. This would also explain his ill-fitting suit. He never needed to buy a new one!

So a CORE KNOWLEDGE point might be: **Jonathan got a job in the gas station at sixteen. Eventually worked his way up to head mechanic.**

How of Behavior: When in an uncomfortable position → he seems to let her know he cares.

WHY?

I believe he probably does care. (How much he cares at this point, I can't determine yet. I'll investigate that as I'm living and exploring the event in my imagination during Emotion with Detail.)

This does speak to the possibility that Jonathan has learned to comfort people in time of need. Maybe he comforts his mother at some point. Maybe when Dad has an emotional outburst. I would make a note of that in my "Notes and Ideas" section. Do you see a specific Core Knowledge point here? Nothing too specific or concrete pops up for me, but feel free to let your imagination fly!

How of Behavior: When Jennifer gives him a sign of encouragement → he seems to let her know he cares.

WHY?

Hmmm ... maybe he cares more than he lets on? Maybe he's never let the love for her go?

Again, I'm not seeing a specific Core Knowledge point with this one, but the idea is a valuable one.

How of Behavior: When Jennifer gives him a sign of encouragement → he seems to connect with her.

WHY?

Possibly he still feels connected to her? Longs for more of a connection?

We're seeing more and more of Jonathan's attachment to Jennifer. And while it's not bringing up a specific and telling event or a Core Knowledge point to me, again, it may to you. It does, however, reiterate the idea that they likely had a deep relationship early on.

How of Behavior: When connecting with Jennifer → he seems uncomfortable with the intimacy.

WHY?

Are the memories too painful?

This seems to support our previous Core Knowledge points.

How of Behavior: When Jennifer breaks the tension with teasing → he seems to lighten up and allow her to draw him back into the room.

WHY?

To me, this seems like an invitation to stay. He acquiesces! Did he always give in to her? Is he used to giving in to people? Just used to giving in to her? Still has feelings?

I get the feeling that Jennifer was maybe the one usually "in charge" during the relationship. What if she was very popular in high school? Hmm ... I like the juxtaposition of Jennifer being very popular with Jonathan being a bit more reserved. Homecoming Queen or cheerleader dates the guy who works in the gas station? While this doesn't necessarily bring up a specific Core Knowledge point, it's always good to make note of little things that spring up in your imagination. Again, this would be good to put into your "Notes and Ideas" section.

How of Behavior: When he chooses to stay in the room → he seems uncomfortable again - and fidgets.

WHY?

Now Jennifer has broken the tension, and he made the decision to stay in the room. Is he kicking himself for it? Feeling like he may be scrutinized? Insecure around her?

This reiterates to me that there was very little closure in the relationship and that Jonathan hasn't spoken to Jennifer in quite some time and, therefore, maybe doesn't know how she feels about him. The fidgeting indicates that an emotion is likely popping up that he doesn't want to let out in this moment.

How of Behavior: When Jennifer playfully teases → he seems to tease back.

WHY?

I get the feeling that this playful banter is probably indicative of their past relationship. It was easy to be around each other; they had fun.

Again, no new or specific Core Knowledge points here, but I would jot this idea down in my "Notes and Ideas" section and be sure to include this behavior in my Emotion with Details.

How of Behavior: When Jennifer playfully teases → he seems to tease back and explains why he pulled her onto the dance floor.

WHY?

Reminiscing in the moment maybe? He certainly remembers it. Was it a significant moment? Was the dance a significant event in terms of their relationship?

If we want to stick with our previous Core Knowledge point of Jennifer having terminated a pregnancy in high school, what if we chose that this dance was when Jonathan found out she was pregnant? Or this was the night they conceived? By no means do we have to stick to that choice. It can all still be flexible at this point.

So a CORE KNOWEDGE point might be: **Jonathan and Jennifer conceived the night of the dance. Or Jonathan learned of her pregnancy that night.**

How of Behavior: When he explains himself → he seems to stop himself as if he is hesitant to talk more (about their past?).

WHY?

Is remembering painful to him? Something happened at the dance? Too painful to remember the relationship that is no more?

I'm gonna say yeah. This supports our choice to make the dance significant in terms of their relationship.

How of Behavior: When Jennifer expresses sadness → he seems to not know what to say and then expresses his concern for her.

WHY?

I think he may still care for her, which makes me wonder about his present relationship. Is it just not the same? Not the same intensity as what he had with Jennifer?

We previously chose that the girl he's now living with was a friend of theirs in high school. We don't have to stick with that choice just because we previously made that decision. She could be anyone. It might be interesting to leave that decision for later discovery during Emotion with Detail. But the behavior does indicate and reiterate his learned behavior of being the guy who comforts people in need.

How of Behavior: When he expresses his concern → he seems to become emotional and seeks to hide it from her.

WHY?

Perhaps he doesn't want her to know how he feels? Or somewhere in the past, he was berated for showing his true emotions?

An interesting choice might be that showing his feelings is a difficult thing for him. That's often a learned behavior from childhood. Maybe there was a significant event with his dad in which he expressed his true feelings and his dad berated him for it. How about:

CORE KNOWLEDGE point: **As a very small child, Jonathan had an attachment to his special blanket, and his dad berated him for it.**

That's something that popped into my head. We can keep it or lose it later. Doesn't matter.

How of Behavior: When Jennifer presumes to understand his feelings for Grandpa → he seems to correct her and freely express his feelings for Grandpa.

WHY?

I think he had a deep, deep respect for Grandpa.

I think we'll discover many reasons why he respected Grandpa so much. Maybe Grandpa taught him many things, was there for him emotionally, listened to him, was patient and kind to him, etc. All these things are wonderful and will support our building of Jonathan's life. Most of these things will be discovered in the Emotion with Details that you do. Do these things bring up one particular, emotionally pertinent or impactful *event* in Jonathan's life that would be considered a Core Knowledge point? Maybe. Maybe not. If you can think of one, by all means include it.

How of Behavior: When Jennifer speaks about Grandpa's feelings for Jonathan → he seems to cut her off and is unwilling to go further with the conversation.

WHY?

Remembering is painful? Is it hard for him to hear this and reconcile that, with

Grandpa's encouragement, Jennifer left town?

If I let my imagination fly a little here, and we decide to stick with the Core Knowledge points we've already established, a strong choice might be to decide that after Grandpa learned of the pregnancy, Jonathan and Grandpa had a falling out. This would be particularly hurtful to Jonathan, given the amount of respect he had for Grandpa.

So the CORE KNOWLEDGE point might be: **Jonathan and Grandpa had a falling out when Grandpa learned of the pregnancy.**

How of Behavior: When Jennifer continues to speak of Grandpa's thoughts about their relationship → he seems to cut her off again and asks not to talk about the relationship between the two of them.

WHY?

Was it really painful to have lost him? What happened to Jonathan and Grandpa's relationship after their break up?

I think this supports our Core Knowledge point from before.

How of Behavior: When Jennifer gives in to him and apologizes → he seems to want to leave and then changes his mind.

WHY?

Is he getting up the nerve to say something? Has he always had trouble speaking his mind or his true feelings? Is this a learned behavior, or is this circumstantial? Both?

This speaks to our previous thought that there was no closure in the relationship. And it reiterates our thoughts that he was likely often berated for expressing his true emotions.

How of Behavior: When he chooses to finally speak his mind → he seems to reluctantly admit that he wasn't enough to make her happy.

WHY?

Jonathan is admitting what he perceives to be his shortcomings. Especially as they relate to Jennifer. Is he always like that? Has he felt like he was "less than" many times?

I believe he probably has on many occasions, going far back in his childhood.

A possible CORE KNOWLEDGE point that just popped into my head might be: **Jonathan tried out for Little League as a kid, but his dad never practiced with him or refused to cough up the money for uniforms and equipment. Jonathan didn't make the team.**

Another non-specific but helpful thought for your "Notes and Ideas" section might be: Jonathan never went out for sports in high school, because he had an after-school job to help his mom make ends meet. People didn't think he was good enough for Jennifer and let him know that.

How of Behavior: When Jennifer exclaims that he did make her happy → he seems to refute this - adding that her leaving was the right thing to do, admitting that Grandpa could see what he couldn't.

WHY?

Is it that he doesn't believe in himself?

I think this speaks to the Core Knowledge points we just made. I'm sure there are many you could find that point to his lack of self-esteem.

How of Behavior: When Jennifer speaks and then hesitates → he seems to let her off the hook, express his respect for Grandpa, and express the disrespect he has for himself.

WHY?

Is it because he really disrespects himself and felt that Grandpa knew more than he did?

Did he not stand up for what he wanted in the past, because he thought he wasn't enough?

There are many thoughts you could come up with. Here are a few suggestions off the top of my head:

Jonathan didn't have many childhood friends come to his house, because he never knew how his father would behave.

There were events with his father that caused him to feel as if he's not enough.

There was intense respect for Grandpa, who likely taught him many things that a father normally would.

Notice I didn't give the above Core Knowledge points a particular timeline in Jonathan's life. These broad types of events or ideas you might come up with may be more powerful if they are discovered in the Emotion with Detail step. I may choose not to use them at all. But I will make note of them in my "Notes and Ideas" section in case I would like to use them. Again, be willing to stay fluid. Be willing to change your mind.

How of Behavior: When he admits that he doesn't respect himself → he leaves quickly.

WHY?

He seems to beat himself up a bit for not fighting for her or expressing his wishes concerning her when they were in the relationship. Does he respect himself more now that he's older?

All great questions to keep in mind. Many Core Knowledge points we've already discerned fit right in. If more occur to you, then by all means, write them down.

Whether you prefer to use the Intuitive approach or the Linear approach to discerning Core Knowledge, let your imagination flow freely.

Trust your gut. From what we've discussed so far, and remembering that it's best to keep it a bit loose by making jogger notes (brief notes that jog your memory), our Core Knowledge might look something like this:

CORE KNOWLEDGE:

- **Preschool/Kindergarten. Lower to lower-middle income household. Dad's drinking is prevalent. Dad berates Jonathan for attachment to blanket? Mother is fearful.**
- **First grade. Shy? Fearful? Doesn't want to say the wrong thing, because he's learned that when you do, you might get hit? Possible embarrassing event concerning his father in front of other children.**
- **Third grade. Jonathan mostly keeps to himself. Not many friends. Tried out for Little League and didn't make the team.**
- **Sixth grade. Dad's beatings are more severe, drinking is worse. Jonathan stays out of the house frequently to avoid the abuse.**
- **Sixth - eighth grade. Grandpa takes Jonathan under his wing. Teaches him much about life.**
- **Freshman year high school. Relationship with Jennifer turns from best friends into romance.**
- **Sophomore year high school. Relationship with Jennifer is getting more and more serious. Much of Jonathan's time is spent at her house with Grandpa.**
- **Jonathan gets a job at the gas station at sixteen years old.**
- **Senior year of high school. Plans to ask Jennifer to marry him. Finds out she's pregnant.**
- **Ecstatic about the news. Grandpa flips out. Encourages Jennifer to leave this town, get an education and follow her dreams (or his). Relationship ends, but with no closure.**
- **Father dies, and Jonathan must help his mother out financially. Works double time at the station to make ends meet. (A Core Knowledge point that occurred to me in the moment and fits quite nicely.)**

- **Now has the job of head mechanic at the gas station. In a relationship with a girl he also knew in high school. She has a child (two years old) from a previous relationship. Struggles to pay bills.**
- **Scene at hand: Seeing Jennifer for the first time in five years. Grandpa has just died.**

I will also want to keep in mind those things that I included in my "Notes and Ideas" section, which might look something like this:

NOTES AND IDEAS

(things to keep in mind that haven't been assigned a specific timeline)

- Fidgeting. When did that first occur?
- Feels the need to comfort people.
- He was often berated for expressing his true feelings.
- Feels as if he is "less than."
- Didn't have many childhood friends come to his house.
- Father had unpredictable behavior and frequent outbursts.
- Often emotionally beats himself up.
- Jennifer was the one in charge?
- Jennifer was popular in high school.
- People didn't think he was good enough for Jennifer and let him know it.
- Playful banter was part of their relationship.
- Grandpa was there for him emotionally, listened to him, was patient and kind and taught him things much like a caring father would.

All this we created from observing Jonathan's Hows of Behavior. We built his Core Knowledge by asking *why* each behavior exists and answering it with an *emotional reason.*

You'll find that a bit of knowledge about the developmental stages in life will be invaluable to your character development. There are many theories on this subject, but the one that I use on a regular basis was developed by Erik Erikson (1902-1994), a German-born American psychoanalyst. His ideas of stages of development are as listed below.

1. Infant - Basic Trust vs. Mistrust (Hope)
2. Toddler - Autonomy vs. Shame (Will)
3. Preschooler - Initiative vs. Guilt (Purpose)
4. School-Age Child - Industry vs. Inferiority (Competence)
5. Adolescent - Identity vs. Role Confusion (Fidelity)
6. Young Adult - Intimacy vs. Isolation (Love)
7. Middle-aged Adult - Generativity vs. Self-absorption (Care)
8. Older Adult - Integrity vs. Despair (Wisdom)

The brilliant Dr. Peter Desberg, clinical psychologist and professor at the University of Southern California, expounds upon Erikson's theory below. These are Peter's exact and much appreciated words:

ERIK ERIKSON'S DEVELOPMENTAL THEORY

When you're considering Base Human Emotions and Emotion with Detail (explained in detail in the upcoming chapters) I think you'll find it helpful to understand a little about the stages of development that people go through. I'm drawn to the work of Erik Erikson whose model of human development will give you a good foundation on which to frame your growth-related analysis.

Erikson's own development provides an interesting example of why he was so interested in the process of identification. Erikson was conceived during an extramarital affair. All he knew of his biological father was that he was of Danish extraction. His mother became a nurse and eventually remarried, when Erikson was three years old.

He was adopted by his new father, but found himself in the awkward role of adopted stepson alongside his three half-sisters who were much closer to his new father. Throughout his adolescence, Erikson thought of himself as an outsider, in school, his local community and even within his family. He was teased at school for being Jewish, and at synagogue for being a tall Nordic blond.

His developmental theory is stated in a series of conflicts that must be resolved before entering the next stage. When people are obstructed in the healthy resolution of early developmental conflicts they have a difficult time with the crises they encounter later as adults. Each stage rests on the one before it forming a pyramid. As you examine Base Human Emotions of a character, understanding how a character may have gone through each stage of development will be a big help in fleshing out his or her current issues. Interacting with a drunk father at three, nine or fourteen years of age would have a different effect on a child trying to make sense of the world.

What follows is a short summary of each stage. Erikson presented each stage as a conflict that has be resolved to move forward. The way it is resolved determines largely how the next stage will be dealt with.

Stage 1 - Infancy (birth to 18 mos.) - Basic Trust vs. Mistrust

This stage has a lot to do with how a child's sense of hope will develop. The most obvious issue during this stage is the nurturing a child receives from his parents. Is he fed regularly or left to go hungry for long periods of time? Is he changed regularly or forced to endure fouled diapers for long periods of time? Does he receive enough visual contact and touch? If the answer to these questions is positive then he will develop optimism, trust, confidence, and security. If not, he may develop insecurity, and become mistrustful of those around him throughout life.

You may think that it's obvious that parents who meet every need and produce heaps of trust would produce the best-adjusted kids, but not so fast. Erikson points out that if every need is always met and life is too peachy, the child may grow up to be too trusting and end up gullible or Pollyannaish. Although it's better to develop basic trust, a little variability is healthy.

2. Toddler/ Early Childhood Years (18 Months to 3 Years) - Autonomy vs. Shame

You're sitting in a chair, go to stand up and a big, burly guy pushes you back down, not permitting you to get up when you want to. First, since this has never happened to you before, you'd be wondering, "What the hell is going on?" This is what happens to each child, only it happens before age two so it's a bit confusing.

As a very young child you are introduced to the world of socialization. You are no longer able to do what you want, when you want to do it. Until then, things were pretty good. If you wanted to scream, you did. If you wanted to poop, you did. All of a sudden, you begin hearing the word "NO." Everybody is telling you what to do and you're finding out that life has rules. It's no surprise that at this age kids develop their sense of willfulness. When you think of the "terrible 2s" kids learn to throw the word "NO" right back to you.

If kids are cooperative during this stage, they have the opportunity to build self-esteem and autonomy as they learn new skills and begin to figure out how to tell right from wrong. Children are learning to assert their independence. They begin walking away from their mothers, selecting the toys they want to play with, and choosing what they want to wear.

If this stage goes well, a child becomes sure of herself. She will develop a sense of pride. But when she hears a chorus of yelling, criticism and scolding for each attempt to try something new, the result is more likely to be shame. When this stage goes badly you will notice defiance, tantrums, and stubbornness.

Sorry for including the F word, but Freud talked about toilet training as one of the major issues during this stage. When this issue goes badly, children are vulnerable and feeling shame and low self-esteem. Erikson says it's important for parents to allow their children to explore the limits of their abilities in an encouraging environment. They should be tolerant of failure. When they are not, feelings of shame ensue.

3. Preschooler: (3 to 5 Years) - Initiative vs. Guilt

This is where the child begins to develop a sense of purpose. Kids begin to show the first sense of innovation and creativity here. The key to this stage is that when they succeed, they show initiative and when they're frustrated trying to reach their goals they begin to experience guilt.

Before the age of three, kids talk, but they really don't carry on conversations. But, in the Preschooler stage, they become aware of adults and want to do what they do. Whether they're playing with dolls or toy soldiers or baseball mitts, they try to act out adult scenes. They want to be like adults. It's also the time when they switch from

"NO" to "WHY?"

This is a time of great activity, curiosity, enthusiasm and play. They begin to plan activities, make up games, and initiate activities with others. If encouraged, children develop a sense of initiative and feel secure in their ability to lead others and make decisions. When parents interpret their child's curiosity as a form of creativity, they blossom. Especially if they are rewarded for that exploration and inquisitiveness.

If a child asks a lot of questions and his parents treat those questions as trivial or a nuisance, or he becomes frustrated trying to get what he wants, the child can easily be made to feel guilty. This becomes even worse when what he wants is viewed as bad or wrong. If parents interpret this behavior as aggressive or inappropriate and punish them for it, this stage leads to discouragement. They may end up lacking in self-initiative.

To protect their child, over-protective parents try to stop their children's initiative, exploration and curiosity. When the child reacts forcefully, parents may punish the child and restrict his initiatives too much.

This stage is also the time when kids begin playing with peers and begin to develop their interpersonal skills. They begin to ask many questions as the thirst for knowledge grows. If parents treat the child's questions as trivial, a nuisance or embarrassing, the child may have feelings of guilt for "being a nuisance."

Too much guilt can make the child slow to interact with others and may inhibit their creativity. Some guilt is necessary; otherwise the child would not know how to exercise self-control or have a conscience. Once again, moderation is key.

4. School Age Child: (6 to 12 Years) - Industry vs. Inferiority

Until this stage, most of a child's world revolved around the home. Now a huge event happens. The child goes to school and meets his peer group. During these next few years he finds out how he stacks up in comparison. How far can he throw a baseball, how good is he at math, how popular is he? He finds out several *thousand* ways that he compares and discovers how competent he is. Can he draw? Play music? Does he have a gift for sports? Is he a brain at school? Can he act? This is when children discover the hand they were dealt in life.

During this stage kids figure out if they are superior, equal or inferior compared to their peers. A sense of competence and self-esteem are developed at this stage that will last a lifetime. The child's peer group becomes significant and largely determines his sense of self-esteem. The role of parents begins to significantly diminish.

The child now feels the need to win approval by demonstrating the competencies valued by both peers and the culture he finds himself in. There is a sense of pride in accomplishments and inferiority in failures.

5. Adolescent: (12 to 18 Years) - Identity vs. Role Confusion

In the fifth stage the child figures out which lunch table she will sit at in school. Does she fit in with artistic students, jocks, popular kids, science nerds, misfits or druggies? Her identity is forming here.

This is where adolescents search for a sense of self and personal identity. This is where they develop a sense of personal ethics and begin concretizing their beliefs. In this time of adolescence kids begin the transition from childhood to adulthood. They become more independent, and begin to look toward their future. Will they go on in their studies or look for a job? Will they live at home or move out on their own? This is where she decides where she fits in.

This is the time to re-examine her identity and try to find out exactly who she is. It is during this stage that her body image changes.

This is also when she explores life possibilities and begins to form her own identity. Failure to establish a sense of identity within society ("I don't know what I want to be when I grow up") can lead to role confusion. Role confusion involves not being sure about yourself or your place in society.

Adolescents begin to experiment with different lifestyles (e.g. work, education or political activities). In the previous stage, she figured out what her talents, abilities and proclivities were. Now she develops a sense of identity based on what she has discovered about herself.

Difficulty figuring out where you fit in is what Erikson referred to as Role Confusion. This can be even worse if you feel people pressuring you to an identity that doesn't feel right. It can be pressure to go to school, go into a family business or being discouraged from pursuing a dream. Adolescents can end up feeling a sense of rebellion and form a sense of negative identity, and feeling of unhappiness.

6. Young adult: (18 to 35) - Intimacy and Solidarity vs. Isolation

At this young adult stage, people have two great concerns: relationships and work. They are beginning their careers, or at least begin working. Career choices have a great influence on which social circles they move within. Young adults are looking for greater intimacy and more satisfying relationships. If such relationships are not found they may develop a feeling of isolation. Their most significant relationships at this stage are with marital partners and friends.

Occurring in young adulthood they begin to share themselves more intimately with others. They explore relationships leading toward longer-term commitments with someone other than a family member.

Successful completion of this stage can result in happy relationships and a sense of commitment, safety, and care within a relationship. Ultimately, it can lead to feelings of love. On the other hand, avoiding intimacy, fearing commitment and relationships can lead to isolation, loneliness, and sometimes depression.

7. Middle-aged Adult: (35 to 65) - Generativity vs. Self-absorption or Stagnation

Career and family are the most dominant events at this stage. Trying to establish stability leads to what Erikson referred to as "generativity." This is an attempt to produce something that makes a difference to society. Inactivity and meaninglessness are common fears during this stage and may lead to feelings of self-absorption or stagnation.

The ultimate goal during this stage is the attempt to find a sense of purpose or meaning in life. During middle adulthood we establish our careers, settle down within a relationship, begin our own families and develop a sense of being a part of the bigger picture.

By failing to achieve these objectives, we become stagnant and feel unproductive. If stagnation occurs, it can cause set-backs, self-sabotage, and sometimes even attempts to drown out one's problems with addictions.

8. Late Adult: (65 to Death) - Integrity vs. Despair

Erikson believed that much of life points toward the middle adulthood stage and the last stage of life is one of reflection. If they view their life as having been worthwhile, they experience feelings of integrity, contentment and fulfillment. They believe they have lived a meaningful life and made a contribution to society.

Those who do not feel worthwhile may experience a sense of despair viewing themselves as failures. They may fear death as they struggle to find meaning in their lives.

As we grow older and become senior citizens, we tend to slow down our productivity and explore life as a retired person.

Erikson believed that if we see our lives as unproductive, feel guilt about our past, or feel that we didn't accomplish our life goals, we become dissatisfied with life and develop feelings of despair, often leading to depression and hopelessness.

Success in this stage will lead to the virtue of wisdom. Wisdom enables a person to look back on their life with a sense of closure and completeness, and also accept death without fear.

This is such a wonderfully helpful guideline for constructing characters. Now you've already done more work on this character than a great percentage of actors would do. If that's true, then why stop there?

Choose excellence, vow to practice it consistently, and soon excellence becomes habit.

I want to examine Jonathan's life even more closely now and see if I can come up with a Base Human Emotion for Jonathan. That's next. Let's dig in.

A QUICK REMINDER OF CORE KNOWLEDGE:

- **This is the history of the character. Make only "jogger" notes on this. (Quick notes to jog your memory.)**
- **Experiment with either Intuitive or Linear Core Knowledge work.**
- **Intuitive work takes clues from the script - dialogue, actions, events, coupled with the patterns of behavior - and expands upon that to come up with specific events that may have occurred in their life.**
- **Linear work takes the Hows of Behavior and asks the general and broad question WHY? Is he awkward? Unsure of himself? Has he always been this way? What big picture, overall issues are indicated by this behavior?**
- **Begin to create events in the character's history that deal with these issues.**
- **Note the milestones in the character's life until you've developed a basic timeline that brings him to the current moment.**
- **For broad or general revelations, make notes in your "Notes and Ideas" section.**
- **Keep it all brief and loose, not too detailed, and feel free to make changes as you discover new information.**

"Watch your thoughts; they become words. Watch your words; they become actions. Watch your actions; they become habits. Watch your habits; they become character. Watch your character; it becomes your destiny."
~ Frank Outlaw

BASE HUMAN EMOTION

The Base Human Emotion is the overwhelming, overriding emotion – triggered by an event that occurred early in life – that leads the character to interpret and perceive the world in a unique and specific way. The character gained this perspective in childhood, and it has been reinforced by significant events as he or she has aged, thereby shaping his/her approach to the world as a whole. If we were examining the psychology of a real, flesh-and-blood person, we would find a complex series of events that led to his or her worldview. But we're going to simplify slightly here, while staying true to human nature, and start with a single formative experience and the emotion that resulted from it. Remember, this is a tool for creating character.

We look at the Base Human Emotion in terms of FEARS or NEEDS. Here are a few commonly used ones:

Let's look at FEARS first. Some examples are (and this is only a sampling):

- FEAR OF ABANDONMENT
- FEAR OF FAILURE
- FEAR OF NOT BEING GOOD ENOUGH
- FEAR OF BEING ALONE

- FEAR OF INTIMACY
- FEAR OF DISAPPOINTING OTHERS
- FEAR OF BETRAYAL
- FEAR OF MAKING MISTAKES
- FEAR OF NOT BEING HEARD
- FEAR OF BEING INVISIBLE
- FEAR OF NOT BEING RECOGNIZED
- FEAR OF NOT BEING UNDERSTOOD
- FEAR OF ISOLATION
- FEAR OF CONNECTION
- FEAR OF VULNERABILITY
- FEAR OF INSTABILITY
- FEAR OF CONFLICT
- FEAR OF BEING INSIGNIFICANT
- FEAR OF CHAOS
- FEAR OF REJECTION
- FEAR OF SUCCESS
- FEAR OF LOSS
- FEAR OF BEING FORGOTTEN

Conversely, there are the NEED-based BHEs.

- NEED TO NURTURE
- NEED TO BE RIGHT
- NEED TO BE THE BEST
- NEED TO PROTECT
- NEED FOR INTIMACY
- NEED FOR COMPANIONSHIP
- NEED FOR TRUST
- NEED FOR TRUTH
- NEED FOR SUCCESS
- NEED FOR CONNECTION
- NEED FOR APPROVAL
- NEED TO BE VALIDATED
- NEED TO BE UNDERSTOOD
- NEED TO BE RECOGNIZED

- NEED TO BE IMPORTANT
- NEED TO PLEASE
- NEED TO BE SECURE
- NEED TO BE TAKEN CARE OF
- NEED TO BE SEEN
- NEED TO BE HEARD
- NEED TO MEASURE UP
- NEED TO MATTER
- NEED FOR ORDER
- NEED TO BE PERFECT
- NEED TO WIN
- NEED TO BE SAVED
- NEED TO BE ACCEPTED
- NEED TO RESCUE

These are just some examples of limitless possible Base Human Emotions. You'll come up with your own as you do this work.

Look at how similar fears and needs can be. They walk hand in hand with one another. For example:

Fear of failure • (is close to) • Need to be successful.
Fear of not being heard • (is close to) • Need to be heard.
Fear of abandonment • (is close to) • Need for connection.

The list goes on. Not every fear-based character will shy away, and not every need-based character will grasp. Sometimes a behavior can seem to stand in direct opposition to an emotion, which makes for one heck of an interesting character!

Science says that by the time we're around six or seven years old, we have experienced almost every human emotion. Of course, as adults, we look back at some childhood events and resulting emotions and more than often giggle at the absurdity of it all. But those traumas weren't so funny when we were experiencing them at that tender age. At age four, I wept with shoulder-heaving sobs when I discovered I had lost my miniature baby doll in the sand. She had been my responsibility. I loved her. She was gone forever. I had failed. Horribly. Funny now. Not so funny then. It made an impact on me.

So for now, we're looking for an event that Jonathan experienced around age three, four, five, six or seven - very early on - that had a strong enough impact to leave an emotional impression. This emotional impression is what we'll refer to as The Base Human Emotion. When this Base Human Emotion was inspired, Jonathan then made a choice or decision to perceive the world in a certain way. Note that the emotion at hand that Jonathan is experiencing in the scene you're working on now may be different from his Base Human Emotion, but the Base Human Emotion will somewhat color his responses in every situation, including the one he faces in the scene.

These interpretations, perceptions and choices of the child create a domino effect where one thing leads to another. So think of the Base Human Emotion like an emotional thread that runs throughout your character's life. People like to debate whether it was really a choice by the child, something he was taught, or something he experienced because of the action of others. It could be either one or all three. But for the sake of our exploration, what is important is that the Base Human Emotion be identified and incorporated.

In building your characters, I don't want you to use your own memories. We're going to create unique memories specific to your character. But for a millisecond, for the sake of example, let's do look at our own lives. What's the earliest memory you can recall? The first one that pops into your head from an early age until around age seven or so. It doesn't have to be hugely significant. It doesn't have to be outwardly tragic. Sometimes these memories are emotionally heavy and sometimes not. Just the first one that pops into your head. Close your eyes, think about it for a second, and give it a whirl.

Now if you think about it, that memory came in a flash, so to speak. Maybe it came complete with details about where you were in a room, or what you wore, who was there with you, what was said and maybe even what you smelled, tasted or felt.

Now take another minute and think about the emotion surrounding the event. How were you feeling in this situation? Is there something about that feeling or emotion that influences or has an impact on your life today? Does that event from the past have some relevance in your life now? If you said no, think about it again.

The reason you remember this early event in your life - often with specific details - is that you stored it in your memory banks because it had *emotion* surrounding it. If I asked you to remember what happened last August 31st, you probably wouldn't remember. Unless it was your birthday, or it was a day that had some powerful emotional significance to you. We store memories and events in our brains in terms of what we experience with our senses - what we see, touch, hear, smell, taste. These memories are stored, because the event has emotional significance to us at the time. The emotion behind this event is the reason we are able to recall the event in detail and are able to feel the emotion when we remember it.

The method schools of thought ask you to recall your own life events in order to bring up an emotion. I am asking you to do it for the character, so that we see the character on screen and not another version of yourself. You will learn how to create your character's vivid life events and actually begin to feel those emotions unique to that character when you experience Emotion with Detail described later. For now, let's continue looking at the Base Human Emotion.

The events that happen in your own life and your interpretation of those events have made you the unique human being that you are. Your life events and perspectives are different from anyone else's on the planet. The same goes for a character.

Before we get to our character Jonathan, let's talk through an example of how this might play out in a person's life. Let's look at a woman named Joanna. To the world, Joanna is a fun-loving, sharp-witted lady. She is extremely well-educated, engagingly attractive, adored by men, and seems not to have a care in the world. Joanna is very possibly a creative genius - she paints masterfully, writes screenplays effortlessly, plays several musical instruments and has a stunning voice. There isn't a fine wine she hasn't tried. Although she never talks about her past, rumor has it that Joanna was born into a wealthy, blue-blooded family in New York. That seems like a good explanation for all the opportunity she has had, although I know plenty of people who were born into great wealth and squandered it or partied it away. I know a guy who had a full scholarship to Stanford and is now a drug addict and homeless.

The truth about Joanna is that she never knew her father. Nor did her mother. She grew up as Jo Jo and was raised by a single mom in a run-down trailer park in Florida. In her early years, she would tell you, she never owned a single piece of clothing that someone else hadn't owned first. Her shoes never fit. More than once, she and her mother ate out of trashcans.

Did she become successful due to sheer will and determination? Where does that will come from? What makes people tick? What compels one person to excel, to overcome all kinds of adversity, while another stays stuck in abject misery?

The path you choose is the journey you take.

A child's early perception of the world is crucial. The unique interpretation, judgment, or perception of events and circumstances causes the child to respond in a certain way. From that unique outlook, the child makes a choice to *act* upon the world in a certain way. Joanna made her choice.

Joanna remembers the first day of first grade as one of the most horrific of her young life. The other kids made fun of her "too big for her" clothes. One little boy laughed as he told the rest of the class that she smelled stinky. No one wanted to sit near her. No one would have lunch with her. No one played with her.

She was alone and ostracized in school. So she would occupy herself by drawing and sketching. She threw herself into schoolwork and excelled in it. She began to want more, to know more, to fly higher than her classmates so that she would never, ever be made fun of again. And she succeeded. Joanna ended up doing so well in school that she had her pick of the best colleges complete with full scholarships.

She *chose* to act upon the world in a certain way. She chose her path.

The important thing to note, in terms of character, is that events happened in Joanna's early life - she was tormented and ostracized. She perceived these events in a certain way and tailored her approach to life thereafter in response. If Joanna were a character, I would say her Base Human Emotion would be "Fear of Being Less Than" or "Fear of Not Being Enough." It was and is her emotional through-line, as it were. The "Fear of Being Less Than" was the motivating factor to act as she acted and moved her to excel.

In real life, there is a confluence of events and circumstances that causes a person to interpret and perceive the world in a certain way. We are shaped by things such as beliefs, expectations, values, experiences, needs, culture, and the list goes on. But for our purposes of character exploration, we will begin our emotional discovery of Jonathan by determining his Base Human Emotion. To oversimplify: The Base Human Emotion is an emotion caused by an event that leads the character to perceive the world in a certain way. When he perceives the world in a certain way, he then reacts to the world in a certain way.

We call it the Base Human Emotion, because it is at the base of the character. It's not the *only* emotion that the character will experience, of course; every character will experience every emotion that exists – love, hate, anger, joy, etc. But the base is the base is the base.

A character may choose to *overcome* his Base Human Emotion. He may learn how to make the best of it, change it, work through it, work around it, manipulate the world around him to support it, etc. But any of these approaches, because they are all responses to the Base Human Emotion, are outgrowths of it. You can't change history, but you can make new and different life choices.

Joanna does not now, as an adult, behave in a way that would make anyone think she began with the idea of feeling less than. She learned how to deal with the world, to survive and thrive. But you can bet that she will never forget those days in first grade. She can remember sitting in the back of the room on the left side. She can still smell the chalk on the chalkboard. She remembers precisely the colors in the faded red and blue dress she wore that day and the gnarled fingers of the teacher's arthritic hands. The reason she remembers those details is that the event was *emotionally charged* for her.

In our lives, we store vivid sensory details of significant events particularly because they are emotionally charged.

In a scene, you'll often find that if a character is particularly provoked or angered or upset, it may have to do with their Base Human Emotion being tweaked in that moment.

For example, it's likely that when Joanne, even as an adult, is in a situation in which she feels "less than" or when she perceives that someone may view her as "less than," she will have a negative inner reaction. She may not outwardly show it, but it's likely that she will feel it.

The interesting thing about Base Human Emotions in characters and in real life relationships is that people will often choose a partner who soothes their Base Human Emotion. In Joanna's case, she might choose someone who makes her feel important, special, valued – anything other than "less than." But if a partner should stop soothing that Base Human Emotion, the relationship often experiences trouble and can even cease to be.

There is no wrong Base Human Emotion. Choose the Base Human Emotion that you feel most resonates with the character. The one that your gut tells you is right. With some characters, the Base Human Emotion seems to fly into your mind. It may glaringly stand out even before you think about your Core Knowledge. This is fine! Let it!

At other times, interestingly enough, you'll start looking at characters, and for a period of time you may find that the same Base Human Emotion will pop up over and over in several different characters. Just let it be. You may be going through a specific phase in your life, and a particular fear or need may speak to you repeatedly. Conversely, there may be Base Human Emotions that never occur to you or never seem appropriate. The whole reason for picking them is that they're from your imagination, from your own gut. So it's important that you don't doubt yourself. Pick one, stick with it and fly. Don't deliberate for hours over it. Don't let yourself get caught up with, "Oh maybe this one's right. No, it's this one. No, I don't know." I know you'll do that in the beginning, but don't let that be a habit. If you can't decide on one versus the other, look to your Core Knowledge for clues. If you still can't decide, pick one and move on.

The Base Human Emotion doesn't necessarily *have* to stem from something really traumatic. Look at the psychological domino effect that can follow even a seemingly innocuous childhood event:

Kevin had just celebrated his sixth birthday. He lived in the same small town where his parents and grandparents grew up. He was particularly close to his grandmother Nana, as she took care of him most afternoons when his mom worked. First grade would begin in several months, and he was excited to begin "big boy school."

Suddenly, life took an exciting new twist. Dad got a new job that would take the family to a new town hours away. Away from friends and relatives. Things would be different now. New town, new neighborhood, new house, new room. Mom wouldn't have to work. During the move, Mom was very organized and left no stone unturned. She talked to Kevin about how much fun it would be in a new house. She took care to warn him that in a larger town he must watch out for "stranger danger." There would be unfamiliar people who might approach him and take him away from her. They might seem like nice, kind men or women. Maybe they would wear suits and look respectable. They might offer him candy or ask his help in finding a lost puppy.

Moving day came and went without incident. Mom was happy to spend more time at home with Kevin. She took him to outings and on all her errands. Everything was new. Even the grocery store was bigger and shinier and full of colorful things he had never seen before. Kevin was securely propped up in the cart seat and had a bird's eye view. What is that strange looking red vegetable that looks like it's wearing a hat? Kevin was too busy staring at it to hear Mom say she had forgotten the ketchup for the hamburgers tonight and was going to pop back over to the other aisle to fetch it.

He looked up. Where did she go? She left? Where is Mom?! The stranger was smiling at him. He was a tall man, wearing a suit and walking towards the cart. This strange man put his hand in his pocket and pulled out a piece of wrapped candy. Just feet away now, he stretches his arm out to offer it to Kevin.

The ear-piercing shrieks of terror that filled the store brought Mom running back to the cart. Kevin was inconsolable. The fear of being abandoned and taken away by a stranger was too much. Even Mom explaining that the man was the store manager was of little help in calming him down.

The next day, Mom thought, would be better. There was a birthday party next door that Kevin had been invited to. The young boy was exactly Kevin's age, so it would be great for Kevin to meet new friends in the neighborhood.

For some reason unknown to Mom, Kevin did not want to go. After much coercion, she walked him, hand-in-hand, next door. The party was already in full swing. Every parent there had dropped their kids off and planned to come back at 4:00. As Mom tried to leave, Kevin clung to her leg in a death grip. He was terrified at the thought of her going. It was just yesterday that she had "left" him in the grocery store, and a stranger had almost taken him! The other children stopped their playing to watch the spectacle. Kevin was in full wail now. Mamma's boy! Sissy! The name calling from the other kids only made matters worse. Try as she might, Mom could not get Kevin to stay at that party without her.

The Base Human Emotion of "Fear of Abandonment" had set in.

School would start in a few weeks. Kevin had by this time made a few friends and felt much better, since they had always come to his house to play. School might actually be fun, he thought. Until he arrived. His class included most of the kids that had been at that awful birthday party. Upon seeing Kevin, the name-calling started again. Oh, there's the cry baby! There he is! Nobody talk to him or you'll make him cry! The taunting and the ostracism was unbearable.

Here is where a child will make a choice. He will choose a *behavior* in order to cope with the situation and his emotions. Will he choose to stay away from those awful bullies and bury his head in the books so that at least the teacher will like him? Or will he choose to be the class cut-up so the other kids will accept him? Choosing a behavior determines a path. One of these chosen paths could produce a world-class physicist. The other might produce a stand-up comic.

I'm exaggerating, of course, and these are just two choices. The character you build may choose to fight and eventually become a bully himself. There are any number of possibilities. But the point is: Driven by a Base Human Emotion, ***the path you choose is the journey you take.*** Kevin experienced the Base Human Emotion of "Fear of Abandonment." So he believed that if he were to be abandoned, bad things would happen. The stranger might take him away. Abandonment triggered danger, so he would avoid it at all costs. This is the way he *interpreted and perceived* this particular event. The resulting *behavior* was to cling to Mom's legs. That behavior produced the taunting from the other kids. Kevin's emotional reaction to the taunting would cause him to choose a behavior that eased that pain.

EVENT

Grocery Store

INTERPRETATION AND RESULTING EMOTION

Fear of Abandonment

BEHAVIOR

Cling to Mom

Which led to ...

EVENT

Taunting from kids

INTERPRETATION AND RESULTING EMOTION

Feeling rejected

BEHAVIOR

Study/Joke

The resulting behavior is to *study* (bury his head in the books) or *joke* (become the class cut up). Studying would serve to *please* the teacher. Joking would serve to *please* his classmates. Note the domino effect that ensued. While we can see that the initial event - "Fear of Abandonment" - led to a "Fear of being Rejected" and then led to a

"Need to Please," the Base Human Emotion that was the springboard remains the "Fear of Abandonment." *It lies at the base of the character.* Remember this domino effect, as it will come into play in later steps.

Another child in Kevin's situation could have looked at the store manager handing him a piece of candy and thought, "Oh good! Free candy that Mom will never know about!" It's the child's interpretation and perception of the event that counts. As I've said before, that perception or interpretation is influenced by many factors in a child's life.

The Base Human Emotion that jumps out at you for your character will be the correct one. You don't want to waste time sitting there questioning and questioning yourself as to whether the Base Human Emotion you chose does or does not fit - you'll feel it. When it's not a particularly helpful one, it won't feel quite right. Sometimes, after you've completed your first Emotion with Detail, you'll realize that the Base Human Emotion may be slightly different than you had imagined it to be. It will be close to what you first determined, but you may find that the particular words you use to describe it may be slightly different. And that's okay.

There are two potential Base Human Emotions that I advise against: "The Need for Love" and "The Need for Power and Control." They may seem powerful, but they aren't specific enough. Every human being is born with a need for love. It's how you go about getting that love that's interesting. The very universality of a "Need to be Loved" makes it ineffective as a Base Human Emotion choice.

Similarly, the "Need for Power and Control" could mean anything. Power and control over what? Get specific! In your scene at hand, does it appear as if your character needs to control everyone in his office? Could it be because if he doesn't, his employees may make wrong decisions, making him look bad? In this case, he might have a "Fear of Failure," which could domino like this: If he doesn't control his staff, they will perform poorly, then he will be seen as being incompetent; he will have failed, he will not be loved, and ... he will die. It sounds extreme, I know. But it's his fear that causes him to behave in a controlling way. You'll do yourself a service by asking why that need is present in the character, and what happened in his/her childhood to cause it. Control is much more a behavior than an emotion, and power is just the ability to control. There will always be a Base Human Emotion underneath "The Need for Power or Control."

The emotion at hand in a scene is not always the Base Human Emotion. It can be, of course, but there's always the possibility that the emotion you see in the scene is a manifestation of the Base Human Emotion instead. In this example of a controlling boss, remember that the Base Human Emotion occurs because of an event early in childhood. Look to what might have happened to him or her as a child that would have caused this seemingly controlling behavior in the present.

In a screenplay, unless it tells you in detail what the childhood of the character was like, the only clues you have regarding the Base Human Emotion lie in the present. Therefore:

A character's behavior, particularly patterns of behavior, are the best indicators of what the Base Human Emotion might be.

Let's find Jonathan's. Look at the patterns we found: Jonathan seems uncomfortable when it comes to expressing his feelings. He also seems angry that he hasn't spoken up for himself in the past. He only lightens up when it seems to be okay with Jennifer. He apologizes a lot when he thinks he's doing the wrong thing or behaving inappropriately. He doesn't show a lot of respect for himself.

There are several Base Human Emotions that would be appropriate here: Fear of Making a Mistake, Fear of Doing the Wrong Thing, Fear of Disappointing Others, Fear of Not Being Enough. All would work. Look at the Core Knowledge we came up with. Do they all fit? Yep. Let's choose "Fear of Not Being Enough." Why did I choose a fear-based one instead of a need-based one? Simply because my gut says he's fear-based. Good! Let's move on. Remember, if you decide to change your Base Human Emotion at any time, you can!

A QUICK BASE HUMAN EMOTION REMINDER:

- **The Base Human Emotion (BHE) is the overwhelming, overriding emotion (caused by an event in the character's early life) that causes him or her to interpret and perceive the world in a specific and unique way.**

- **The BHE is formed in childhood and reinforced over the course of the character's life.**
- **Read aloud the Hows of Behavior. Look for patterns to emerge.**
- **Consult your Core Knowledge for help.**
- **Assign a BHE in terms of a FEAR or a NEED.**
- **When in doubt, ask which one occurred first.**
- **The "Need for Power or Control" and the "Need for Love" are too broad and vague.**

"Could a greater miracle take place than for us to look through each other's eyes for an instant?"
~ Henry David Thoreau

EMOTION WITH DETAIL

An actor can use initial, gut instincts to be somewhat believable in a role, but the most provocative, compelling and intriguing acting is in the nuanced performance, the unique character we see on screen that surprises us with its reflection of humanity. So far through this process, we've developed an understanding of what makes Jonathan tick. But to carry this through to a powerful performance, it's necessary to now LIVE as the character through Emotion with Detail work.

By the time you've done Emotion with Detail work on Jonathan, you will know how he thinks, what he hungers for, what angers him, what makes him joyful, what his hopes and dreams and desires and wants are. You'll know how he loves, or how he doesn't. And rather than knowing all this information on an intellectual level, you'll know it on a gut level. You'll feel it as Jonathan feels it, not as *you* would feel it.

You will create it using the beautiful right side of the brain, where your imagination lives. When your imagination is in full gear, you are drawing from an infinite well, as it were. When we limit ourselves to our own singular experiences, we draw from a finite and limited well.

Remember that as human beings, we store memory by what we see, touch, hear, smell or taste. We particularly remember an event if it has emotional significance. We do the same thing for a character. *You will live, in detail, in your wildly creative and imaginative right brain, an emotionally pertinent event in the character's life, incorporating all that the character sees, hears, smells, touches or tastes.* That's why we call it Emotion with Detail.

In a nutshell, you will be:

- Closing your eyes for better focus and concentration. In order to temporarily escape from your present circumstances and place yourself in the world of the character, closing your eyes helps your imagination to soar a bit.
- Speak out loud. Voice the character's thoughts or inner monologue. It's helpful to note your emotion at hand - how you're feeling in the moment.
- Speak in the first person. Say "I" instead of "he" or "she."
- *Create events and scenarios, placing yourself - as the character - in this moment and experiencing this event in the present time. Avoid creating the event as if it's a character memory. Instead, you, as the character, are living in this moment, experiencing the event as it unfolds and all the subsequent emotions that arise from it. You're not watching this movie - you're in it.*
- Sometimes it helps to jumpstart your imagination by beginning with a small object that belongs to the character or is pertinent to the character.
- Allow your imagination to create the circumstances surrounding that object.
- Expand the room or locale that the character is presently in.
- Give all that you create an emotional reason to exist. (For example, I'm not just drawing a picture of a horse. I'm drawing a picture of a horse for my little sister. She wants a stuffed one for Christmas, and I know that Mom doesn't have enough money to get it. I'm making it purple because that's my sister's favorite color.)
- Take note of what you see, hear, smell, taste and feel and what emotions you are experiencing at the time.
- Allow one Emotion with Detail to inform the next one. Note the domino effect.
- Do not write these down. You cannot live it and write about it at the same time. I want you to experience it.

Now getting a little deeper with all that ...

The first Emotion with Detail event that you create will be for the purpose of discovering the emotional resonance of the Base Human Emotion. Therefore, it should occur around age three, four, five, six or seven. From there, you will create further events as the character ages, experiencing the ways in which his responses to the world are shaped by the initial Base Human Emotion. As Jonathan grows up, he will change and grow over time. His past experiences influence his choices and thereby alter his future experiences. You'll essentially grow him up to the present day, and in doing so, you'll actually create a whole, human, fully realized character.

No part of Emotion with Detail is written. It's actually important not to write it down. In the time it takes your brain to create it and your hand to write it or your fingers to type it, chances are you are already editing it in some way. It's quite difficult to be living in your imagination in your right brain while at the same time you're engaged in a left-brained, result-oriented task. You can't *live* it and *write* it at the same time. If you are doing Emotion with Detail effectively, you'll find no need to write it down. There are actors who are able to recall Emotion with Details that they created a decade ago. When you create them for your character, you readily remember them as easily as you recall your own memories.

Is this dangerous, you ask? To create and live through tragic events of the character? No. Your brain knows the difference between make believe and reality. As a child, you could easily play pretend and then quickly snap back into reality when your parents required you to. Part of the beauty of using Emotion with Detail to fully grasp and feel specifically what a character feels, is that when you are done, you are able to readily let it go. You don't have to hold on to that emotion. You don't have to let that emotion interfere with your actual life. Consequently, when you are on set or at an audition, you will readily be able to access it again. It will be there when you need it. Think of it as visiting the vibration of the character rather than owning that vibration or emotion.

When you first begin Emotion with Detail, you'll want to close your eyes and speak it out loud. I say this in the beginning. As time goes on and you become quite skilled at it, you'll find your own variations. But for now, for your first ones, close your eyes and speak it out loud. It will ground you, keep you focused and keep your mind from wandering off into thoughts such as what you'll be having for dinner tonight.

You will be speaking the inner monologue – or the innermost thoughts and feelings that the character is experiencing in the moment. And I do mean in the moment. As you create these events, *seek not to watch them from afar as if you're viewing a movie.* You want to avoid thinking of it as if it's a past experience that you are recalling once again. You want to feel it right now. With your imagination, experience it in the moment through the character's eyes and point of view – as it's happening. Truly be in it. I want you to live it. So incorporate, as much as possible, all that you see, feel, taste, smell and hear.

Every human being, at any given time, has all of the senses in play. Touch, taste, sound, sight and smell. But one of these senses might be strongest for you. You may be a more visual person than you are auditory or more tactile than you are visual. Research shows that certain smells can elicit powerful emotional responses. I've found this to be particularly true with some actors who have trouble bringing up the emotion by only seeing and hearing things. We're all wired differently. The more you do Emotion with Detail work, the more aware you will be of which of your senses might be strongest. When you discover it, seek to infuse your Emotion with Details with abundant details of that particular sense.

You'll start by *experiencing* the particular events that caused the formation of the Base Human Emotion. Because you start with the exploration of the Base Human Emotion, you see and experience the character's world through their early childhood eyes. Think about how a young child of that age sees the world. When we're young, we sometimes feel at the mercy of the world. We are told what to eat and when to eat it, what to wear, where to go and what to do, when to sleep and when to wake. The world impacts us. It's only when we get a bit older that we realize that we have the ability to impact the world. So you will begin by seeing what the character's world looks like through young eyes and all that entails.

I don't write the story or plan the *specifics* of the Emotion with Detail event and then try to experience it. I prefer it to be a surprise. So I start with a concept I'd like to explore. For example, I might begin an Emotion with Detail by asking my imagination to explore the concept of what my character feels like and experiences when she's feeling left out. Or I might explore the concept of what my character experiences and feels like in a situation where she feels proud of an accomplishment. And so on. My imagination will lead me to events in which these concepts realize themselves.

It's okay to follow your Core Knowledge as a good guideline. But it is just that - a guide and not your character's bible, so to speak. That's a good reason to keep your Core Knowledge loose - more like a skeletal outline. Don't feel like you need to lock yourself into something. Of course, if an event is mentioned in the script, then you must do an Emotion with Detail on the event (or specific flashes, which I will cover later) in order to be fully invested in what you're saying. In our Jonathan example, this would include Emotion with Details on the Winter Formal, their song, etc. Checking back with your Givens is always a good idea to see if something might have slipped your mind. I'm often surprised at things that I forget.

Know that sometimes when your Emotion with Detail idea is *specifically* planned out (and sometimes that's necessary, because the event is mentioned in the script), you will have the tendency to anticipate the outcome. If so, the emotion that springs up may not be as powerful as you might have hoped. For example, if you're doing an Emotion with Detail about being dumped by a girlfriend/ boyfriend/ partner/spouse, and you plan *in detail* what that event looks like before you experience the actual Emotion with Detail, you'll know *exactly* when the breakup moment is coming. You'll anticipate it, and there's a chance it won't hit you with the same force as it would if it were a surprise. It's far better to simply plan the concept - "I'm going to explore what the end of this relationship feels like" - but leave the *specific details* of the events out until you do your Emotion with Detail of the event. Try surprising yourself. Maybe the breakup doesn't actually happen during this Emotion with Detail. Maybe it happens on the next one.

To begin creating the character's world, start out small and expand. I find it helpful to start out imagining an object that the child is holding in his/her hand. Then my imagination will justify why "I" am holding this object at this particular time. The imagination begins to bloom as I build a scenario around that.

Once the imagination starts to open up, I will place other objects in the room and give them emotional reasons to exist. For example, if I've built that my character has a brother - one that my character doesn't particularly like or is, at the moment, upset with - I might imagine a half-deflated football underneath my bed. I will make it my brother's ball, which I took from his room. It's the ball Dad gave him. He's really proud of it and is upset that it's gone. Dad never takes me out to play ball with him. Even if I am a girl, I wish he'd spend time with me, too. So in essence, I've given that object - the football - an emotional reason to exist.

By giving objects that are pertinent to the character an emotional reason to exist, you will ground your character in their world. You're exploring their world, not your own. So create it anew.

Everything you create will be from your imagination. Because your life is not the same as your character's life, you will want to invent and create the character's world. Therefore, the character's childhood home will be different from your own. Classrooms, house, bedroom, friends, parents and siblings should be different from your own. If you were to use your own childhood events, surroundings, parents and so on, you would be demanding that your mind relive a personal memory. You would be drawing from that finite well of your own personal experience, not the viewpoint and unique experience of the character.

When you first begin Emotion with Detail, you might find yourself picturing things or places from your own life. This is common. But it's the character's world we want to live in. So when you find yourself back in your childhood home, for instance, simply change some of the physical details. You'll notice lots of elementary schools tend to look similar. If you can't get the picture of your own childhood classroom out of your head, change where the windows are or where the blackboard is. Or create something interesting and pertinent to the character. For example, you could place something on the classroom wall that's meaningful to the character. If you keep picturing your own childhood bedroom, do something like change the color of the bedspread or the light fixture above your head, etc.

If you find yourself picturing a bedroom that looks remarkably like that of one of your childhood friends, should you change it? Not necessarily. But if that friend's bedroom was particularly significant to you growing up, I would consider changing it, because you will begin to have specific, personal emotions relevant to your life as opposed to the character's life.

Don't have your character avoid experiencing things or events, just because you have experienced similar things. As long as it's not the same exact event with the same exact details that occurred in your life, it's perfectly okay. You are inventing this character through *your* eyes and *your* imagination. Simply create a different world in which they experience it. Anything your imagination invents is going to be informed by something that you have seen at some time or another, whether from a book, online, a movie, a video, etc.

We all have things in common, right? We all have a reference point of what "mother" feels like - or at least what a parent or care-giver feels like when you are a child. It's how that person is making you feel that's important. When I'm creating a character, I will want the character to, of course, have a mother that looks, and, I'm sure, acts like someone *other* than my actual mother. The character's mother may have similar emotional qualities to my own mother, and that's okay. What's important is that I understand and feel the *essence* of this character's mother. With any relationship that the character has with other people, it's okay to feel the essence of that person and work on knowing how these other people make *my* character feel.

Now hopefully, your own mother has never been in Jonathan's particular situation with an abusive, alcoholic husband in the home. If she has not been in this situation, if you try to imagine that your own mother is being abused, your brain will instantly tell you that it isn't true. This is the trouble I have with using "as if" exercises. ("As if" this is happening in my personal life to someone I love.) Your brain automatically creates an experiential distance, because you're creating a situation that muddles reality (my own mother) with make believe (she's being abused). I've used it in the past and found it to be either profoundly painful or confusing, at best. If your own mother *has* been in this particular circumstance, your brain will try very hard not to go there, because it knows the pain that is about to come.

In the feature film *Arrival*, Amy Adams plays Dr. Louise Banks, a linguist who has been hired by the military to find out why twelve alien space crafts have arrived on our planet. What do they want from us? (If you haven't seen the film – spoiler alert coming!) In brief scenes throughout the film, we follow Louise's relationship with her young daughter until Hannah dies of an incurable disease. In real life, Amy is the mom of a beautiful daughter. Rather than using "as if my own daughter had died," Amy created a most compelling and powerful performance through Emotion with Detail combined with Flashes. She created her character's daughter Hannah – her life and their life together as a family – from birth until her painful death. If you've seen the film, go back and watch it again. You'll see subtle, masterful and beautiful moments. By using Emotion with Detail rather than her own life events, Amy can walk off the set and have a full and happy life. I think it's safe to say that Amy certainly moves an audience with her work.

In creating my character's parents, siblings, friends and others, I never actually put a face to these people. I might create what their hands or hair look like, what they might be wearing, the smell of my mother's perfume, the texture of my father's shirt – things that inform me in some way.

Now there are some actors who absolutely can put a face to the person they are creating in their Emotion with Details, but I find that this trips me up. When I'm on set, and the person I've created looks totally different from the actor playing the role, it throws me a bit. Some actors can do it without a problem. I will create a face for that person in my Emotion with Details only if I absolutely know who has already been cast in the role.

Let's get back to our Jonathan character. The first Emotion with Detail that we always want to do in the beginning is the exploration of events that formed the Base Human Emotion. We've chosen "Fear of Not Being Enough." In order to experience what not being enough feels like, we would have to first experience what feeling good enough is like. Right? When I know what *being enough* feels like, then *not being enough* is painful and uncomfortable - something to be avoided and feared.

You can't know what you've lost, until you know what you've had.

In order to create a moment that made an impression strong enough to actually change your character's outlook, you'll need to start him out feeling one way and then give him a reason to be altered.

See how that would work for both fear-based characters and need-based characters? If I were using "Need to Please," I would first have to investigate what it felt like when I *did not please* my parents or friends or siblings so as to produce the *need* to do it.

So let's think about the Base Human Emotion of "Fear of Not Being Enough." First we will create an event in Jonathan's life in which he felt loved and felt like he was enough - and then let him experience what it feels like to take that feeling away. Review and give it a try.

- Close your eyes for better focus and concentration.
- Speak out loud. Voice the character's thoughts or inner monologue. It's helpful to note your emotion at hand - how you're feeling in the moment.
- Speak in the first person. Say "I" instead of "he" or "she."
- Rather than creating these events or scenarios as if your character is remembering them from the past, place yourself in the moment. Experience them in the present, as if it's happening now. You're not watching this movie - you're in it.
- It's sometimes helpful to begin with a small object that belongs to the character or is pertinent to the character.
- Allow your imagination to create the circumstances surrounding that object.
- Expand the room or locale that the character is presently in.
- Give all that you create an emotional reason to exist. (For example, the coffee table was an amazing find at the flea market. The two of us bought it when we were dead broke, madly in love and first moved in together.)
- Take note of what you see, hear, smell, taste and feel.

- Allow one Emotion with Detail to inform the next one. Note the domino effect.
- Do not write these down. You cannot live it and write about it at the same time. I want you to experience it.

Below is an example of an Emotion with Detail that was recorded by an actor and transcribed. Here the actor is exploring the moments in which Jonathan feels like he is enough. Each ellipsis (or ...) is an actual pause (when the actor was imagining or feeling something not spoken).

It's Saturday afternoon...and I'm sad...I wanted to get a baseball pennant today to put on my wall cuz Mama said I could fix my room up...but Dad said I couldn't get a pennant cuz we don't have any money to spend on stupid stuff like that...I'm in my room right now just sitting on my bed cuz me and Mama don't get to go to the baseball store now...I didn't cry in front of Dad when he told me...I wouldn't dare...he would have spanked me...but Mama knew I felt like it.

There's an old tree right outside my window...it's the monster tree cuz it looks like a monster...there's a little bird on it just pecking and pecking at something...he's all alone...kinda like me...I wish I could go over to Jack's house...He has so many baseball posters and pennants and baseball cards everywhere...He has the perfect room...My room is just boring...I have a wooden bed...the same bed I've had since I was really little...I have a little white bedspread that has nubbly things on it like you see at a grandma's house...Jack once thought this was my grandma's room...I don't even have a grandma...I wish he had invited me over to play with him today but he invited Matthew over instead cuz I don't have any baseball cards and Matthew has a gazillion of 'em...The walls in my room are white and there's an old painting of fisherman guys...It's not a real painting...my uncle gave it to me before he died...I don't remember him...but Mama still talks about him and cries...she misses him a lot...My floors are wood and I have a little circle rug by my bed for when it gets cold so my feet don't get cold when I get out of bed...I am so, so, so, so bored...

Maybe I'll draw something for Mama...she likes it when I do that...I have a little wooden desk that used to be Mama's when she was little...I like it though...and even though it was a girl's desk it doesn't look like one to me, even if Dad says it does...it's white and has green glass knobs on the drawers...Mama says that if you write down a wish and stick it in the drawer, then it'll come true...I can't write so good yet so Mama helps me...I have one wish in the drawer...Someday both Jack and me are gonna be famous baseball players and even play on the same team!!! His dad plays with him all the time and he's really good...I'm good too but I don't get to play so much... my dad thinks baseball is a stupid game...I wish he liked it and would play with me...but when he gets home at night he's really grumpy...sometimes he gets home really, really late after I'm in bed...anyway...I'm just so sad now...I really, really wanted that pennant...I already told Jack I was getting it too...

"Jonathan!!!!!" Mama's calling me...

"Yes Mama?"

"Come in here, please!"

"Coming, Mama!"

I'm opening my door...Ahhhh...I smell chocolate chip cookies!...yay!... my room opens up to the hallway and the living room is right there...everything's always perfect in the living room...we have a brown couch that's really scratchy if you sit on it in shorts...there is a little wooden coffee table in front of it with magazines on it... always just three and Mama makes them look like a fan...there's a big yellow ashtray on the table that is always, always clean cuz Dad smokes cigarettes but he doesn't like butts in the ashtray so Mama always cleans them out really quick...I smell cookies!...the kitchen is to the right and the closer I get the more I can smell them...I turn the corner and Mama is standing there in her apron...it's white with red and blue flowers on the bottom of it...she's had that apron ever since I can remember... Mama's beautiful...she's so little...sometimes I think she's gonna break...she has really pretty shiny dark hair that she always wears back in a ponytail...her hands are really small and skinny and you can see the veins that pop out...

"Thank you, Mama!"

"I hope you like them. I have another surprise for you too. We can wait for the cookies to cool down and you can see if you like..."

"Sure, Mama, what is it?"

"Look here."

There on the kitchen table is the red felt that Mama uses for Christmas decorations...

"Your dad can't get mad if we make our own pennant, now can he? We don't have to spend any money at all, because I bet we have everything we need right here at home to make one."

"Really? We could do that?"

"Sure. Do you want to start now, or do you want to eat your cookies?"

"Let's do it now! And then we can have our cookies to celebrate!"

Mama unrolls the felt...there's all kinds of other different colors rolled up inside – blue, green, white...

"Hey those are the colors of the pennant I wanted!"

"I know. Now if you'll hold it down on the sides, I'll draw an outline of where to cut."

I'm holding it as tight as I can. Mama has a ruler and draws the lines so neat and perfect...She takes her time...she goes slow...she's so careful...she's done!

"Can we cut it now, Mama?"

"Sure. Go slowly, now."

This time she's holding it tight for me so I can cut straight. This is really hard...maybe I should use two hands...It's almost cut out...I'm so so excited! I get to have a real pennant!

"Good job, Jonathan! Couldn't have done better myself! Look how straight and beautiful!"

We cut out all the other stuff that goes on the pennant...now we get to glue it...I dot the glue on the backside of each piece...not too much cuz it'll run out the sides...

"Wow! Look, Mama, it's a real pennant!" I am so happy...and I love Mama so much...she's the best mama anybody in the whole world could ever have...

"Can we hang it on my wall today?"

"I don't see why not." I love Mama's smile.

"Are you crying, Mama?"

"No, baby, these are tears of joy. It makes me happy to see you happy. Should we dig into those cookies?"

This actor started out with an emotion and was simply sitting in the bed. He did not start with a single object. Is this okay? Of course! Starting with an object is only a suggestion that I find helpful. I don't even have to relate it, in the beginning, to anything. The object could be a pencil, a book, or a shoe – anything! If you do choose to start with an object, simply justify why you are holding it or looking at it, and let your imagination fly. Different actors start with different things. I know a very accomplished actress who always begins with the character's feet. She says it makes her feel grounded! Good. Whatever works for you. I also liked the way this Emotion with Detail incorporated inner monologue thoughts in the moment. There's even a smell in there!

Did you notice that there are moments when this actor mentioned things that were not exactly in the moment but were past remembrances? Sometimes, that's necessary in order to set a situation up. In creating the world, we may need to include helpful flashbacks in order to fully realize the importance or significance of certain objects or scenarios. An example would be when the actor said, "...I wanted to get a baseball pennant today to put on my wall cuz Mama said I could fix my room up...but Dad said I couldn't get a pennant cuz we don't have any money to spend on stupid stuff like that..." He's talking about what Mom said in the past and Dad's subsequent reaction to it. That's very helpful and doesn't take us out of the moment at all. This is also what Jonathan is thinking in the moment. The point is, you will want to set up your world. In doing so, you may want to flash back to events or instances that help explain or justify or give emotional resonance to objects or situations.

In this Emotion with Detail that we just heard (read), we have a nice bonding moment between Jonathan and his mother. The actor has done a good job of starting out small with lots of details in the bedroom and giving Jonathan an emotional reason to be there. He was there out of boredom and sadness, because he couldn't get the pennant today. It seems the idea of baseball popped up in the moment. Good! Because later you can take that dream away from him to further reinforce "The Fear of Not Being Enough."

Would it be wrong to avoid using the baseball reference if you also loved and played baseball as a kid? NO! It's a natural reference point. Just avoid using your personal childhood baseball coach, the exact visual of the ball field you played in, the exact uniform you wore as a child, etc. Create for your character fresh, new and imaginative details that are not *exact copies* of the details from your personal life experiences. In many, or most, of the characters you play you'll discover that you share common ground with them. If you were a dancer in real life, could you not play a dancer? Of course, you can! You can't pretend you don't know anything about dancing! That's ridiculous.

Choose to invent and create details that are not exact copies of your own personal experience.

Now the bond with Mother and Jonathan is established, and the world that Jonathan lives in has been created. He feels that he's enough. Now rip that feeling away. The actor continues:

I'm in my bed...It's so cold tonight...My dad took away my blanket last week because he says that I treat it like a blanky and until I stop I can't have it back. It's blue and soft and cozy...I miss it so much...All I have is this scratchy sheet. It smells funny like that Clorox stuff Mama washes white things in...I won't tell her though cuz it'd hurt her feelings...

I'm glad I have my warmest pajamas though...Mama got them for me for my birthday. They're really, really soft. They're my favorite because they have baseball stuff on them...My pennant looks beautiful on the wall...It's hanging right at the foot of my bed...I'm happy that my bedtime came before Dad got home...that meant I got to have a story...she read my favorite book "Casey at the Bat"...if Dad's home he sometimes wants her to be with him and she can't read to me...

Mama's always different when he comes home. She gets really quiet. She tells me to be quiet a lot too when he's home in case I do something wrong and it makes him mad. He's scary when he's mad.

Anyway, I'm glad I'm in my room right now...but I'm so cold without my blanket...My room feels really still...I'm getting kinda scared...I wish I was already asleep...the wind is blowing outside...that's when the monsters come! The monsters on the ceiling! Mama says that when the wind blows, the streetlight from outside shines through the trees and makes scary shapes on the ceiling. That's what Mama says...that it's just the streetlight. My cousin told me once that that's not really true, that it really is monsters on the ceiling and that they'll just wait for me to fall asleep and then get me and that Mama just said that so I wouldn't be a scaredy cat...Ahhh! There's its arms! AHHHHH!! The overhead light comes on...

"What, Jonathan?! What?! Are you alright?"

"The monsters are back Mama! Look!"

"Sweetheart, that's just the streetlight showing through the trees. There's no such thing as monsters, pumpkin."

She comes over to my bed and sits down with me...she's holding me...I feel safe and good now...I love the way she smells at night when she washes her face and puts that stuff on...

"Good gracious, sweetie, you're shivering to death. Let me get your blanket."

"No, Mama. Dad will get so mad."

"I'll take it off of you before he gets home. Let's just warm you up for now."

"Thank you, Mama. I love you."

"I love you too, honey. Would it help if I read 'Casey at the Bat' one more time?"

"Oh, please, Mama, please. Thank you!"

She's opening the closet and reaching way high up to get my blanket... She's going to my desk and she gets the book...she's covering me up and tucking the blanket in all around my body with an extra tight tuck at my feet...she lays down with me...My head is on her chest...I'm safe now...safe from monsters...

She's reading...I'm not listening, I just like the sound of her voice...I'm so warm...and comfortable...and safe...

There's silence...

"What's wrong, Mama?"

She's just staring straight ahead. She looks really scared!

"What's wrong Mama!"

She whispers, like she's really scared, "Shush, baby. Quiet..."

I hear the front door open. We are both frozen...I hear keys thrown down on the coffee table...It's Dad...I look at Mama...she's just staring straight ahead like she's frozen...

"MARIA!! MAAARRIIIIIA! WHERE THE HELL ARE YOU NOW?!!

"What do we do, Mama?"

"Just stay still 'til we hear him go into the kitchen. Then I'll put your blanket back in the closet. Just stay as quiet as you can."

We are so still...I'm afraid to breathe...

"Stay still."

...I can feel my heart...Something falls in the living room...something is crashing and breaking into pieces...Dad screams a cuss word...He's yelling things that don't make sense...Please Dad...please go into the kitchen...What is wrong with him? He seems so mad and we haven't even done anything yet...

BLAM! My door crashes open...Dad falls into the room...Mama is in front of me in the bed...Dad stumbles again...what is wrong with him? His face is all red and sweaty and he can't stand up...He's looking at us...his mouth is hanging open and drool is coming out of it...his eyes are so red...

"WHAT THE HELL MARIA?!"

Mom is trying to ball up the blanket and hide it...Oh no...Dad peeks around her and sees it!...

'WHAT THE HELL DID I TELL YOU! HUH?! WHAT THE HELL DID I TELL YOU BOTH?! YOU WANT TO MAKE A PUSSY OUT OF THIS BOY!? HUH? HUH? ANSWER ME WHEN I TALK TO YOU!"

He's right in her face...Spit flies out of his mouth...he is spitting in her face as he screams...

He hits her so hard blood flies out of her mouth...

"Mama! Mama! Please don't hurt her..."

Dad stumbles back...wipes his face with the back of his hand...he's stumbling everywhere...he knocks over my desk chair and falls into the wall... he stops a minute and looks at my pennant on the wall...he's just standing there staring...but almost falling over...he looks over his shoulder to us...and screams...

"WHAT THE HEEELLLL DID I TELL YOU?!!!!!"

He rips my pennant off the wall and tears it...he runs over to Mama and jerks her up by the arm...he's dragging her out of the room...shoving her...pushing her...slapping the back of her head...he shoves her to the front door...takes his foot to her back and kicks her outside...he turns to look at me...I run to Mama...he slams the door behind us...

It's so cold out here...Mama puts her arm around me...

"Come on honey...Let's go...quick now..."

We run down the sidewalk...we're getting in the back seat of the car...

"Why can't we just leave Mama?"

"I don't have the keys, honey. Just stay down low...We'll just stay here for a while..."

She watches the house...She holds me tight...She's shaking...her left eye is swollen shut...her right one barely open and purple all around...my sweet mama...If I had been strong enough...she wouldn't be hurt right now...

If I were brave enough to be in the dark by myself she wouldn't have come in and given me that stupid blanket...

Now let's suppose that you've completed this Emotion with Detail to explore the Base Human Emotion of "Fear of Not Being Enough." After you experienced it, you say to yourself, "Wait a minute. That wasn't 'Fear of Not Being Enough.' That was more along the lines of 'Need to Please'" (or any number of Base Human Emotions that pop up in your mind). Is it wrong? Do you have to redo your Base Human Emotion or redo your Emotion with Detail now? No. What you call it or name it isn't important. What is important is that you now have a springboard, a base from which to grow him up. Call it whatever you like.

You'll notice in the above Emotion with Detail that the actor voiced the other person's dialogue out loud. He finds that speaking it helps to ground him a bit. Some actors only imagine that they hear the other person's voice, finding that voicing it out loud throws them off. Either is fine. Play with it and see which way suits you best.

Every actor is different. I know actors who must be on the floor when they do Emotion with Detail. Some actors find the need to always be active and physically moving the whole time. Whatever suits you best is exactly what you should do. It doesn't matter. I wouldn't walk around with my eyes closed, though.

Here's another alternative to always sitting: As you're out and about in your day, take a minute to drop into the belly of your character, then try to view the world through his or her eyes. If you're in the supermarket checkout line, rather than thinking your own thoughts, try to think the thoughts that your character would think. Have opinions as your character rather than yourself. Before shooting began on *Catch Me if you Can*, Amy Adams put on her prosthetic dental braces, parted her hair down the middle, and in her best Southern accent, trooped out to a department store as her character, Brenda, to shop for, as her character would say, "big girl panties." What fun!

When you first begin Emotion with Detail work, know that you may not feel something miraculous every time. It's okay! You shouldn't expect to. It takes a little time to get used to doing it. Every character is going to feel somewhat different. Some are more difficult than others. Each character has a unique complexity. You'll master it. But only if you put the effort into it. Relearn the beauty and joy of imagination. Rediscover it. The Emotion with Detail part of the technique is an excellent brain trainer.

How long should your Emotion with Details be? It's completely up to you. If you find that a five-minute Emotion with Detail gets you to the emotion you're looking to discover, then fine. You're done with that one. If you find they last longer, then let it be. Some people do twenty-minute ones. Others less. The point is to *feel* something – let an emotion spring up.

Where do you go now that we've completed the Emotion with Detail that establishes the Base Human Emotion? Well, we know that Dad is none too nice. Mom is afraid of him. And you feel like you're not good enough to protect her. Maybe take yourself to first grade now. Maybe you're sitting at your desk in school. See it. Describe it out loud. Then start inventing, creating, imagining. What class is it? What time of day? What does the light look like in the room? Are you hungry? Is the teacher asking you a question? Are you taking a test? Where is your desk located? This would be a good time to give these things an emotional reason to exist. For example, it's not just any desk in the classroom. You're sitting next to a specific bully who's giving you a hard time. People are making fun of you and whispering; maybe even a friend of yours is joining in with that.

What choices do you think Jonathan will make in first grade? Would he be more likely to be withdrawn? Would he retaliate and be a bully? I would say he's a fairly cautious and maybe shy kid, because even as an adult, he seems to be unsure of himself. Put him in first grade as the shy kid and see what happens to him.

This Emotion with Detail will inform the one that follows, and so on and so forth. Refer to your Core Knowledge as a guideline if you want, knowing that it's perfectly fine to veer from it if need be. Keep making incremental movements forward in the character's life. Take care not to skip over huge chunks of the character's life. For example, you don't want to age the character from five to eighteen in a single leap, because there are too many important changes in the intervening years. Those events could very well have an impact on how your character feels and behaves in the present.

The beautifully talented Rachael Taylor, who brings us the character of Trish in Marvel's series *Jessica Jones* has this to share:

> "A lot of the work I do with Warner is creating a very specific back story. VERY specific! The word back story isn't even quite right. The work you do with Warner is as detailed as real human memories. For example, on 'Jessica Jones' we worked on the depth of the friendship between my character, Trish, and the character of Jessica. We built up 'memories' from when Jessica moved in with me as a teenager so there was a sense of deep history there. One of my favorites was a 'flash'; sitting in my mother's kitchen with Jessica as a teenager, eating ice-cream at night. *[A 'flash' being a specific moment within the Emotion with Detail.]* So simple but we really 'lived it' in great detail. As an actor, I was surprised at how many times I returned to that simple flash when shooting! Such a simple little moment between two teenagers, but it gave me access to that deep sense of historical friendship that was so important to the character."

So don't skip the developing years when you're building the character. You'll discover juicy bits that you might use in the most unexpected places. In working on that character, neither of us would have realized that the seemingly innocuous childhood moment that Rachael describes would turn out to be such a powerful one.

If you're stuck, try choosing a circumstance in which the Base Human emotion will be *challenged* by someone or *soothed* by someone or some event. If Jonathan's Base Human Emotion is "Fear of Not Being Enough," explore a situation in which a specific person causes him to feel as if he is not enough. This person tweaks his Base Human Emotion, so to speak. When your Base Human Emotion is poked or tweaked, you'll find yourself being particularly emotional in that moment. (Seems that family members have a particular knack for knowing what our Base Human Emotion is –

albeit usually on a subconscious level - and finding a way to tweak it or push our buttons.) Or create an event in which somebody *soothes* his feelings of not being enough. It could be a teacher, a friend, Grandpa.

Keep in mind that you are creating a personality over the course of a series of events, just as a human being's personality evolves over the course of his childhood and into adulthood. Note the domino effect that happens. *Therefore, even though he may view the world through the filter and lens of the Base Human Emotion, every Emotion with Detail does not necessarily center around the Base Human Emotion.*

Every Emotion with Detail you do will not be tragic, just as every event in our own lives is not tragic. So be sure to incorporate Jonathan's joys, likes, dislikes, fears, triumphs, hopes and dreams, etc. in order to create a whole person.

This is very important: *Don't command yourself to "feel" something.* Just live in the Emotion with Detail, moment to moment. It's only then that you will feel. Don't try to chase the emotion. Anything you chase flies away. Chase a dog; he runs. Chase a lover; he/she runs. Try to catch a feather falling through the air, and the force of the wind repels it away from you. Keep voicing that inner monologue out loud, and something will occur to you. Get lost in it. See where your imagination takes you. Do not force it, but instead, let it occur to you in the moment.

FLASHES

After you've grown the character up a bit, you'll find that long Emotion with Details won't always be necessary. You'll be able to feel something or come to know something about the character's inner life through the use of Flashes. Flashes are quick moments in time that your character experiences. Why would you not need to do lengthy Emotion with Details? Because you already know the character to a degree. For instance, when you're building Jonathan, and you've done Emotion with Details on meeting Grandpa when you were younger

– being in Jennifer's house, spending time in the sanctuary – you already have the experience of what all that feels like. You wouldn't need to go back over the minute details of the house, the sanctuary, Grandpa or Jennifer. It's all familiar to you. Place yourself in a space that's familiar, then create and live through a quick moment in which something impacted you. It doesn't have to be a major event, and it doesn't have to take a great deal of time. It could be something like this:

It's my fourteenth birthday. Jen And Grandpa are making me wait in here (Grandpa's sanctuary). They told me to keep my eyes closed! It's really cold out here. Should've brought my jacket with me.

I hear them at the door. Jennifer's giggling. She and Grandpa are whispering and giggling! The doorknob must be stuck. Rattle...rattle...whispers...giggles...BAM! The door flies open. Jennifer flies in! No! She trips! She's gonna fling the cake in the air! I catch her – and the cake – at the last minute. She's got chocolate frosting all over her face. God, I love her.

"It's awful Jonathan. Just turned out awful!" She giggles.

"Oh, yeah? How awful could it be? And it's my favorite!" She giggles more. Grandpa turns his face away, his shoulders heaving in silent laughter.

"Oh, it is. Just trust me. I'm really sorry. I really...(laughing)...really... tried..."

I stick my finger in it. Taste it. "No, it's...it's..."

"No! Don't lie! Liar!" She giggles and throws some frosting at me.

"Oh, you didn't! No, you didn't!" I smear some on her cheek. She chases me now. Grandpa says, "Not in here, you two! Take it outside!"

I run outside, and she chases. It's on! It's a full-on food fight!

See? That's a sweet little moment or *Flash* that strengthens their relationship. Nice.

Flashes are great for creating quick memories of events when time constraints might not have allowed you the luxury of creating complete Emotion with Details. Ryan Reynolds's stunning performance in the feature film *Buried*, directed by Rodrigo Cortes, is a great example of how effective quick Flashes can be. In this film, Ryan's character is an American contractor working in Iraq when he is taken hostage by insurgents and buried alive in a coffin. The hostage-takers have placed a lighter, a knife, a flashlight and a cell phone in the coffin with him. The cell phone is there so the hostage-takers are able to speak with him to demand that he call the State Department and secure a rather large amount of ransom money. In his attempts to do so, he also calls various people in his life. At one point of hopelessness, he calls his aging mother, who is now in a nursing home and suffering from Alzheimer's. He knows this will likely be the last time he ever speaks to her. An emotional scene to say the least. We had worked on, and loaded, most of his character's relationships. Because of the time constraints of this particular project, it was necessary to work at lightning pace.

It was a Wednesday morning. We had prepared for the day of shooting the night before, but as is common on set, circumstances change. We walked onto the sound stage that morning to discover that, because the shooting schedule had changed, Ryan would now be shooting the scene in which he would talk to his mother for the last time. The problem was we hadn't had the time to load many significant memories of this mother. Ryan politely asked the director if we could take a few minutes off set. Rodrigo, being the amazing director that he is, said sure.

Because Ryan had done so much of the Emotion with Detail work on his character already, it was quite easy to add specific "mother" events. We fast and furiously loaded "memories" (quick Emotion with Details or Flashes) of Mother. All those moments that she was there for him, the time she rescued him from the tree house, the laughter they shared, the lessons she taught him, the words of encouragement, the times she had his back, times she stood up for him when others didn't. Ryan put twenty minutes to good use. Then he walked on set and laid down some magic. This performance would go on to win him a nomination as Best Actor in a Drama for the Goya Awards, Spain's equivalent of an Oscar.

Flashes can be tremendously helpful when coupled with Emotion with Detail or when you're in a bind. When Amy Adams was shooting *Sunshine Cleaning* with Emily Blunt, the two girls were given a brand-new scene at the last minute, right before they were to shoot it. Amy had a choice - either let that little "hitch-in-the-giddyup" throw her, or simply focus on the task at hand. She chose the latter, and I think it's safe to say, it served her well. She invented a powerful Flash of herself with Emily's character when they were young. The resulting emotion made that scene fly. If you haven't seen the film, check it out.

Use Flashes to fill out, add to or enhance moments in a scene. Below is an account from the fabulous Shiri Appleby, who plays Rachel Goldberg on the series *UnReal*, where she describes using Flashes to flesh out a particular unsavory event in her character's life:

> "The Flashes part of the technique made going to dark places safe, and as an actress who is often asked to go dark, I feel so grateful to have this method in my arsenal. Warner and I have prepared every page of the series *UnReal* together. We know Rachel Goldberg's life thoroughly. And each season, the work we are doing has gotten deeper, because we've flashed so much of her life experience and have a true understanding of why she is the way she is.
>
> During the third season, my character decides to confront her past and knock on her rapist's door. Not exactly heartwarming stuff. When the idea was presented to me, I simply wanted to avoid it and wish the story line away. I made these feelings known to Warner, and she promised me it would be fine, we would do our flashes and build the story out so acting the scene wouldn't cause me any personal pain.
>
> Rachel is a character with a strong "Need to Connect," because she was raised by a psychologist mother who kept her love at bay from her daughter. The big emotional trigger and turning

point of Rachel's life was this rape. The story goes that when Rachel admitted to her mother that one of her mother's patients raped her, her mother, fearing for her career, started putting Rachel on antidepressants to numb her of the experience. She never allowed Rachel to feel safe and grieve, and refused to be there to comfort her daughter through it.

Together with Warner, we built out a very specific Flash. It went something like this: I walked upstairs and saw the man in the bathroom. He looked at me and I looked back at him. He had been downstairs talking with my mom, and I was really curious about who he was. When he looked at me, I felt noticed. He looked at me like I was beautiful. I went into my room, and he followed me. He asked me, "Can I make you feel good?" and that's all I've ever wanted to hear my whole life so of course I said yes. He walked in my room and had me lie down."

And the Flash went on and on. I was able to identify at what exact moment the act turned the corner and stopped making Rachel feel comfortable and why. I knew exactly how the man went too far. Initially he had soothed my Base Human Emotion of needing to connect, and then he got abusive when he flipped me over and used me as a pin cushion. I knew how the act ended, how disconnected my body felt lying on the ground and the courage it took to confront my mother. The Flash work helped connect so many dots of Rachel's life and allowed me to feel her pain in a safe way.

By the time it came to shoot the scene, I knew this moment so intimately and exactly how it was going to rattle my emotions. I knew how to control it and what the trigger was to let it all out. This allowed me to be safe in my playing and not walk into the scene fearful. My own life experiences were never going to come into action. There wasn't any way to abuse myself. I walked into shooting confident, because I had done the work and could bring up the emotion by quickly going through my Flash."

Now you might say, "This sounds more like an Emotion with Detail than a Flash." But the amazingly talented Shiri knows the character so very well and has played Rachel for an extended period of time now. She doesn't need to do long Emotion with Details. She's able to accomplish what she needs to in a Flash.

Know that dozens of Emotion with Details aren't always necessary. If you've got the time to do lots of them, then perfect! If you've got less time to prep, do as many as possible. Do, however, seek to do, as extensively as possible, Emotion with Detail on events that are mentioned in the script. In our script here, the Winter Formal would be a particularly important one to explore. Most of all, let go, and let your imagination soar!

Below, you'll find the transcription of actual Emotion with Detail work on Jonathan from wonderful actor Wes McGee. Under normal circumstances, you would certainly do your Emotion with Detail work in private. But Wes was kind enough to share his work with us. I was there to witness and have made a few comments and suggestions. Enjoy!

My name is Jonathan. And I'm, I'm seven. I'm seven years old. And I'm sitting in the far back section of my mom's station wagon. I can feel the rumble of the road shake through my body. And as I hide these – behind the seat.

And I have a really big parka on and it makes a whoosh noise and it rubs up against the seat. And I put my hand up against the seat. When I put my hand up against the seat, it comes back down. It comes back down to make the whoosh noise. My mom's driving up front. She knows I like to play in the back. There's, uh, like a Dolly Parton song playing. And I had already asked her that I – if I could go pee when I was at home earlier.

And I couldn't because she said I already had three layers of clothes on because it's so cold outside and I couldn't get out of my clothes so I'm waiting to get to school to go pee. And I'm playing with, uh, a Gumby. A little green Gumby guy. And he's the only thing – he's smiling at me and I wave his hand at me really slowly. And his arm is bendable and it has sort of a rubbery green skin.

And I can feel the car turning slowly into the, the parking lot of the school because my weight starts shifting towards one side of the station wagon. It's a left-hand turn. So I'm floating to the right a little. I can hear the creak of the, the shocks as it hits the curb to get in. My mom says, "Jon, boy. It's time to go."

I don't really say anything. "Honey, I know you're back there."

"Okay, Mama. I'll get out – can I get out through the, through the back side."

"Yeah, Hun. I'll roll down the window. But be careful. I, I've seen kids fall out of there and hit their head."

"I'm tough, right? I'm gonna be tough just like Dad told me to be tough. I'm not a pussy."

"Don't say that word. Don't, don't ever repeat that word at school."

"Yes ma'am. Dad said it though."

"But it doesn't mean you can say it."

Okay. So the glass goes down. Slightly. And the back of the station wagon opens up. And I grab my, my little – my little back-pack that has cookie monster on it. And I put it on. And I close the window.

And I do wanna go give my mom a kiss. But I don't wanna be a wimp. So I close the back gate. [SOUND EFFECT]. I walk to-wards the, the crossing guard. She says, "Hey Jonathan."

"Hey Ms. Darby." She walks me into school. It's snowing out. And then the cold is brisk upon my face. Still have to pee pretty badly. As soon as I get in I'm gonna make sure I get this thing off. But I'm starting to kind of grit my teeth a little bit.

So I walk upstairs. There's about five stairs after I walk down probably twenty feet of concrete. And the building is big and red brick. Two stories tall. It's sort of a 1940s look to it. Sort of the, uh, not really art deco but just very much like brown stony. And I walk up to the big gates.

And then to the door and a big whoosh of hot air hits me because they, they've been heating the – they've been heating the school to make sure everyone's warm and just a loud noise. And kids run around and it kind of smells like – that smell kind of hits me almost in the back of my throat. It's almost [PAUSES] like a smell of construction paper and, and, and cookies. Maybe even cleansing material. Cleansing fluid. And I walk down the hallway really quickly.

And we go into class. And I'm going towards my class. And everyone has to stand in line. For the bathroom because I was gonna try and go in. But the bell rings and I was late. So everyone runs into the – and we start running to our classes because we have to get in there. We don't want to get D-R's or disciplinary referrals because we'll have to go to tell our mom and then the principal and no one wants a spanking because I don't want a spanking. I don't wanna ever get hit again.

So I'm running to the classroom. I start taking off my parka and my – and I take off my [PAUSES] parka. And then, [STAMMERS] and there's like, a sweater I zip down. But I still have, like, three pairs of pants on. So I sit there I see the teacher. And she kind of looks at me because I was running late. And I, I had this feeling of, of embarrassment for running late and I don't want her to be mad at me.

So I throw my book bag up under my desk and sit down. And, uh, she says, let's take out our readers now. Thank you for making it, Jonathan. Some of the kids laugh at me. So, pick up the books and I, and I put it on the desk that has, like, a little pencil holder up top. And, uh, right next to the pencil holder, I've [STAMMERS] etched in a J for my name.

I like this desk. So I gotta take out the book. I can see all my, my friends pulling out their books. But they're not really my friends. It's just people I know. I don't feel very close to them at all. I just – young people that – six and seven years old. First grade. The sound of books slamming onto, to tables and desks. Opening up... opening up the book.

Miss Childers says, "Okay, we're gonna read from the reader today. Page 13." So I flip to page 13. [STAMMERS] Okay. Billy, would you please start. So I hear Billy reading. I really gotta go to the bathroom and it's making me afraid because my cheeks are starting to get red.

I'm gritting my teeth. And I don't wanna say anything to her because I don't want her to see I'm weak. I don't want her to think I'm a pussy. He's reading but I can – I'll hold it for another twenty minutes. I'll be able to go to the bathroom when we're done reading. I can do it. I can hold it in. When he starts reading about the apple, and I'm not really paying attention. Everything's just sort of, like, wah, wah, wah. It has a – almost a Charlie Brown teacher noise because I'm starting to feel so much pain inside. Oh, just hold it. Hold it. My face is hot because I have so much – with all the clothes on. "Jonathan?"

"Yes? Yes, Miss Childers?"

"Will you read out of the book?" I'm afraid to read. I'm not very good at it. My mom won't read to me anymore. I'm so afraid that's – I, I can't. I can't hold it anymore. A warm sensation starts going over the top of my legs. I just wanna cry and run but I'm, I'm cold. And [UNINTELLIGIBLE]. Just stay still on the desk.

"Jonathan, will you please read? What is wrong with you?" I can't – I can't speak. Then there's a loud stream that starts hitting the floor. And I just wanna catch it. But I can't move. "Oh, my God, Jonathan, stand up now." I stand up. And everyone just starts laughing at me. And [SNIFFS] my pants are soaking wet.

And it's warm and it's sticking to the side of my leg that's quickly growing cold. It's – [STAMMERS] "Come up to – come up here right now. What did you do?" I just – I don't – I can't say anything. I can't say anything. I don't want her to get mad at me.

"Go outside now!" And so I'm standing in the hallway. When the door opens up, it has, like, safety glass. It opens up. It creaks open and it slams shut.

And I'm shaking with embarrassment. I never wanna go back in there. I'm not. I'm not a pussy. I'm not.

Here's another at the same age. Notice how Wes states who he is and at what age. That's his particular trigger. He's telling his mind that he's ready to explore.

I'm Jonathan. And I'm seven years old. And I'm walking very slowly out the back of the school. And it's warm outside. It's warm. And there's a ramp that I'm walking down that's made out of wood. I think it was made for the handicap people.

But everyone else is running down the stairs. I like walking down the ramp. It makes a clunk noise with my shoes. And I touch on the grass and it's nice and green. There's a huge field surrounded by trees. Baseball stop is on the far end. It's probably about 100 yards away from where I'm standing.

There's a play set to the right. It's made out of big chunky wood. Big galvanized steel chains and black rubbery seats for the swings. There's already people on it. Different grades. Already swinging on it. I think it's the third graders. Their recess is right before ours. They're being called in.

And I think I see one of them whispering to another one and pointing at me. But I keep walking. I have on a light blue Converse. And I'm kind of looking at them as I walk down with my head down. I can see everyone playing baseball. I love baseball. I definitely, definitely wanna play baseball.

But I rarely get picked for the team. So today, I'm sauntering over just slowly going over because I, I don't think they're gonna pick me. So I'm walking through the outfield and I see all the kids run past me really quickly. One guy flips me on the head really hard. [SOUND EFFECT] Laughs and runs by.

It's funny. I'm kind of taller than most of the kids, but they still pick on me a lot. I could see the green trees all around. About 50 to 60 yards to my right. And I could see them swaying in the breeze. It's kind of lonely. Look at the trees. Trees are just slightly swaying. And I can hear people – girls squealing in the background. And I, I think they're on one of the play sets.

So I walk over and all the kids are starting to line up in the infield. Billy, Kevin stand up near home, home plate. And they're standing there looking at everybody. They're almost always the captains. Billy's usually very mean to me. Kevin, he's all right. He's a good guy. He wears his Boy Scout uniform and I talk to him about it a lot.

So they're both standing up there. And I think there's probably about fifteen of us that are just standing there in line. Billy starts out first. He calls out two guys' names. "Ted! Sam! You're on my team." Kevin points over. "Uh, Brian. Brian, Bill you're on my team."

So it goes back and forth, back and forth and they're calling everybody, and I'm starting to get this sinking sensation. And I'm not gonna be able to play baseball again. So it's between me and the kid who's a little heavy. And he always has, like, chocolate on his face. And his name's Simon. So it's between me and the heavy kid. The fat kid.

I look at his stomach. And it's kind of protruding from his shirt. Everybody's wearing shorts. So I can see the fat – his fat knees. He's a slow runner. I'm so much faster than him. So it's Billy's turn to pick. "Simon. Not picking the pee pee kid." Everyone laughs. I just stand there.

I'm standing near the pitcher's mound. I grab a baseball and I throw it as hard as I can at the backstop. [SOUND EFFECT] Kevin sees it. "No. I'm gonna take Jonathan. Okay. Jonathan, I think you should pitch."

"Um, okay." So, I'm on the mound. And I have the ball. And everyone's calling me pee pee kid. And cheering from the dugouts. And I throw my first ball towards the batter who's up. And I hit him. He goes to first base and he looks at me like he's gonna kill me.

"Don't you ever hit me again with the baseball, pee pee kid." I'm getting more and more anxious. They throw the ball back to me. So I breathe. And then my head is just going all over the place, and I throw the ball. It goes way over his head. [SOUND EFFECT] Oh, God. Just control it. Kevin says, "Jonathan, if, if you don't wanna play pitcher, it's fine."

"No, just give me one more chance, one more chance." Oh, God. It's unbearable. I'm looking down. Everyone's just laughing because I'm pitching horribly. I'm concentrating as hard as I can. I throw it. [SOUND EFFECT] It's a strike. [CHUCKLES] Everyone's like, wow. He throws the ball back to me. I catch it. I, I smell my glove.

Something comforting about smelling the leth, leather. But my head goes crazy again. It goes way outside. "All right. Jonathan, it's okay. [STAMMERS] You just go out in the outfield. All right?"

"I – but I'm –."

"No, no, it's okay. We're not – I'll pitch." So Kevin takes the ball. And I'm so embarrassed. I blew the chance. I blew the chance to be a good pitcher. To be someone so well respected.

And I walk out slowly into the outfield. And I just walk over to the play set, because I don't wanna be there anymore. I'm slowly walking up. Girls start singing. [SINGS] "He peed his pants. He peed his pants." All I wanna do is hide. All I wanna do is hide. I go to the swing set. And I go sit in the sand box by myself. And I watch them play baseball from a distance. [BREATHES]

It's important to note that as Wes is doing it, he's actually creating and seeing much more than he voices out loud. That's quite common with someone who's done it for a long time. In the above Emotion with Detail, I asked him to tell me one little detail that he didn't say out loud. He replied, "Clover patches. I saw clover patches. The little white clover flowers." Now that's not necessarily an emotional thing, right? But it serves to anchor the moment. Details can make the moments more concrete. There were many, many more details that he visualized but didn't say out loud. You'll also notice that he seeks to put in smells, sounds, etc. It's really beneficial to try to put in all five senses. Not all five will ring out to you, but do give it a whirl. You'll find that certain ones will trigger your emotions more than others. Here's another from Mr. McGee:

[BREATHES] Okay. I'm Jonathan. And I'm on the bus that's taking me home from school. It's a big yellow bus, and I'm sitting near the front. And these vinyl plastic seats. And a kid from another grade is sitting next to me. Doesn't really say much to me. He's reading a comic book. Looks like Spiderman. But I'm just staring out the window. Wishing I would've played baseball. And one day they'll figure out that I'm actually pretty damn good.

As long as they don't call me pee pee boy. So, I'm just kind of looking at the seat and there's a piece of dried up bubble gum. It's blue. Here comes my stop 'cause we're, we're passing the street that's, uh, Blair Street. I could see the sign. It's like a wooden street sign. The bus driver, I can see her curly hair. It's kind of grayish. And sort of a big, big, big curls.

She has glasses on. She's a happy lady. Ms. Titus. So, I'm off at my stop. It pulls up. I get off. And I run as hard as I can to my back yard. And I just crouch down and take my backpack off. And breathe. Look around at all my surroundings that are safe to me.

There's the shed. There's the lawn mowers and chainsaws that my dad uses. And then right next to it is a bucket of baseballs. I found all these baseballs near the high school. But they were out, they were out in the woods and I was going out in the woods and they were obviously home runs or fouls or something.

They're not in great condition. But they're my baseballs. But I do have one that was in really good condition. They must've just lost it. So I walk up to this bucket. It's made out of wires. I can hear the pines and straw crunching up under my feet. The whole back yard is basically pine and straw. Except for the area my dog runs around. It's just all dirt. And that's probably about – [STAMMERS] and it's on the other side of the yard.

And I pick up the baseball and I look at it. I squeeze it hard. It's really firm. Hard ball. I'm looking at the red. They got the red and white. The red stitching and the white leather. And it says Spalding on it in blue.

And it has a nice weight to it. It's nice and balanced. It's almost like a brand-new ball. I'm so proud of this ball. Pick it up and I open up the shed and I pull out my glove, which I'm not supposed to keep in there because my dad says he doesn't want me to. And I go over to the barbeque and I grab a piece of charcoal. And the bar – and the barbeque [PAUSES] is, like, it has four metal legs that come down.

And a little ash area I'm able to stick my hand up into. Pull out one piece of charcoal. And the grill still smells like some kind of old beef or steak. And I'm actually kind of hungry. Should probably get a snack in a second. But I've got the baseball. And I've got my glove and the charcoal and I go over to the wooden fence and I draw a big circle.

Big circle. Just enough for a strike zone. It's perfect. And I back up, and I say, "Now on the mound, Jonathan Turner! Pitching for the Philadelphia Phillies!" And I look at that circle. I shake off the call sign from the catcher.

And I say to myself, it'll always be a strike. And I am not a pee pee boy. And the anger swells up inside of me. [BREATHES] And I throw the ball as hard as I can. [SOUND EFFECT] whack. Hits up against the wood. The wooden fence [SOUND EFFECT]. It leaves a small mark so I know where it hit.

It bounces back. I go over and pick it up again. [BREATHES] The anger stretches up inside of me again. [SOUND EFFECT] Boom. It hits the gate – the fence. Strike. Right down the pipe. Hard as I can. Leaves a little indention. Maybe a little crack in the wood. I pick it up again. I do this at least eleven times. Bam. Bam. Bam. Bam. Hitting it.

Over and over again. Strike zone. I never miss. I never miss. [BREATHES] The last one I have, I see Billy's face. I can hear the birds in the trees. Smell the cool air. As soon as I – as soon as I see

Billy's face, my anger grows so much. To the point [STAMMERS] I feel like my ears are hot. I feel my ears on fire. They, they must be bright red. And I throw it as hard as I can. Boom. It goes through the fence. [LAUGHS] I broke the fence. Oh, no. I broke the fence. I hear my dad pulling up in the driveway. Oh no. Oh no.

It's starting to get dark out. Hopefully he won't see it. I run. And I, I run around the fence to go get my baseball. It's a big hole. Run hard or Dad's gonna see it. He's calling my name. "Jonathan!" Whew. My dad's here. I have to go and answer. He screams again at me. And I run back around slowly.

"The – Did you put a hole in the fence?"

"Dad it was –"

"You get over here right now!" His face looks like the devil.

"I – Dad, I just was trying to prove that –"

"No! You get over here right now!" He grabs me by the arm. It hurts. He's squeezing so hard. And he swings and hits me right in the, in the butt. And then he hits me in the face. [CRIES]

"I just wanted show people."

"You aren't showing anybody – body anything!" He's just so angry at me. He's squeezing my arm so hard. I think I'm gonna pass out it hurts so bad. And my mom screams "Leave him alone! Leave him alone! Drop him right now!" And she, she has a bat. And he, he's like, "What do you think you're gonna do with that?"

And he drops me. And she says, "You just leave him alone." I'm just holding my arm and breathing. My pitching arm and it hurts really bad. And he takes my balls and he throws them in the trash can. And I don't want – don't want him to throw them away.

[BREATHES] [CRIES]

At this point, Wes took a break and continued another day with this:

I'm Jonathan. I'm lying in my bed. I can see the first amount of sunlight starting to come through the window to the right of my bed. Tossing and turning all night. I – I hit the ground, my arm hurt so bad when my dad threw me down. I – My arm. It's so hot when I touch it. It feels three times bigger than the other arm. [SNIFFS] Ow. I wanna call my mom but I don't want my dad to know.

I can't lay on it. It's, uh, barely slept. [BREATHES] It's gonna be such a hard day at school. I don't wanna go. I don't wanna go to school. So I slowly take the blanket off me. It's a cold morning. The house is so quiet. And I step down off the bed.

And I can't – I have my arm tucked really close to my rib cage because I don't want it to move. I look at it and it's purple. It's purple just below the shoulder. It's pounded just a little bit it's pounding and the small pulsation.

Ow. Okay, so I'm trying to straighten it out so I can put on my shirt. [STRUGGLES] It hurts so bad. I – I can't let them see it. He'll call me a pussy and I don't wanna be a pussy. [STRUGGLES]. I don't wanna tell my mom. She had a bat yesterday and I don't want her to fight with Dad. And so finally I have the shirt on and I button it up with one hand, because my other hand's starting to swell. I put on my pants with one arm. [BREATHES]

And so I – put my shoes on and everything and I put my backpack on my left shoulder, because my right arm can barely move. [SNIFFS] So I'm gonna go to the bus stop early, because I don't want them to see me. My parents will think I'm acting weird. It's cold. There's crickets. I think it might be about 6:30. And I look at the clock, it's 6:32. It's on the stove downstairs as I walk through the kitchen. The kitchen's eerie and quiet. There's no lights on at all. It's almost kind of scary. Oh, my arm. And I walk up to the front door. And I unlock it. Makes a small creaky noise. [SOUND EFFECT] I stop. I don't want anybody to hear me. I open up the screen door. Very slowly it creaks, very slowly it creaks. And I spit on the hinges so it doesn't creak. So it easily opens. I close the kitchen door behind me and I close – the front door which is right next to the kitchen. I close it behind. The screen door closes. And outside, it's really chilly. I should've brought a jacket. I can hear the crickets because it's still slightly dark out.

The glow of the sun is just past the forest that's on the other side of my street. Just wanna start walking slowly because it's gonna be about an hour until the bus gets here. I'm so hungry. I'm so hungry [UNINTELLIGIBLE].

So I'm standing at the bus stop. And I feel so alone. I look at the dirt patch from all the kids that were standing there usually. But I'm here by myself. I take off my book bag. Look through it. Actually have a half of a peanut butter jelly sandwich from yesterday.

Oh, so I eat that really quickly. Tastes so good. The bread's slightly moist from the jelly. It's really sweet and delicious. My mom makes such a great peanut butter and jelly sandwich. But it's hard to swallow because I'm – my stomach's upset from the pain in my arm. It's such a horrible feeling, my stomach's upset and I'm hungry at the same time.

It's so – And finally the bus shows up. And I'm standing far away from the other kids that have finally started to come and stand next to the bus stop. And I walk away from them so they don't see me, see that I'm off and on crying. It's about five kids. And the bus pulls up. Thank God, because it's probably warm in there. Yes, it is. I step up on to the steps and I can feel the heat from the bus hit me in the face. It's that smell of diesel fuel and – it's – dirty kids. But also a clean smell. The bus driver looks at me and says, "Hello Jonathan. You okay, honey?" I don't say anything I just walk to the back of the bus.

So now I'm at school. Thank God, the bus was warm. And my arm feels like it's tight like a sausage because there's so much swelling. And my hands look kind of fat like tiny sausages. Sitting in my classroom.

And my teacher sees that when I put down my backpack, I make a really – like a wincing – like a yelp. "Jonathan, come here, son."

"Yes, Miss Childers."

She asks me about my arm. "Let me see your arm, son."

"It's fine. It's fine. It just – got stung by a bee."

"No, no, no. let me see it. Honey, that – that's broken. That, that – oh. Let me – I'm taking you to the infirmary right now."

"No, no, no."

"No, you're, you're coming with me. Leave your books. Everything's fine." And so we're briskly walking down the hallway and the speed is hurting my arm. I'm crying. It makes me feel so stupid. I'm being taken from class again. [STAMMERS] the nurse's station.

We walk up to the nurse's station. I can see the nurse. She's in a white apron. And her name's Ms. Tuttle. And she looks at me with this really soft smile. And her touch is so gentle. As we walk into the, the infirmary, the nurse station. And there's a small vinyl bed that she tells me to step onto the stool and sit on it as she pulls the paper out.

"Okay, now." Her hands are warm and soft. She looks at my hands. Blood is starting to pool near my, my knuckles. "Oh." She says, "Oh, honey. Okay. Let's get you, let's get you an ice pack. I'm gonna call your mom –"

"Don't call my mom! Don't call my mom! She'll tell my dad!" [CRIES] "Please don't call my mom."

"Oh, Jonathan. Okay, Jon – well. Well then, we'll call your mom when we get to the hospital."

"Don't, don't, don't."

"We're taking you to the hospital. I don't care what you say. We're gonna do that. You're a strong little boy. And I'm really impressed by your courage. But we're taking you."

"Oh, okay. Okay."

"Now you just lie down. Just lie down on this bed while I get everything ready."

I lie back and the paper kind of crunches on my head. She gives me two very large pills and they're chewable. And I crunch on them. And I drink some water. I'm so tired I just, I slowly go to sleep. As I feel her pull a blanket over top of me.

And he takes a break and begins again here:

I'm Jonathan. And...I'm in fourth grade. Um...in my mother's car with her. In the early morning. It's one of those special mornings where she picked me up after her all-night job. I don't have to take the bus because sometimes the bus can be loud and...too hot in the summertime. So, so she showed up right when I was getting ready for the bus stop. She had gotten off work early so we're in the car now. It's a little...Chevrolet Omni hatchback. Kinda rattles when the, when the A-C goes on but thank God there's A-C, because it's so hot. I'm happy to be next to my mom. The car kind of smells like French fries. She's taking me to school.

I gave her the note that said Ms. Tuttle actually wants to talk to her. Ms. Tuttle is...the nurse that I...she's just...She's been such a caretaking angel to me. I love Ms. Tuttle. [CHUCKLES] She lets me take home cotton balls when...if I'm – if I stay late after school. Because nobody can pick me up, she lets me play with the cotton balls. So my mom's gonna drop me off and talk to Ms. Tuttle.

I'm not sure what they're talking about. But I think it has to do with my after school and what I...what I can do to keep me out of trouble. So they're approaching the, uh...the complex which is really big. There's a...few trailers for the school – and the elementary school that have – hold classes.

And then a main building for the high school. And the middle school...is the one that's farthest in the back. I, I can see the high school. It's obvious that it was the, the main building that was built. And it has columns and a...a breezeway where you can be dropped off by the buses. The American flag is high on its pole on the right-hand side of the building with the lawn. The lawn has a few random boulders. It's a nice school. It's red brick.

A few of the columns are made out of stone. So my mom...we, we pull up to the parking lot.

She looks so tired. She's been working, like, a twelve-hour shift. [STAMMERS] and she smells like French fries. [CHUCKLES]

We both get out of the Omni and close the door. It's early morning. Still really muggy. Start walking toward the school. Ms. Tuttle is right there waiting for us. Talks to my mom. And I hear her and she – Ms. Tuttle holds my hand...almost as if she's my aunt or my grandmother. She has such an affection for me. She's such a wonderful, gentle way of holding my hand. And I smile big at her. And she says, um, "Hey Cindy. I [STAMMERS] the idea that I have for Jonathan...is that, uh, uh, my husband – of course you know. Um, Mr. Tuttle. He runs the auto mechanic program vocational wing in the high school. So, what I propose is that Jonathan..."

"Yes!" I say yes immediately. [LAUGHS] "I would love to go work back there and go hang out..." Even though she hasn't said anything to me. I just know that she wants me to go hang out with her husband in the, uh, auto mechanics wing.

"Jonathan, let me finish. Okay. Well, a lot of the boys get to go back there and work on their cars. And Mr. Tuttle has a lot of work to do back there and I think Jonathan would have a good time... because I have watched him. He, um...he's really good with wiring and stuff. The other day when he was helping me at the nurse's station, he fixed my radio."

My mom smiles big. She's, like...I can see a tear go down her eye. She's just...she says, "Thank you Anne." And she gives my mom a big hug. My mom gives me a big hug. And then I walk into the building. And she walks me to my – to my homeroom. We started changing classes since third grade to get us ready for middle school. Well, fifth grade. Fifth grade is when you start middle school. I'm kind of excited about that. So I walk in.

And I don't care what anyone is thinking right now. I get to hang out with Mr. Tuttle and play with cars. I love cars. In my backpack, I keep a little Matchbox GTO 1967...I don't let anybody see it. I don't want it be taken away. It's one of my most prized possessions. It's a convertible. For the whole day, I'm sitting and watching the clock ready for...ready for the final bell to sound so I can...run to Ms. Tuttle, because she's gonna walk me there to her husband.

The bell rings. And I am so excited. Ah, I can barely stand it. I'm the first one out the door when I'm usually the last one behind packing up my stuff. [SNIFFS] There's so much energy and love that's just running through me right now. [SNIFFS] So she holds my hand. And I run up the, to the nurse's station. Past all the kids, all the different grades are being left out. Such a hustle and a bustle going – bustle going on right now. And I'm trying not to hit anybody's backpacks. They don't get mad at me. [UNINTELLIGIBLE] run up and, and, and, and knock [SOUND EFFECT] on the glass of the, the nurse station.

And she's – looks at me and smiles. Opens the door. She says, okay. Let's go. So, we're walking down. It's a very big campus. It's – high school, middle school, and elementary school together. So. Walk down a very long wing. And I can see all the different kids. I can see the horticulture kids. Who have all their little sprouting...I don't know what they are, but they're little sprouts of green plants walking by that they're obviously so proud of. And I can hear the clop of her...uh...her shoes. On the linoleum floor. She [STAMMERS] continue, continues to hold my hand. So we knock on the big...big grey metal door with safety glass. We open it up and it's a...a classroom. Looks more like a...an auto...an auto mechanic shop. It's, it's great. I mean, there's about eight desks over to the left when you first walk in.

But then to the far back, two very large steel roll-up doors so cars can drive into the classroom. And there's, uh, one – there's one car that's up on a lift right now. It's a truck – it's a Ford 50 – F-150 I think. It says it right there on the left...right above the wheel well. There's Mr. Tuttle is, is sort of a...a plump man. Stands up from his desk. His small...square-ish glasses. "Well, this must be Jonathan."

I just smile at him. A little shy. But something about him reminds me of, like, Santa Claus or something.

"All right. Well, we got a few things we're doing back here today. We're gonna start off. We got a broom. [SNIFFS] Let's just sweep up around here. I think that would be fantastic."

That's not really what I wanna do. But I sweep. And I see two boys tinkering with, uh...with a...with a roundish thing that's on top of the engine. On the other car...looks like a small four-door sedan. Nissan. And they're having a hard time getting this thing on. I walk up to him and I, I look into the engine. They kind of look at me and...They're nicer kids. They're around fourteen or fifteen. I say, "What's that?"

"Well, it's a...trying to install this new, kind of, uh, this new air system on a car trying to make it go faster." I can tell they're having a hard time. I lean in really close. Put my hands up on the...the white papery filter. It has, like, a...a rubbery kind of surface on it. On top of it and on bottom of it. There's a little plastic thing that they forgot to take out. So I slide it on. Boom. Take the wing nut, the little nut that looks like it has wings on it and spin it. They both look at me with their mouth open.

"What grade are you in?" [STAMMERS]

"I'm in, I'm in fourth grade." [LAUGHTER].

"Well, glad to have you back here. What's your name?"

"Jonathan." I feel so good inside.

I feel so received and...and just needed. I can smell the gasoline and I can just feel the heat from the car. It all feels so...comforting. And then they close down the hood of the car and crank it. Runs like a champ. Mr. Tuttle's watching the whole thing. [LAUGHS] he's just standing in the basement.

"Jonathan...I think you're gonna have a fun time back here." And I look at him and smile. [BREATHES]

I like this, because it's an example of when Jonathan feels good about himself. He feels like he's enough. Wes jumps a bit in age for his next one.

[BREATHES] I'm Jonathan. And I'm thirteen years old. I'm

thirteen. Hm.... Ah. Eighth grade. Hm. And I'm...I'm sitting in my room right now at home. I have a...a blanket that's opened up and I have a carburetor that I'm rebuilding...that Mr. Tuttle gave me.

All the little intricate pieces on...on the...on this old blanket and towel that my mom let me use. Feels like...my hands are kind of greasy. Probably should've done it in the garage. But...I don't want my dad to see. I don't want my dad to get into anything. So the...smell of gas. I have all my windows open so the...the fumes will go out. And I can hear my mom downstairs turning off and on the sink. Scrubbing a pot. Sponging some dishes. The clank of it hitting a drying rack. Another clank. We're steadily working together. We're both busy. It's nice. I'm really figuring out this carburetor. Mr. Tuttle's gonna be pretty...pretty excited when I'm done with it. I'm hoping I can have it put together before my dad gets home. [PAUSES] Nope. Here comes my dad. [PAUSES]

It's about, about 9:00. About four hours after he gets off work so he's...he's probably drinking. By how fast he hits the driveway, yeah. I'm pretty sure he's drunk. My room's at the front of the house so I see the...the amount of how -- the headlights jump in the air a bit and the tires and the shocks kind of make the car jump a bit. So... it's almost sort of violent entry. Blaring some...country music song.

Shuts off the car. Closes the door. He's singing really loud. [SINGS] "Hey good lookin', what'cha got cookin'?"

"Mike,' she says. "You missed dinner."

I hear him say, "Cook something else!"

"Well, it's in – it's in the oven what we had." So, I hear him open up the, the oven door really quickly. [SOUND EFFECTS] Violently you can hear the springs open up of the door.

"What's this shit?"

"It's the lasagna that me and your son had for dinner that you were four hours late for." I get up, I can hear sort of the, the fear in my mom's voice. I walk down the hallway. He's got her. "Make this better...woman."

"I took a lot of time to make that thing..."

"Well, it's all dried up and shitty!"

"Well you shouldn't've been late."

He takes this casserole dish and jams it in her face [CLAPS]. Boom. The casserole dish breaks and cuts her face. "Look what you made me do!"

Oh, God. Oh, my God. Her face is bleeding so much. "You son of a bitch."

"What'd you call me?!" He takes her and slams her up against the...the oven, and she hits her head on the...on the fridge. Oh. Okay. She's out cold. And blood's sort of pooling around her from the cut from the glass – and the casserole dish. I'm looking at him. I'm like, "Dad what did you do?" [HEAVY BREATHING]

"You son...you son...No, we, we gotta take her to the hospital. I'm not mad at you, I'm not mad at you, I'm not mad at you."

I know not to make him angrier. "Let's just – can we...?"

"She slipped and fell, son. You saw that. You saw that."

"Now, okay. I understand. Understand. Let's just...let's put her in the car and [STAMMERS] let's take her to the hospital. She's bleeding a lot, Dad. Hey, I'm gonna get a towel and put it on her face." And I'm holding her face. She looks so pitiful sprawled out on the – on the kitchen floor. [CLEARS THROAT] He just looks wild. He looks...crazy. "But...all right, Dad. I'm gonna – I'm gonna drive. If you don't mind. I'm, I'm gonna drive the car and you hold on to Mom, okay?"

He looks at me almost like he's a little boy. He says, "Okay." He knows I've been driving with Mr. Tuttle after school. I've been driving the cars around in the parking lot of the high school. Okay. I can do this. And I'm driving. And he has my mom in the back seat. And as the blood...bloody towel that was a white towel that's almost red now. [CLEARS THROAT] She's out cold and her face looks sort of blue-ish. Sort of pale. I'm driving as fast as I can without getting in...getting in trouble.

And then we're close to the hospital. And I run inside as quick as I can. And they...the automatic doors whoosh open [SOUND EFFECT]. And the next ones [SOUND EFFECTS]. Like the, the... that smell of, uh, of disinfectant and shit that's in a hospital. And I see all the people that are sitting in the emergency room waiting to go in.

I'm like, "My mom. My mom. My mom!"

"Bring her in son. Bring – bring – wait, wait I can – [STAMMERS]." One of the orderlies – one of the nurses points to one of the orderlies and follows me. She – they see all the blood that's on my hands and on my face and they take off running – we're in the middle of the hospital. Then to the, to the – through the waiting area – and then we go out to the car that's just sitting there in the – in the – where the ambulances park.

And, uh...my dad's slowly pulling my mom out and she's limp. Puts her into...puts her into the wheelchair and the orderly says, "What happened?" [STAMMERS]

He just says, "She -- she fell and hit her head."

And then, then, I – I'm like, "Yeah. She fell. She fell and hit herself." He looks at me with the devil's stare like don't say anything.

And I want to so bad. [CRIES]. I hate him. I hate him so much. And then he... [BREATHES] They take the wheelchair and speed it by.

They speed by everyone. They, they take her immediately into surgery. My dad's just looking at me. This...dopey half-drunk expression. Blood all over his shirt. And he's filling out paperwork. And I'm just sitting in my chair. I'm just sitting there. Oh boy. With my head down.

A nurse takes my hand and walks me to the bathroom so I can wash my hands off of the blood. My dad almost killed my mom. [CRIES] Oh boy. I look at myself in the mirror. I should tell the police. My dad will kill me. He'll kill me. So I come out.

He says, "She's – they said she's gonna be okay. She has a fractured skull. They gave her some blood so she'll be okay. So we, we can go home now. We can come back in the morning."

[PAUSES] So I get in the car next to him. He, he wants to drive now. He stops at a liquor store. I'm sitting in the car and I just...I can't...I can't be here. I can't. He comes back with a brown bag and a bottle. And we get back in the car and we start driving off.

Driving mom's car. There's a picture of me on the dash that she keeps there. [PAUSES] He's drinking the brown liquor. As we get home, he starts saying it's her fault. It's her fault. I say nothing. I just say...I sit silently. We pull up into the driveway. And he says... [PAUSES]... "We'll get her in the morning. I promise." He's finished off half the bottle of liquor at this point. Walk in the house. He opens up my...my bedroom door and sees that – the blanket I've ruined with grease.

"What the fuck is this?!"

"I was fix – I was fix..."

"I – I see what you're trying to do. You've ruined this blanket that I bought with my money that I earned!" He's raging. He's running at me and I…I refuse to stand still and I run out the back doors as fast as I can. And I trip and I hit the ground. And I'm on the ground and it – I've cut my, my – the top of my head. And it… it's starting to bleed into my eye. But I still run. I'm wiping away the blood. I'm running and I'm running. And I don't know where I'm gonna go to but he's so drunk he can't run.

It's probably about…four, three or four in the morning right now and I'm running. I'm running. It's cold out and…running as fast as I can. I can hear crickets. I hear crickets all around. The wind's in my ears because I'm trying to run as fast as I can. Going through the woods and…snapping branches. Getting through the woods. And it's dark so I have to go…a little slower now because it's darker inside the, the deeper parts of the woods.

No longer the street lights are helping me. And I…and I go to the pond. I see the pond that's deep in the woods. I can see the moon reflecting off of it. I can hear him yelling from far away. He doesn't know where I am. [BREATHES] I'm so tired. [SNIFFS] I'm so tired.

There's a small…dock…out on the pond. And I walk out on the dock. It moves and floats with my weight. I look down and I see the moon staring at me in the pond. And I pray to God that my mom will be okay. The moon smiles back at me. I walk back off the dock to a grouping of bushes that are really thick now. No one will be able to see me. And I have my hoodie on and I pull my hoodie over the top of my head, zip it up. Pass out.

I wake up. The heat of the sun, it's about…7:00 I think. The sun's still pretty new in the morning sky. And it wakes me up with the brightness. It's shining directly at my face. I see all the…far side of the pond. A young girl and…an older man, probably in his fifties. Maybe sixties. Just sitting quietly together. She's holding a rod that he just sent the bait out with that – his, his fly.

It's like they might be using worms. She just sitting there with a ponytail. She looks like she's about my age. They both sit on...white buckets. My face is so caked with blood so I go over to the pond and hopefully trying to...not let them see me. I wash my face a little bit with the pond water.

He looks over at me and [STAMMERS]. Puts up his hand... his – the back of his hand at me and sort of waves over to me like... come, uh, come here sort of motion. And I've seen him before. He has a...old truck and always has the girl with him. So I walk across the pond. He looks at me and says, "Morning. Good morning. Doing a little fishing this morning?"

"No, no. I was just taking...I was just taking a walk."

"Do you wanna do a little fishing?"

"Nah, I'm a little hungry. I...think I need to go get some breakfast."

"Well, I got an egg salad sandwich right here. You don't mind if we share with him, do you? Do you Jenny?" She kind of looks at me. Smirks. "What happened to your head?"

"Oh, I...I, uh, I was just running through the woods last night. And I hit a tree."

"You hit a tree?"

"It was dark."

"Well, you don't run through the woods if it's dark."

"Yeah. You're right. It's probably not a good idea. I learned my lesson." [PAUSES]

"You like a Coke with that?" the old man says.

"Yeah. I'd like a Coke." [SNIFFS] [PAUSES] He has such a safe presence. And she...she sits – sits so close to him that you can tell, he's just a good man.

"Well, we got one more rod in here if you wanna sit down with us." Not wanting to go home, I jump at the opportunity.

"Well, I've never really done this before."

"Wow. A boy your age, you should definitely know how to fish." [LAUGHS]

"Okay. Uh. You show me?"

"Course. Okay. Take a line." He shows me how to fish and I...I have my rod out there. Everything's just quiet. And he looks at me. I can see him out of the corner of my eye looking at me. He looks like he has some type of sympathetic face.

Dragonflies bat -- buzz by. Bounce from cattail to cattail.

"I'm Jonathan."

"Oh. Jenny likes to call me Grandpa. This is Jennifer. Nice to meet you."

This is good, because he went from "Bad Daddy" to kinder, gentler Grandpa. He stops for a bit and then continues:

[BREATHES] I'm Jonathan. And I'm – I'm thirteen. I'm, uh, at the vocational wing of the school – the high school. And I'm...uh... up under an old Volvo. I can see the axle and the oil pan and I have a monkey gun wrench – a crescent wrench. And I'm opening up the oil plug. It's everything – I feel so worthwhile and needed here.

They let me do just about anything I want. Um...actually I came to school with Mr. Tuttle today. I called him after...I called him and I called up miss...I called Mrs. Tuttle after I had...my mother got into the hospital. And they came and picked me up from my neighborhood. They let me stay with them. So I drove to school with Mr. Tuttle today.

Here comes the black oil oozing over the top of my hands. Gotta quickly put the pan up under there to collect and I come out to get some new oil. Couple of kids over there, like, uh...um...sand crate -- sand papering. And, uh...it looks like a brake drum, trying to clean up the brakes. Listening to a little, uh, Rolling Stones in the background. These guys are all older than me and are much, much more my friends than anybody I know in my grade.

And I still keep to myself. I can concentrate better when I'm by myself. And I, I hear, uh, a knock on one of the corrugated doors. I turn around [STAMMERS]. I look up and there's a glare of, of light coming in through the bays. And it's, and it's Grandpa. It's the guy [LAUGHS] who...taught me how to fish yesterday. Uh...he walks up to Mr. Tuttle's desk. Shakes hands [STAMMERS]. "Hey Jim, how are you?"

"Great, great. I think I got those, uh...got that part you needed for your Cadillac. Oh, that was a, uh...solenoid. Uh, you, you've been fishing?"

"Yeah I went yesterday." And he glimpses over his shoulder. Obviously he feels me staring at him. "With that kid right there."

"Hey there, sir."

"Jonathan, right?"

"Yeah. It's [LAUGHS] – yeah. I'm Jonathan."

"How's the head, brother?"

"Uh…it's good. Got it all patched up. Um…no more bleeding. Thank you so much for taking me in to…to…to fish the other day. Your, uh, granddaughter, Jennifer. She's…she's pretty cool."

"Yeah. We're going fishin' tomorrow. So, you're more than welcome to come."

"Uh, well, I was staying with the Tuttles."

"No – no, you –" Mr. Tuttle says, "No, you…you go with him." He's says they're old war buddies and that he lives in the neighborhood.

"Wow. Okay. Uh…that would be great. [STAMMERS] So, what, what time are we thinking about going fishing tomorrow? I – I – I'm trying to do all this stuff for the Volvo here so Mr. Tuttle can…"

"No, Jonathan, don't worry about it. You're still thirteen years old and this is not your classroom. I know you love it over here. But you need to go fishing. It's good for ya."

Then Grandpa looks at me and he says, "We'll have you another egg salad sandwich and another Coke."

And that sounds really good to me. I walk up over to the desk. Grandpa puts out his hand. Wipe off my own hand. He says, "I know it's a school day, but we'll just do a little fishing before you have to come to school, how's that sound?"

"That sounds awesome." So I shake his hand. And he walks out.

Mr. Tuttle says, "That's a good man right there. You stick around with him, you'll be all right."

"Yeah, he was really nice to me yesterday."

"And I can write you a note if you want to come in a little later tomorrow for school. Uh...spend some time fishing. You had a rough weekend."

"That sounds great Mr. Tuttle. That sounds real great."

So the next morning. I'm waking up...and then I'm, I'm getting off the bus at school. From school. And I'm – this would be the first time I'm going back home. My dad's not there. And at the bus stop... there's Grandpa in his Cadillac with Jennifer. And he says, [CLEARS THROAT] "Grab you a back pack with some clothes and a toothbrush. You oughta stay with us for a while." Mr. Tuttle must've spoken to him.

"I don't think I can do that."

"Son, I'm not gonna discuss it with you. It's what you're gonna do. [CLEARS THROAT] Just, uh...be quick about it, all right? Nobody wants any problems." So I, I open up the...the door to my house. It is absolutely trashed. It looks horrible. I'm walking into my room. It's been trashed. I go to my underwear drawer and I grab some socks and underwear. My toothbrush. One of my duffle bags...and I pack it all in there. Doesn't look like my dad's been here for a bit. But I gotta hurry before he gets home. Or if he just shows up randomly. And there's my carburetor just busted all over the place. Grab my baseball hat. Put it on. My jacket. And walk out the door. Open up the Cadillac door. Sit down.

Grandpa says, "It'll be easier for you to get up and go fishing with us in the morning. You stick with us anyway." Cranks up the old V8. Does a U-turn. Starts heading towards his house. Jennifer's in the front. Gives a smile back at me. I guess she thinks it's okay I'm gonna stay with them for a while. Turns up the radio loud. Cadillac just floats. It's like a boat. It's so comforting.

He says, "Uh, we got – we got a bed set up for you in the garage. It's an old cot I had. Brought it back from Germany. I was in the war. And, uh...think you could stay here for a few nights. I think it wouldn't hurt – wouldn't hurt anybody. Especially until your mom gets out of the hospital. It'd be okay. I'm sure she'll be fine with it." And I guess that that's true because Mrs. Tuttle and Mr. Tuttle know Grandpa pretty well.

We pull up into the driveway. Open up the car door. We all get out. Slam...slam the doors. He's like, "You hungry?" Shit, I'm always hungry. We walk into the house. And it smells like tobacco and cinnamon. Just the sense of warmth and safety just comes over me.

"Yeah, go ahead and go out to the...the garage and, uh, throw your stuff down. Wash up. We'll have some, we'll have some supper."

Sounds great. And, and his wife...his wife greets me. Shakes my hand.

"I guess do I call you Grandma?"

"You just...you can call me...you can call me Lisa. Okay. Or, uh...Miss Lisa if you like."

"Oh. I'll call you Miss Lisa." It feels better. Looks like she's working up a storm. Fried chicken. Mashed potatoes. It looks like they might've been expecting somebody.

So I go set my stuff down in the garage. There's no cars in it. It looks like it's just been this place where...someone sits at and watches television and just, kind of...messes around. Looks like a man cave. Old...torn up [SOUNDS LIKE: "barka"] lounger. It looks like a newish TV with antenna. And then my cot over in the corner. I bring my duffle bag over. Set it down. Sit down on the, on the cot and I'm just overwhelmed. [BREATHES] Thank God I didn't have to go back home. So I stand up and I go over to the sink that's in the...in the kitchen and I wash my hands. [SNIFFS] Open the door. Walk out and everyone just smiles at me.

And he jumps forward a bit in time:

I'm lying on the cot. Which is actually very comfortable. It's kind of cold in here. But they got a space heater near my feet which is nice. You can hear someone rumbling in the kitchen. But I look around and I see the old chair. And it looks sort of like – it's that, uh...material where it almost looks like it's plaid but then it's rougher, sort of...not corduroy. But...it's just – almost looks like a Triscuit but made out of...fabric. And I go over and run my hand down it. It's rough. It's pretty early in the morning so I'm sleepy. But I slept really, really good. I'm standing around in my boxer shorts and underwear just kind of looking at...everything that's there on the wall. That bass is huge. It must be twelve-pound bass on the wall that's...Grandpa must've caught. He has a whole, like...a few paddles and a canoe that's hung up on the ceiling. It's a high ceiling. Probably about twelve feet. It's like vaulted almost. There's a rug. [LAUGHS] that's a bear. That's a bear head? Wow. This might be the coolest room I've ever seen.

I can smell coffee wafting in from the kitchen. [LONG PAUSE] Huh. It's still dark out. And I'm pretty sure that's Grandpa. We're getting ready to go fishing. So I, I throw on some jeans. Pull them out of my backpack. A few of my shirts are stained with...something that my dad put on them. Don't know what it is. I'll ask Miss Lisa. She'll clean 'em for me. Sure enough, Grandpa opens up the door.

"Up and at 'em soldier?"

"Yes sir. I just gotta...uh...put on my shoes and I'll be ready to go."

"Okay. We'll, uh, I got your egg sandwich. And, uh, Jennifer, she's almost ready to go too. So, uh, grab, grab those poles for me and that tackle box. And we'll – then just bring them out to the

Cadillac." I hurriedly grab the three poles which kind of make a clack and rattle noise when I pick them up. And I pick up the, the tackle box. It looks like it has a little bit of dried fish guts on it. And, uh...open up the door. Walk outside. He, he's opening up the trunk for me. Put it in, put that in. Here comes Jennifer. Just with a huge smile on her face. [LAUGHS] And, uh...pink little rubber band in her blonde ponytail – swinging. She's got on a blue polo shirt. She smiles at me and she hops in the side passenger door. And I hop in the back. Grandpa jumps up in the front. All the doors thud. [SOUND EFFECT] He turns the key and it rattles. And the starter, it just goes [SOUND EFFECT]. I think I know exactly what's going on. But he – he tries again. Pumps the gas. [SOUND EFFECT] Oh man. Ugh. He gets out. [LAUGHS] A little angry. But it's funny the way he's... the, the way his, his temper rises. He's just sort of, like, clinching his lips together. Making 'em tight and just sort of, hm. scratching his head.

And then...opens up the...opens up the hood and looks inside. And I...I open up the door. She – Jennifer says to me, "Where do you think you're going?"

"I just wanna look in there. See what's going on."

"Okay smarty-pants. Sure." So I close the door. Walk over.

And he says, "Uh...I saw you workin' on them cars. What do you think's going on here?"

"Well, you put in that new solenoid? Yeah. Hm. The starter sounds like it's okay. And that clicking noise means it's probably the battery. But the battery looks like it's new too. So, I'd have to say it's the alternator, sir."

"The alternator, huh?"

"Yeah. So, if there's any way we could jump it, and we could run it around a bit...we could be able to, uh, maybe charge up the battery and it'll be okay for later. We can bring it into the shop."

"How do you know so much about cars?"

"Just comes to me real easy." So I, I...grab a spare battery that he had in his garage that I saw. Got the two jumper cables, put them on the battery. Boom. Car starts up. "Now we're gonna have to drive this around a bit if the alternator's bad. So, uh, let's get to fishin'."

He looks at me, he's like, "Son. Gonna really enjoy having you here." [LAUGHS]

"Well, as long as there's fried chicken every night, I'll be great." [LAUGHS] He's just making me feel so at home. So at home. Then Jennifer gives me a big smile. But then it also kind of sloughs it off like you think you're so awesome. [LAUGHS] Sit back of the...in the back. Closes the door and we head off to the pond.

And Wes leaves it for the day, and picks back up with this:

I'm Jonathan. I'm thirteen. And, uh, [PAUSES] and I just finished watching, uh, Jeopardy and Wheel of Fortune with Grandpa. He's really good at answering questions. Or questions that are the answers in Jeopardy. And I've walked into the garage that I'm – is my temporary housing. It's a little cold. And I step down the two brick stairs that get me down into the, uh, garage cement floor that's been – the AstroTurf that's been put on the ground as a carpet. And I take off my shoes, put my feet on the AstroTurf. I kind of scrunch up my toes on the green grass, the fake green grass. And it's cold. Gets cold in here. So I get myself ready for bed. Take off my pants and fold it up and put it on the shelf that has the spray paint and different tools. It's right at the foot of my cot. But they cleared a little area for me to put my stuff. And I turn on the small space heater with a little click [SOUND EFFECT] to the right. And it starts to hum. [HUMS] The warmth immediately starts to come out and touch my feet. The glowing orange from the heater.

Sit on the cot with a squeak. My belly's full from spaghetti. We had spaghetti and meatballs. I still got that acid taste in my mouth – [UNINTELLIGIBLE] tomato. And my belly's so full. [BREATHES] it's time for me to lie down for a second. I think it's 10:30.

So I lie down before brushing my teeth and the comfort of the room and the buzzing of the heater makes me fall asleep. Right before I do, there's a knock at the door. It's Grandpa. And the door opens up squeaking a little bit.

And he sort of says in a tone – it's a little softer than the usual sounds. "Jonathan?"

"Yes sir?" I pop up out of my sleep. A little groggy still.

"Son, you mind coming with me into the kitchen?"

"Sure."

"You, you know, actually I'll come in here and sit down next to you on the cot. It's nice and quiet in here."

It's dark. And he, he flicks on one of the lights that keeps it still kind of dim in there. And there's moon light that's pouring through the, the garage door glass. He walks over. And the AstroTurf gives him kind of a scratchy noise when he walks. And I want –

"I'm gone sit down next to you. So, son, um. I just got a call. From the hospital. And, uh, yeah. You know, your mother just passed away from complications from, um, a brain injury she sustained."

[CRIES] [STAMMERS] "She was oh – she was okay the last time I saw her. Are you sure?"

"Yeah, son. If you need –" And I grab him and I hold him before he can even reach for me and I'm holding him close to me.

[CRIES] "I wanna see my mama. I wanna see [STAMMERS]."

"Well, we can't do that now, son. I'm sorry. I'm so sorry. I would bring you back to your father. But at the moment, son, I think you should stay here. In this bed. We'll be praying for you and I'll sit here next to you as long as you need me to tonight."

[CRIES] "I can't believe she's gone. No, there's no way she's dead –"

"Yes, son. I'm sorry. It's hard to believe."

"She was –"

"I'll – just...Come here buddy, it's okay."

He just starts stroking my hair. Just like mom used to. And then I see Miss Lisa come out. She sits next to me. She doesn't say a word but holds me close to her, too. [CRIES]. And I look up at the doorway, there's a silhouette. It is Jennifer.

And we make eye contact. And she's crying for me. [CRIES] She's crying. Looking at me. But the two warm bodies next to me make me feel much better. [BREATHES] So, I finally fall asleep that night.

But, throughout the night, Grandpa and Jennifer open the door to look at me. She stayed up with – with Grandpa. Brought me a wet towel every now and then to sponge my head. And right now, she's sponging my head. The cool towel is on my head. She says to me, "My, uh, my mom had died too, you know that?"

"Yeah. I know. I know she did. Does the pain ever go away?"

"Well," she says that, "the memory's always there but the pain starts to fade."

And I say, "There's no – this pain hurts too bad. It hurts too bad." She holds my hand.

She squeezes it and then sits next to me on the cot. Grandpa stands in the doorway and watches. She's wearing a flannel nightgown. And the room is dark. The towel feels like ice but it's so refreshing. I put it on my eyes because they're so hot. And she holds my hand. "Thank you, Jennifer."

"It's okay, Jonathan. I understand."

[PAUSES] "Yeah."

After a short break, Wes goes right into the funeral:

I'm standing next to my mother's grave. I'm wearing an itchy suit. Granddad was – Grandpa was nice enough to take me shopping. Because I didn't have a suit. He said I'll need one. "Every man needs good suit."

And there is brass fix, fixtures. There's these pulleys that are next to the grave. There's nylon. Nylon, uh, straps that are going across these brass, sort of, hoists. It really feels like the whole town has shown up.

I could see Mr. Tuttle and Mrs. Tuttle across from me. But I don't really wanna look at anybody. Because I don't wanna tell them what happened that night. And I wanna tell them what my father did. I see my father stumbling up the hill. No one really looks at him.

He hasn't shaved and his suit looks too big for him. I'm afraid that he's gonna hurt me. He looks at me. He doesn't care who's around. He says, "Where you been boy?"

Grandpa stands up immediately. "I think you need to back off, sir." He's making a, a scene in front of my mother's grave. And Grandpa briskly walks over to him and grabs his arm and starts making him – walking him down the hill. He's trying to fight Grandpa telling him to let go of him – or that he's, he's – he keeps moving his arm. But Grandpa's grip is really strong. And he won't let go of him. He keeps ushering him down the hill.

I can hear him saying something drunk. Words that are just coming up. "You ashamed of – your son, your family." You could just hear certain things of Grandpa just loading into him. Walks him down the hill. And finally – my father falls down. And falls in a puddle. Just lays there. [CHUCKLES] Beat – just beaten. The whole thing is so scary to me.

[BREATHES] Jennifer takes my hand because she sees my face. She squeezes it hard. She actually interlocks her fingers with me and it makes me – My, my heart sort of melts at that moment because it feels like we're connecting on this level. I – this – I – this sense of this love and this connection and just a crush. Uh, uh, my heart just sort of flutters when she interlocks her fingers with mine. And then pulls me close to her hip.

She has a navy-blue dress on. Several tombstones are nearby. Mr. Tuttle's helping my Grandpa now. He's not my grandpa. But he feels like my grandfather. Mr. Tuttle stands midway in between the funeral's procession and Grandpa and my father.

They both stand there both on guard. As the preacher says his final words. They stand there as my father walks away, gets in his car and drives off. I'm watching the casket. And as several strong – several men, two of the boys I knew from electro mechanics and auto mechanics class help pick up the box. The casket. Six people put her up on the device to lower her down. [SNIFFS] Then I go touch it. But I feel safe with Jennifer. She's keeping me closer to her. She walks up to the casket with me.

And I tell my mama good bye. [CRIES] The casket slowly sinks into the ground as the pulleys start lowering it down slowly. The preacher says something, "Ashes to ashes, dust to dust..." Grandpa comes back up the hill. Resumes his place sitting next to Miss Lisa – Miss Lisa gives me a look of strength and encouragement. As I throw the first bit of dirt on top of the grave. [SNIFFS] And then we all get in Granddad's Cadillac – grand – Grandpa's Cadillac after many people come up and give me a hug.

Mrs. Tuttle gives me the biggest hug. Pretty [UNINTELLIGIBLE]. Enveloped by her bosom. Mr. Tuttle. He, he sort of smells like mothballs. He pulls me in close. I think my back cracks a little he squeezes me so hard. But it doesn't matter.

I want them all so close to me. Jennifer says let's go. And her and I just walk off and they allow me to. They allow me to walk away, with her. She says, "I'll always be here for you Jonathan."

"I'll always be here for you Jennifer."

We walk to the far side. Under a big oak tree. We sit. Huge oak tree. The roots are entangled all over the ground. It's like splotches of grass and dirt. A little bit of mud from the rain that happened the day before. There's a small bench under the tree that we sit on. [SNIFFS] and she gives me, uh, a piece of Wrigley spearmint gum. I unwrap it slowly and its sweetness just trickles down my throat as soon as I start chewing it.

It's comforting. She holds my hand, she never lets go of my hand. Even when she's pulling the gum out of her small purse. I don't, I don't know...

With that, he ends it. Eek! He did two big emotional ones back to back. Sometimes that's hard to do, and sometimes you'll find you'd rather do it and get them over with. Notice how he combined the loss of his mother with the bonding with Jennifer. That's a time saver.

Because of his need to save even more time in his preparation, Wes then chose to use Flashes as a way to connect more moments. He feels he's got a really good sense of who Jennifer is now and who Grandpa is to him, so he'll quickly visualize short *moments* of events. These moments are captured quickly, without all the details that lead up to the events. Flashes are visual spurts - quick images. They are less detailed and much shorter than an Emotion with Detail. The more you do Emotion with Detail, the easier and more powerful your Flashes will be. Like anything, it's practice. So referring to his Core Knowledge notes as a guideline, he might quickly visualize something like this:

- Dad actually went to prison. Because all that behavior at the funeral makes it seem as if there's some foul play there. And from that, an investigation happened. It was proven that Dad dealt her the blow that ultimately killed her - that made her hit her head. So he was tried and convicted. He's going away for the rest of his life, which leaves thirteen-year-old Jonathan to fend for himself. So the Tuttles, being educators, take Jonathan in. Let's have them live like maybe five doors down from Grandpa and Jennifer. Or at least close enough to be able to walk there.
- Jonathan lives with the Tuttles now. See him at their house. Visualize moments of kindness that the Tuttles show him.
- Grandpa teaching him how to tie a fishing hook.
- They are all out to dinner, and Grandpa insists that he pulls the chair out for Jennifer to sit down. "Now pull the seat out for her. Now, okay, now make sure the seat goes under her - but don't knock her down." Also, that Jonathan stands when a lady leaves the table. And again when she returns. Maybe there's lots of laughter and gentle ribbing going on.
- Grandpa gives him boxing lessons. Maybe at the pond. He teaches him how to defend himself against the bullies who still remember him as pee pee boy at one time.
- Quickly visualize a fight. Jonathan gives a swift pop to the nose and the bully goes down. Everyone is impressed. "Whoa!

Jonathan! Alright!" He notices Jennifer watching all this.

- You'd next want to do some quick Flashes on bonding moments with Jennifer. Some of Wes's ideas:
- Mutual love for fishing. Going together to the pond without Grandpa. Sitting on the blanket, opening up the picnic basket.
- Playing hookie somewhere.
- Listening to music and dancing.
- Defending her against her jerk of a boyfriend.

If you've decided at this point to keep with the Core Knowledge points that are established (note that you absolutely don't have to if your Emotion with Detail has taken you on a slightly different journey), you would now want to investigate whatever feelings are wrapped around Jonathan and Jennifer when the deep friendship turns into a love relationship. For that, I would recommend a full-on Emotion with Detail. Following are Wes's thoughts, spoken out loud, of what he would like to do in that Emotion with Detail. Yet, as he spoke, much of it turned into an extensive Flash and then into an actual Emotion with Detail. Interesting...

> Let's say that, as a freshman, Jennifer is dating a senior boy. And he seems like a nice enough boy. He's from a really good family in town. One of the wealthier people in town. And we know Grandpa's not one of the wealthier people. Kind of middle class, right? Let's see [STAMMERS] he's from wealthy, wealthy people. He makes good grades. He's seemingly a good guy. Grandma maybe only allows a kind of supervised dating. I, I bet you, I might be over at the house when he comes over. Let's give him a name. Bobby.
>
> So, Bobby's a seemingly good guy but he does not like me hanging around at all. And maybe he says a little something. You know, when Grandpa and I are in his sanctuary watching TV, watching a football game. Maybe he, he kind of comes out there and disses me in some way. Maybe because Jennifer's a freshman, he's allowed to only see Jennifer at the house. And Jennifer keeps wanting to come in with me and Grandpa to watch the football game.

Bobby doesn't want to spend all of his time here with me and Grandpa. He sees how close we are. How easy we are with each other. And it becomes a jealousy thing for sure. To see that kind of thing happening, right?

But she's head over heels, you know, about him. Because he's like the most popular guy in school – I mean, he's the quarterback. He's the guy every girl wants. The total jock, which I am not, only because I'm too busy doing other things. [BREATHES]

And then I could see him, you know, the, the – that they're allowed to go to the movies together but only if Grandpa, he goes too. Which he thinks – which Bobby thinks is stupid. He's a senior in high school. That's just – [SOUND EFFECT] you know. Then we find out that Bobby cheats on her big time. And she's devastated. And cries her eyes out. Bawls her eyes out. Is afraid to tell me. And for a day or two she won't tell me what's wrong.

She just cries and cries and cries. And finally I say, "You know, let's go fishing. We hadn't gone fishing in so long. Let's go fishing." And so, I take her out just like when we were kids.

And I let her cry. And she finally tells me. He cheated. And she cries and cries and cries. And I hold her and I hold her and I hold her. And she's like, "Why can't he be like you? Why can't he be a gentleman like you? Why can't he be honest like you? Why can't he pull out the chair when I sit down. Why can't he –" You know, this whole long litany, this whole long list of why can't he be like you? But then she looks at me, like, different in that moment. I realize it in that moment and she realizes it at that moment that, oh, it's suddenly turning from really good friends to there's something more here. But I don't kiss her that day. I want to, but I don't. Because that'd be inappropriate.

So, maybe Grandpa lets us go to the movies by ourselves. Probably does. There's trust there. It's Friday night just to – you know, ease the pain a little bit. And it's fun. And, and I'm there at the movies and – it kind of feels like a date. To me. And to her, too, but nobody says anything.

Because this has always been normal. It's always like I've always opened the door for her. I've always been like I'll, I'll try and pay for what I can pay for. You know, let her go first. So it's not anything that's out of the normal. But the look that she's giving me – it's a different feeling now. I'm looking at her through different eyes.

Like she actually really put on [STAMMERS] perfume. And, and, like, the, the – the clothes that she knows that I like, I think that's really pretty. She did her hair a little different. And it – it's kind of a thing where you're sitting at the movie and her hand moves to hold mine. It's like, oh. Am I supposed to hold her hand? And, holding it this time means something much different than it did when we were kids. She knows that I'm ner – nervous. So nervous. And the screen is blurry because I can't even think right.

And. And she whispers really soft in my ear. Hold my hand. And I really quickly just kind of – or I actually just slowly move it over top of hers. And. Interlock the fingers. And I look to her. She doesn't look me in the face at all even though I'm looking at her and she's smiling.

And there's, uh, uh, she's – there's a – I can see it [STAMMERS] – the, the light of the, the chapstick. Whatever she has just glistening off her lips. There's a certain amount of radiance that's coming off of her that's making me hot all over. And then she finally stares at me.

And then, I – we get closer and closer. And I think my skin's gonna explode. And I kiss her lips. And I breathe her in, and yeah... there's fireworks. There's the explosive stars.

And then we sit back. Sit back quickly in our seats like, what did we just do? But the biggest smiles on both of our faces. We don't say a word until the movie ends. And we walk outside. We can't stop kissing – once we go out to the alley just cause we don't want anyone to see.

Here we see Wes in conversation about Jonathan, discussing Flashes or Emotion with Details of future events he might explore if given the time. There are moments where he segues into some pretty specific and helpful visualizations.

And now I'm afraid to tell Grandpa. That's freshman year. I think it becomes a point where I, I have to tell – that both of us have to go to Grandpa and say that our relationship has changed. But we'd both be scared to do that, right? So I would probably tell him in the, the sanctuary.

I think we'd both tell him together. A lot of fear involved because you don't know how he'll handle it and I think I make a point of telling him, you know, "Sir, I would never disrespect Jennifer. Um, I just want you to know, you know, that I will look after her. And everything you ever told me about how I should treat a woman, I will definitely treat her that way."

And there's like a moment of silence where he's just sort of like, no expression. And a big smile, and then he says, "I was waiting for that to happen."

The kind of thing where it's accepted. He makes me start going to church with him. [LAUGHS] And the Tuttle's weren't really very [STAMMERS] religious. And so it's every Sunday, you know, church and then, and then lunch after church. Yeah. Yep. [LAUGHS] We go to like the local sort of, S and S cafeteria for food. Like everyone gathers there for the, the Southern cooking.

Grandma doesn't like cooking every Sunday. Like, it's sort of the Sabbath. She doesn't wanna, like, it's a good excuse not to cook. So the S and S cafeteria...that's, that's where the football coach comes and everyone just kind of like comes and almost – Grandpa's sort of the patriarch of the town. He must have done something that was, like, sort of like heroic for the town. I feel like he was a World War II hero or something. There's a lot of respect for him. Whole lot of respect. Like, maybe, like, some kind of pilot. Or like was part of an elite regiment that made it into Berlin or something like that – where people are like he – he's a hero – they're actually gonna – they gave him the key to the city. Or maybe he was one of the last returning men of his unit from that town.

So it's sort of sad but at the same time he was the hero. He doesn't talk a lot about it unless you ask him. Unless you ask him. Hence the American flag on the wall.

Maybe that flag was given to him, um, at the same time he was awarded some medal. Some kind of – Silver Star maybe. Maybe he saved his whole infantry. Like, putting his life on the line by running up onto a tank and throwing a grenade inside. Something, something – so it's just really heroic where it's like – there's a banner parade.

I do refer to him as the only decent man I've ever really known. Maybe Grandma gets sick and I see how he's by her side day and night, day and night. Maybe I stay at the house in the guest room a couple of times to help out. I cooked food and stuff. Helped Jennifer cook. So it becomes like, uh, a happy little family where Grandpa appreciates it, Grandma appreciates it.

At sixteen I get a job at the gas station. I figure I'm still living with the Tuttles. And maybe feel obligated to help out bill wise. Or want to get my own car. So at sixteen I start working.

Plus I'm able to bring in parts for the stuff Mr. Tuttle needs for his classroom. I'll bring in stuff for him. Maybe he gets me that job. So doing local mechanic work. Maybe a lot of different jobs. Don't care too much for academics. Grandpa talks to me about going to college because I think he's very, um, interested in Jennifer going to college. Probably talks to the both of us about it. And I think how she does well in school, me not so much because a lot of my time spent focusing on work after school. I don't really have a desire to go to college.

If I get certified in welding or something like that, I can make twenty-five bucks an hour. And I'm like, that's the life. I don't need a salary. I don't need a stuffy accountant job. That would, that would choke me down and all you ever told me to do was be out in -- be out in the woods. Why would I wanna be something different? If Jennifer wants to go to college, that's fine. I'll just follow her wherever she goes. I can get a mechanic job anywhere.

So maybe our relationship turns sexual our senior year. Yeah. God, it's hard not to. We've gone through so much together.

After a short break, my conversation with Wes:

Warner: I think it would be important to do an Emotion with Detail on the first time the relationship became physical.

By the way, it's not cheating on your girlfriend/wife/partner; it's character research, and it's okay! Feel the emotional bond that it creates. Any event that's actually mentioned in the script - such as the reference to the school dance - would definitely be made much more powerful by doing an Emotion with Detail. That will make it live!

When you refer to "our song," you'd need to know why it's your song. Create an event in which the two of you determined that. That will give it an emotional reason to exist and will have more impact. We could do that in a Flash if you're short on time. But if you have time, it would be good to do an Emotion with Detail on it, because Jonathan gets choked up about it in the scene, right? I mean, he can't continue the conversation when he starts talking about it.

Let's say that Grandpa said to you that it's kind of stupid to rent a suit. Nobody this year is wearing tuxes. So, it's probably smarter to spend the money and buy it rather than spending the money on a suit that you gotta give back.

So, Jennifer goes with you. You drive to the next city over, which actually has decent stores. That could be a nice Emotion with Detail to do or maybe even just a Flash of you guys making a day of it and feeling kind of – I don't know – big and important, you know, as you're driving to the city. It's kind of a big deal to drive to the city. You feel all grown up and kind of like a couple.

There's a particular restaurant that Grandpa talked about that he used to go to when he was younger, when he would court Grandma. Maybe you stop at that restaurant. It's run down now, but it's still making an attempt to be romantic. You know? After you've bought the suit. And she's already got her dress. It's white – with a navy-blue sash.

So, now she's had her dress for all this time. And she thinks that you should get a navy blue suit, because it goes with her sash. So you find one that you actually like and can afford. So there's not so much money left for dinner. But if you had to eat crackers, you would. You would at least have enough for a root beer float I imagine. I'm kind of flashing on it as we're talking. With the romance and love that you have. I don't know – maybe you pulled over and had sex in your car on the road trip. I don't think that was your first time. But I do think that you are each other's firsts. Let's say it's about a week before prom, and her dress is a little snug. She's really upset, because it has that sash. So she's really upset that it's too snug, and she can't figure out why. She's just been – acting weird all week. All week.

And now it's prom night. You go over to pick her up. There's something off about her. You bought a wrist corsage for her – to match her dress. Like a white rose and baby's breath. Maybe a little bit of cheesy '80s lace. A little bit of greenery. It's definitely showy. And she's like, "Oh, Jonathan! Thank you so much!" Something feels off. You can't quite figure out what it is. And you tell her how beautiful she looks. Grandpa's taking pictures as you guys smile and pose.

From here, Wes takes off with a mixture of Flashes and Emotion with Detail:

> It's funny she's not wearing any, any of her rings. I've given her one or two of those rings. Like, the going steady ring. She's not wearing it. And I don't really ask anything about it. She just says it's not fitting. And I'm confused about that. It's the kind of thing where she's always been so, so thin. And I'm like, maybe kind of hurts a little bit. I don't say anything about it. But she wears it

around her neck instead. Because I, I look around for a little bit and I'm like, oh, okay. She has it around her neck.

So Grandma and Grandpa take pictures and whatnot. And, and I'm all smiley, smiley. And Grandma cries and Grandpa has a little bit of a tear. I walk her out to the car, open the door. I mean, it is so shined and polished and waxed. I guess I belong to this family now. And I think I definitely now have a great need to belong.

Maybe Grandpa's actually given me the Cadillac at this point. Once I hit sixteen, I took great care of it, and he wanted to get himself a truck. So he gave me the Cadillac. Which is something he bought with his GI bill. It's a dark color. Dark burgundy or, like, one of the classic colors of '84 because I thought, this is the time period I have been thinking about when I'm doing it. And it has sort of a leather back top on it. You know, an old Alvarado. But I fixed it up real nice. It runs amazing. It's a V8, hums. And, uh, I get to take her in it, and I've done so many great things to it. Waxed it twice in the sun. I think my right arm kind of hurts from circle, circle, circle, wipe, wipe, wipe. You know? All hand wax. So, my beast is ready to take over my – the chariot is ready to take you, to take you to the ball, my dear. You know, that kind of thing. I'm so proud of my car. And we're, like, listening to all the great top 40 stuff that's happening on the radio on the way to prom. I almost feel like we meet friends before, because now I'm actually starting to belong more. Because of her. Being with her, she's like the captain of the cheerleading squad. You know. People tend to think you're cool, if the person who's cool hangs out with you.

So we meet our friends up at, like, a McDonald's because it's the place to meet in a small town, because there's all of three restaurants. And we have a burger and fries beforehand. And she – All the guys are in their suits. And all the girls in their dresses. We're all sitting there feeling important in all our finery. But still, I have a quarter pounder with cheese. Large fries. She gets chicken nuggets because she likes those the best. And I like to have them too, because it reminds me of when they first took me in. It was, like, the fried chicken, right? Fried chicken is such a comforting thing.

Wes takes a break and then comes back with:

Okay. So. Here's, uh. [PAUSES] [BREATHES] We are in the back parking lot of a Piggly Wiggly. It's right across the street from McDonald's. And everyone looks great. [STAMMERS] our cars are all pulled nose to nose to nose. My Cadillac's there, just shining. And Jennifer is, is radiant.

She – her dress sort of comes off one side of her shoulder and then leaves the other one bare. And she has such a beautiful brown shoulder. And that leads to the, uh, leads to the corsage that she has on her left arm we put on earlier. And [LAUGHS] we're all having such a great time. And passing around, uh, a small bottle of, uh, Jim Beam bourbon. Not too much, because Grandpa would have my ass if I was drinking and driving.

So I only have, like, a few sips and the other guys are having a few more. So I just end up kind of finishing my large coke that, that's icy and it's running over my fingers. And I have Jennifer in my arms to my left. The whisky comes around, I pass it to her. I keep noticing that she doesn't put it to her mouth at all. She kind of smells it and kind of looks around but then passes it over to her friend Bethany who has baby blue dress on. And she's sitting on the bumper with Scott and his F-150. And then across from us is, uh, is Bradley and, and Tonya. And, uh, they both have an F-150.

But, uh, they call me the mayor because I have a, a Cadillac. And the excitement of being able to go and celebrate with Jennifer. And all these people calling me The Mayor. I just – I kind of love that. I definitely belong. Um. Only – it's, it's about 8:00. We should probably head over now. Okay, great. Um, Jennifer's face is kind of, kind of sullen especially with how – I mean, it's still smiling, but it's a little sullen compared to everyone else.

But I don't mind. She looks lovely. All the makeup looks just – she just looks like a queen. So, we, we hop in the Cadillac and start driving over to the high school. And they've turned the gymnasium into, into this, this – I think they said it's a jungle theme for our prom or under the sea. I don't know. I haven't – I didn't really pay much attention and I walked past it this – today.

Um, and I'm driving, and she's holding my hand. I look down I give my boutonniere a little smell. It's a white rose on my navy-blue suit. It smells nice. [LAUGHS] Wow. This is probably as good as it gets right here. I love this woman. It just feels so connected to her right now.

I can smell the Armor-All inside my car. The leather treatment. I just – I feel like a million dollars. But now I actually see Jennifer's face is no longer smiling now that we're alone. The tears actually – it's coming down her left cheek.

"Baby, what's wrong?" And she kind of shakes her head. She doesn't really wanna say. She looks down almost like she's ashamed. "Baby, it's okay. Jennifer, you can tell me. Did – Did you not make it – get into the school you wanted to? Did – you know, I'm gonna come wherever you go." I pull up next to the tennis courts in the high school. And I shut off the car. I can see, like, one or two tennis balls that are still left in the high school tennis court. I turn off the radio. And my seats make, like, a squeak noise as I turn to her. "Honey, this is, this is one of the best nights of our life. What's going on?"

She turns to me. She says, "Do you love me, Jonathan?"

"I love, love you more than anything in the world. I will do absolutely anything for you. You know that. Baby, you're scaring me. What's going on?"

"Well," she said, "that, uh, I've, I've missed my – missed my period."

"So what are you saying? You – Saying you're gonna have [STAMMERS] what? I don't mean to be stupid. I'm sorry. So what are you, what are you saying honey?"

"Well, I took a – a pregnancy test. It was positive." [LAUGHS]

"Oh. Baby. Baby." I pull her, I pull her close to me and I pull her in tight. And I can smell her perfume on her neck and her neck is just so – just smells so good and she's – she's put on, I think, cocoa butter and it's just – she's just – uh, just having her in my arms is just – pulling her close to me. Oh, I feel like this is my purpose. Having her close to me is my purpose and this Cadillac right now in this high school parking lot. What? [LAUGHS]

"Gonna have a baby? You're gonna have a baby? Oh. My baby. My Jennifer baby, baby, baby." Oh. I pull her close to me as hard as I can and she starts laughing and crying at the same time. [LAUGHS] "Oh. Now don't mess up your makeup. We still need to go dance." Yes. Yes. I'm gonna be a daddy. I'm gonna be a daddy. [SNIFFS] "Okay. Okay. Have you told anybody else?"

"Well, just – Well, just, uh, Bethany and Tonya. Stacy."

"So all the girls know and you're finally telling me?"

"Well I wasn't really sure how you..."

"Okay. Well, I'm glad you told me now. Oh. Uh. [CLAPS] Clean your face up. We gotta go inside. We gotta, we gotta celebrate. We gotta celebrate. That's why you weren't drinking the whisky. [LAUGHS] I love you so, so much. I love you so, so much. I love you so, so much."

So I hop out of the car really quick, close the door. Run over to the other side and slowly open my Cadillac door. It creaks just a little bit. The window shines, she looks up at me. With these eyes. Oh. And she gives me her hand. I slowly lift her out of the car. "I was wondering why you didn't have my ring on your finger." [LAUGHS] I close the, close the door with a thud. [CLAPS] Just so proud right now. Everything I want is right now. Everything is – everything I want is right now. I just wanna scream. [CHEERS] And then our, our feet go gently across the gravel parking lot. We walk and I hold her tight, tight. In my arm. She's interlocked with my arm and she has her shoulder – has her arm – her head on my shoulder. And she's just resting there as we walk in.

"I love you, Jonathan."

"I love you, Jennifer. I love you so much." And so we walk up to the double doors. And, uh, one of the teachers from the high school is there and standing next to her is Mr. Tuttle. And he's actually taking tickets. "Hello, sir."

"Hello to you, too. It's gonna be a fine night. They really transformed the inside of this place."

"Well, I can't wait. So, uh, let's get to it." We open up the doors

"Well, you guys have, have a good time. But not too good of a time. Mr. Jim Beam."

"Oh. God, what? No! Not – that, that's mouthwash!" He smiles at me. So we open up and the music's just pumping through the door and it's a big wood door. Double wood doors that lead into the gymnasium. And this is where I've come to watch basketball games a lot.

And there's this, this color. It looks like it's blue with, with sort of disco lights flashing around and [STAMMERS] it's a David Bowie song, "Let's Dance" is playing. I'm like, "Should we dance to this?"

She's like, "I think I can dance for the first few moments of having this baby." She smiles. "Then let's dance." And we go over and we find where everyone's waiting for us. And everybody gives us a big greeting and a big hug.

Everyone's kind of lit up. So it's a little bit exciting. Um. And it's dark in there. And, uh, uh. Everyone's just looking at us. I feel like I'm the – I feel like I'm the king of the high school. Even though I'm not on the, the, uh, the court, I feel like I'm much bigger than anybody. Much more special than any of these people right now because I have such a great gift. Great gift.

And then the song. Cindi Lauper. After we've been sweaty and dancing and dancing and this suit's hot as all get out but I don't wanna take it off – the jacket – because it was a good price but at the same time I don't want anybody to spill any punch on it. So I'm just dancing to the point of me smelling. I smell like a bit like [STAMMERS] old horse I've been dancing so much.

And, um, the slow song comes on. "Time after Time." I look at Jennifer and she looks at me. "I guess this is officially our song, Baby." She pulls me onto the floor. I'm holding some Boone's Farm somebody gave me in a red cup. A little bit of it spills on me. We laugh.

And she just pulls me right up to her. She puts her chin in my chest. Puts her right ear on my left – on my – my right shoulder and just lies there. And her body just relaxes into me. Her whole warm body just lies close to me.

I pull her real snug tight into me and I, I feel my hands across her. Her. [UNINTELLIGIBLE] It's a coldish back because that – she's been so sweaty it's just sort of like cold now. And we sway to the music. She looks at me. I look down at her. I just give her a big reassuring, loving kiss. To let her know I am here. I will always be here. Without any words. And she lays her head back down. We finish listening to the song "Time After Time."

[HUMS TIME AFTER TIME]. The whole place is just packed. We're lost. We're lost in the crowd.

Wes ends his Emotion with Detail work for the day. On a separate day, he explores telling Grandpa:

Okay. [LAUGHS] I'm Jonathan. And I'm eighteen years old. [BREATHES] I am nervous as shit. I – Been trying to like, just doing deep breaths all day. Just trying to clear my lungs because they've been getting tight. They're pretty tight right now. [BREATHES] Grandpa loves me [LAUGHS]. But I don't know if I acted like a gentleman getting her pregnant. Oh boy. Okay. I'm sitting in my Cadillac right now and I can feel my feet connected to the floor board. And they're heavy. And I called Grandma – Grandpa earlier and asked him if I could talk to him around 5:30 or so. I got off my job early. I've been watching the clock ever since. I'm looking at my, my clock on the dash on my car right now. 5:25. 5:25. And he's – this is – okay. Yeah. Man. Oh boy. I'm excited to tell him. I'm excited to tell him. [LAUGHS] I'm gonna ask him to be my best man. Yeah. I can smell the gas that's on my shirt that actually I – spilled a little gasoline on my t-shirt. I didn't even go home to change. I just got in the car and drove on over. My hands are clutching the steering wheel. It's 5:28. I look in the mirror and I look at myself and I say, "I can do this. I can do this. Jonathan, you're a man!" [LAUGHS] "You're a man. You're about to do something awesome." Okay. [CLAPS] [LAUGHS] He loves me. He loves me. Okay. I open up the car door, it makes a little creak noise.

I slam it behind me. The same familiar street. I parked just outside the mail box. The mailbox is in front of my car. And I start walking up the lawn. I'm stretching just a little bit because I'm [BREATHES]...I'm a little nervous, just a little nervous, just a little nervous. I step up onto the, to the porch. And it's a brick porch with, like, cement and I can smell the azaleas that are blooming outside. There's a honeysuckle that's intertwined and on the rail. I smell the double sweet smell from azaleas and also from the honeysuckle. It's calming for me. [BREATHES] It's calming. And I, uh, I open up the, uh, screen door. It creaks. [SOUND EFFECT] And I – and I give a good knock. [KNOCKS] Okay. All right. I hear him unlatching it through the door. He looks at me.

[LAUGHS]

"How are you, sir?"

"Hey J, come on in. come on in." I close the screen door behind me and it slams a little bit. "Don't let that slam."

"Oh, sorry about that. I – I remember, I'm sorry. I'm not thinking, sir. Sorry. It's, it's – it's hot outside." And so I close the door behind me.

"You want a little ice tea before we do our talk?" [LAUGHS]

"Yeah. I'd love some ice tea. I'd like a little iced tea. That'd be great."

So he pours a big glass of ice tea for me in the kitchen. And I can hear them, the ice tinkling on the side of the glass. There's a little, uh, palmettos on the side of the, of the glasses. He shuts the, the door after putting up the, the sweet tea. It makes a thud [SOUND EFFECT]. "All right, let's walk out to the sanctuary. That's where men talk."

"Yeah, let's do it." So, uh, he opens up the door. Unlocks it. The handle kind of jiggles and makes the brassy noise that the door knob makes. And he puts me at ease. The nerves aren't really there right now. He's just such a calming force in my life.

So, we walk in, walk down the steps there and, uh, the door just closes behind us. The nerves crept back in. It feels like an interrogation room now. Even though this room is so special to me. It just feels like it's a lot of pressure. So I, I go and, uh, there's the, there's the chair. There's the chair. There's – Got a little duct tape on the arm. It's silverish. But it's brand-new. It must be brand-new duct tape. He made it look nice. Nice as duct tape can be. And, uh, I sit in the, uh, the small rickety chair that I pull off the, the, wall. A small wooden chair with a – five wooden spokes in the back. It's worn out. It looks like he might've gotten it out of a, a flea market.

And I set it down near the head of the bear rug. I don't know where the heck he got this bear rug. Never really asked him. I guess I just assumed he killed him. [BREATHES] He sits back in his chair, actually props his feet up. Makes that thud noise with the little handle inside. And I look at him, I'm sitting straight up in my dirty shirt.

Light beams in from the, the windows that are on the garage door and he's got a fan just oscillating back and forth to cool us off. "All right Jonathan. What's going on? What's going on? Let's talk. Man talk. You thinking about a business? You want a little money? I thought definitely one day you'd definitely come to me for that. I'm happy to do that." [LAUGHS]

"Uh, well, maybe, maybe someday now that we're talking about it. I'll, I'll take some money from you." I take another big sip of the iced tea. It's sweet. Refreshing. Goes down my throat. I keep it in my hands because it's nice and cool and how hot it is outside.

"All right. So spill it, son."

"Well, you know, I, uh, I graduate high school soon."

"Yeah, I'm proud, I'm proud of you for that."

"And, uh, you know, I, I feel like I've become a pretty good man and I really, I really owe it all to you." He looks at me, doesn't say a word. "And, um, I've been doing pretty well. In fact, I'm, I'm one of the, the head mechanics and I'm making a little more money and I've been putting it away and – You know, I've, I've been with Jennifer for a long time now. And, uh, I can –" I'm looking at him and yeah, he's not moving. He's like a statue.

"And I, I think it's about that time, sir, and I ask you, the man who's given me so much, I ask you for one more thing. Can I have your granddaughter's hand in marriage?"

He just stares at me. "Oh. Jonathan, Jonathan, Jonathan, Jonathan. You know I love you like a son. I love you like a son." I hear the door open up. It's [STAMMERS] it's Jennifer.

"Hey you guys."

"Uh, honey, we're just in the middle of something here."

"No, [STAMMERS] I think I should be a part of this."

"I really think – okay. I think you're right, honey, because yeah. Uh, even though I am – I'm trying to be a man here, doing the right thing." [LAUGHS] "Uh. Yeah. Sit down next to me, honey." So she grabs another chair, it's like a fold out nylon thing.

"So you know about this, Jennifer?" Grandpa says.

"Yes, sir. I do."

"You know how I feel about you going to college."

"Well, I'll, I'll, I'll still go to college. I mean, there's a community college in the other town."

"Honey, you are not community college material. It is not where you want to go. All the time you put in and all the time that you put in high school it's not [STAMMERS] – it's not gonna benefit you with anything. It's not gonna benefit you the way that you wanted your life to go! And I've seen the things that you want and the life that you wanna live and the way you wanna live it. And I am –"

"Well, sir, [STAMMERS] I really need to – my duty as a man. And I – there's some certain responsibilities that I need to take a hold of right now and this is the responsibility that I think is the most important to me in my life."

"Jonathan, what are you talking about? Responsibility." He looks at Jennifer in this sort of cold look.

"Well, sir, I, I – I have, uh, I have some – Something I tell you and I think it's only or – it only makes sense that, that we get married."

Jennifer says, "Grandpa, I'm pregnant."

Oh my God. It's – oh boy. It needed to be said. It's on the table. It's on the table. It's on the table. Grandpa...his face turns red.

"Jonathan, I trusted you, son. I trusted you. I trusted you like you were my own flesh and blood and you turn on me like this? I never should've let you two go off like that."

"Grandpa, no. I love him. We love each other."

"He was – no, Jennifer!"

"No, please, Grandpa!"

"No, you listen to me! Jonathan, you're not good enough for my granddaughter."

"Sir, I, I don't think I can accept that."

"There is no question about what's gonna happen here. There is no accepting. What I say is what is going to happen. Jonathan, get out of my house! You – I can't talk to you, Jonathan."

"No, sir, please I love her –"

"GET OUT OF MY HOUSE!"

I stand up slowly. Jennifer's crying. "But, sir –"

"Not another word! Not another word. Not another word. You get out of my house, Jonathan, I – we will talk later on. But for right now, I need to talk to Jennifer."

"Sir, no. If you – there's, there's a [STAMMERS] decision to be made."

"There is no decision! You are children. I will talk to my granddaughter. Get out of my house!"

"Yes, sir. Yes, sir." I feel my face just flushing with embarrassment.

I run out of the house. I run out. I jump in my car and I turn it on. I don't wanna leave yet. I don't wanna leave yet. I don't want to leave yet. I am good enough. I am good enough. I am good enough. I am good enough. [CRIES] I am good enough. God damn it. God damn it. God damn it. I crank up the car. Like, and haul ass. I'm going as fast as I can. God damn it. God. [CRIES]

He's talking to her and he could be absolutely saying anything. Making her not love me anymore. [PAUSES] And, uh, [CRIES] just seeing him that disappointed in me is crushing. And I'm just sitting here at the pond. [CRIES] I'm just sitting here at the pond and I'm angry and I'm angry and I'm so hurt.

And looking at the tadpoles and nothing has any meaning to me. Nothing has any meaning because all the meaning has been taken away from me. Anything that had any kind of – he could be saying anything right now. Oh my god. Right? He could be saying anything right now. [CRIES] No.

What can I do? What can I do? What can I do to help – there's nothing I can do. There's nothing I can do. He won't let me talk to her. He – please. I need to be able to see her again. I need to be able to see her. I have to see her tonight. I have to. I have to know that she – she's not gonna leave me.

So that was emotional. Because he's fairly spent and emotionally raw right now, he was able to use some Flashes that had impact. Here's what he visualized in quick spurts or Flashes and going in and out of Emotion with Detail:

So I can't see her that night. I call her to talk. And she's like tomorrow, tomorrow. And she keeps saying she loves me, she loves me. She won't...she's like, later, later, later. Let's just – but tell me. Just tell me, Jennifer, just tell me. And she's like, I love you. I love you. At least I've got that. Yeah, yeah. I got the promise of the fact that she loves me right now. And I know that to be true.

But then, the next day comes and I call her and she can't see me. Grandpa's sick or something like that or Grandma's sick – Grandpa's sick. And I feel guilty because it's [STAMMERS] he was, he was probably so distraught. He has heart problems anyway, right? And then, um, [BLOWS NOSE]. Maybe, maybe she's gotta go away. Like, like, for a week somewhere. She says it's a family reunion, and it had already been planned. She must have forgotten to tell me she says. For a minute, I fear that she might do something with the baby, but then I think – that's not her. She would never. And she loves me so much.

And they come back and finally I see her – she sneaks out to see me. Or she just leaves the house to see me. I don't go over there. Because Grandpa's not – he doesn't want me around the house. Won't, won't take my calls.

And I talk about the baby like, oh, you know. We're together. Maybe go to the pond. Like maybe we can, we can run away together. And this look comes over her face. Oh, god. Oh god.

She says, "I lost it. I lost it."

"What do you mean you lost it? What do you mean you lost it Jennifer?"

"Gram –"

"No."

"Grandpa took me down..."

"No, no. [CRIES] No..."

"I'm so sorry."

"No..."

"I didn't have a choice, Jonathan."

"What do you mean you didn't have a choice, you could – [CRIES]"

"I'm sorry. I didn't have a choice."

"Okay."

"But I love you."

"We, we could run away. We could leave. We could leave. And I'm going to take you. We're going to leave. Can you go and get your bags and pack? And then we can leave. I've been saving up money."

"Just let me get into school. It – just let me start school then you can come. Okay? I'll just..."

"Okay. I'll come there to school with you."

"Well, let me just start because Grandpa's gonna take me and you know he'll never allow you to go too."

"Jennifer, you're making it seem like you don't want me around."

"That's not true. That's not true. I just don't wanna rock the boat any more than we've already rocked it. You know, I think if he saw you in here, he would just flip out. You know how volatile he can get."

"Yeah, yeah, I do."

"I, I couldn't take that. So just let me start school. And then. Then you'll come."

"I – How about I just come with you now?"

"Jonathan, you know you can't. You know you can't."

"Jennifer, I love you. I love you so much."

"I love you too."

[CRIES] "Then let me go with you."

"You – you know Grandpa would never allow it. You know he wouldn't. [PAUSES] Just let me start school."

And so I let her. And I try to call her. A lot. Sometimes she doesn't answer. Maybe she makes the excuse of studying all the time. She says how hard it is. It's so different from high school. And maybe I arrange to come see her for a weekend. So I go, and it's really, really awkward. I'm planning on staying in her dorm room with her. But she's got a roommate, so it's just really weird. I end up sleeping in my car. The campus cops come and make me move. I feel alone, awkward and just not wanted...Maybe I go find a liquor store, and sit there in my car and get wasted. Then decide I'm gonna go talk to her. It's late at night. I go to her room.

Knock – knock on the door and I'm drunk and probably – that causes trouble. And I think it's a massive feeling like, I do not belong here. Because I don't. I'm the mechanic from high school and now she's the college girl. And I feel it. I'm not good enough.

So this is tweaking this character's Base Human Emotion in a big way.

> Maybe she actually she does come down from her dorm. She's like, in her night clothes. And she's like, "I can't talk to you here. It's, it's late. I'm tired. I told you not to come here." One of those kinds of nights it's just – You could just tell you're losing someone. And eventually she says, "I'm, I'm seeing someone else." I would go home depressed, hurt, maybe angry, but definitely confused.

At this point, depending on how much time Wes had left to spend building the character, he would either do Flashes or Emotion with Details that allowed him to experience what life is like after Jennifer. How long after this last event is it that Grandpa dies? I would say at least several years. She's out of school and in the job force now. So it's important to explore what life is like now. What job is he in? Still working as the mechanic in the same shop? Does he have a relationship with someone now?

Whether you've followed along with Wes's Emotion with Details and Flashes and his building of the character or you've done your own building of Jonathan, look back at the scene now. It looks remarkably different now, right? It would be difficult for you to play Jonathan in a one-note way now. We never want to "play at the scene." Instead, we are able to create nuance and texture in a character by building the life, experiencing the life and then dropping this fully formed life into the circumstances of the scene. Just like real life works.

DEBRIEFING

You'll find that occasionally it's difficult to let go of an Emotion with Detail. Even though your intellect knows that you are separate from the character, your body may hold on to pain, tension or discomfort after the scene or after the Emotion with Detail is over. Debriefing after doing a particularly uncomfortable, distasteful or horrific one is very important. If the need arises, try giving yourself an almost ritualized way to end the experience. For example, take a nice, deep, cleansing breath, and as you breathe in, say to yourself, out loud, something along the lines of, "I now breathe myself in, with all the joy, abundance and full life I so richly have and deserve." As you release the breath, state again your willingness to let the character and all the character's pain go. "I now let go of _____'s experiences, and all the tragedy, horror and heartbreak of what he/she has suffered." You can repeat this several times until the feelings you're having are gone. The mind follows the body, and the body follows the mind. So for me, saying it out loud is another way of telling my mind and body what to do: release those feelings! I know an actor who debriefs by washing his face after an Emotion with Detail as a way of washing the character off for the time being. Whatever works for you is fine.

Respect the fact that your job as an actor may be hard to "leave at the office," and take the time and care to let it go. It's important to learn not to carry the burden of the character around with you on a daily basis so that it does not bleed into your life. Don't worry that you won't be able get the character back. You will, quite easily and on a moment's notice. Trust me, some Emotion with Detail work you will actually remember for years to come.

Congrats! You've completed "full-circle homework." You began on the left side of the brain with the analytical Givens and Hows of Behavior and segued into the right side of the brain with the Whys, Core Knowledge, Base Human Emotion and Emotion with Detail. What a joy it is to create a rich, nuanced, textured and unique character unlike any other and unlike any other actor is capable of creating.

A QUICK REMINDER OF EMOTION WITH DETAIL WORK:

- **Start out at age three, four, five, six, or seven.**
- **Speaking out loud, create and live the emotionally pertinent event that created the Base Human Emotion. Remember, you may have to set up this moment. (For example: You can't feel loss until you know what you've had.)**

- **As you speak the experience out loud, refer to the character as "I."**
- **Speak the inner monologue out loud, as well as actual conversation.**
- **Live the event as if it's in the present rather than narrating it in the past.**
- **Experience it rather than watching it, and relate in a way that feels natural to you.**
- **Let your imagination flow freely.**
- **Create and hold in your mind the character's surroundings. Start out small, perhaps with an object. Justify why your character is holding it or using it. Or begin in the child's bedroom, for instance, and expand from there.**
- **Give details an emotional reason to exist.**
- **Incorporate as many of the senses as you can – what you see, hear, touch, taste, smell.**
- **Do not force the emotion to come.**
- **Let one Emotion with Detail inform the next one; allow the domino effect.**
- **Move forward in the life in order to live as many moments as you can.**
- **Build in necessary relationships and events.**
- **Go slowly and create as much detail as possible, loading the character with emotional fuel.**

"The true sign of intelligence is not knowledge but imagination."
~ Albert Einstein

FROM PREP TO SET

PREPPING WITH TIME CONSTRAINTS

This is something I hear quite often: *"I have an audition tomorrow, and I don't have time to do 'full-circle' homework. What do I do?"* Or you're on set tomorrow, and you just wrapped your last movie a day ago. In other words, you have no prep time! It happens. First determine how dramatic, tragic or complex the character is. This will tell you how deep to go in your Emotion with Detail work should you have the opportunity to do more later on.

For auditions, read the scene as if you have all the time in the world and are not in fact panicking. Read it from an objective viewpoint, avoiding at all costs thinking about how you're going to play it. I know that's hard, but you can do it. Determine what kind of scene this is and what is central to making it work. Is it a relationship scene? A break-up scene? A fight scene? A deep revelation? What's the relationship that lies at the core of this scene? Is it with a lover? Brother/sister? Parent? Friend? Take time to do some quick Hows of Behavior to determine specific character traits, paying attention to patterns of behavior that emerge. From those patterns, quickly pick a Base Human Emotion, and stick with it. Then build a loose and quick Core Knowledge. Create several brief Emotion with Detail events that explore the central elements you've identified. When you are adept at Emotion with Detail, you'll be able to accomplish this with Flashes only. Do a brief Emotion with Detail on any events that are actually referred to in or during the scene. You may not have time to create the character from childhood on up. You may have to hit only the highlights of the character that are given in the scene or explore the relationships in the scene, but you will have worked more specifically and added more dimension than you could ever have done by playing "at" the character.

One of my students told me an interesting story that I think helps clarify this concept. A professor walks into the classroom and sets down a large, cylindrical glass vase on his desk. He fills the vase to the top with golf balls and asks, "Is it full?" The class responds, "Yes." He then pours a bag of gravel over the golf balls. "Is the vase full now?" The class responds, "Yes. It is now full." The professor smiles and produces a bag of sand from underneath his desk. He pours the contents over the golf balls and gravel. "It's certainly full now!" the students exclaim. "Maybe," he replies. "But what about now?" he asks as he pours water into the mixture.

Seeing something as full is actually subjective. Indeed, the vase was full to the top with golf balls. It was also full with gravel, and then with sand, and even more full with the addition of water. In an audition, we often feel like we haven't had enough time to do as much work as we'd like. We feel that, like the glass vase, our character isn't full enough. But if you have time to do even a small portion of the work, filling it up with "golf balls" only, know that you've done more than most. Do all you can do as time permits, and let the rest go.

For auditions, ask yourself, "Why did casting choose this scene? To show what aspect of the character? What books this job?" Then choose those aspects of the character to focus your limited time on.

In looking at the scene you're about to shoot or about to audition with, remember that *we never enter a scene in quite the same way as we leave it.* A simplistic example would be: If this is a relationship scene in which we see two lovers at odds or in a fight with each other at the end of the scene, consider that the emotions at hand in the beginning of the scene are different. Are they cautious with one another? Happy? Hopeful? If the scene is well written, you'll be able to see the difference. This will be true for most scenes, not just relationship scenes. Find the emotional differences at the top of the scene versus the end of the scene.

Pre-performance (I hate that word), note where the scene turns and changes. But in the moment of doing the scene, you must, of course, be willing to allow yourself to actually take the journey of the character from one moment to the next. You must let go of anticipating that this turn or change is coming - that something is about to happen. Also, be keenly aware of not playing the emotion that comes at the end of the scene in the beginning.

Most of all, remember that when you are acting, you must be thinking character *thoughts* rather than *personal thoughts* during the scene.

MEMORIZATION

Have you ever said, *"I'm scared I won't remember my lines, so I memorize them right away"*? And then later said, *"I feel like I'm stuck in my head during a scene"*? Well, one of those things can certainly cause the other.

This may seem counterintuitive to some, but take care not to memorize your lines before developing your character.

You will find teachers who would advise you otherwise, but I feel strongly about this. When you memorize lines in a rote fashion, without emotional fuel behind them, prior to character exploration, you are forcing your brain to store those lines in the rote memory section of the brain. This is a different section of the brain than the section that stores images, concepts, and memories to which you are emotionally connected.

Rote memory is perfectly designed to store information such as dates, multiplication tables, symbols and such. These are usually stored by repetition with no thought or value placed upon them. We store this information in the rote and repetitive section of the brain so that we can quickly retrieve the necessary facts.

But if you store your lines in the rote memory section, how do you think they will sound? A parrot comes to mind. Ask anyone – I don't care where they were raised – to say the ABC's out loud. I guarantee you that they will say them in the same singsongy "A, B, CEEE, DEE, E, F, G..." So if you memorize your lines through repetition, without building the character first, you have stored those lines in the rote memory section of your brain. They have no meaning. When you need to retrieve those lines, they will come spewing out of you easily. But now you are trying to attach meaning to them at the same time. That's a lot of work and can be confusing. Maybe impossible. It makes it twice as hard, and completely frustrating, when a director tries to get a slightly different and subtle emotion out of you. Your brain is too busy trying to remember and feel at the same time. Human beings aren't wired like that.

Build the character first; do your full-circle homework. *After* you have built the life of the character through Emotion with Detail work, go back and look at the lines. They will hold a different meaning for you than they did upon first look. Now that they have emotional significance and resonance, they should be much easier to memorize. Your character will want to say the words – will need to say the words. You'll allow yourself to walk as the character walks. You'll think, breathe, speak, and react as the character does. You will free yourself from the page, get out of your head, and get inside the world of the character.

When it's time to put your character in front of the camera, focus on these next and final steps in the process: *Flashes* (if needed), *Prior Circumstances*, *Prior Moments* and *Prior Instant.*

FLASHES BEFORE SHOOTING

(Reconnecting with the Character)

Many actors wonder about dropping into character when it's time to shoot. If you've done full-circle homework, the character will be there for you. The experiences you've lived as your character will stay with you, and you will no sooner forget your Emotion with Detail work than you could forget the truly emotional moments in your own history. When we think or speak about our personal past experiences, we have an emotional reaction to those moments. Since we follow human nature in this technique, I want you to do the same for your character. Previously, we discussed the ability to use Flashes to create character memories when time constraints don't allow you to do full-on Emotion with Details. We're going to use Flashes in a different way here. You'll use them to reconnect to your character when necessary.

In the Emotion with Details you've already done, you'll notice that a particular moment in each one of them stands out to you. Or there will be a point in time when you were particularly moved. This poignant moment is much the same as a Flash that you learned to create earlier. The moment makes such an impression on you that it becomes a touchstone for reconnecting with your character. Briefly recall or "flash" on these particularly poignant moments, and you should start to feel the character again. The same thing tends to happen in real life: when you recall something that happened to you, you remember it much like a flash of an instant - short, vivid moments of the event. Think of a Flash as being like a mini version of an Emotion with Detail.

While it's not always necessary, if you want, you can flash on the character from the beginning, starting with the formative experience that created your BHE. Or you can flash on something that relates to the scene you're about to shoot. For example, if the scene you're shooting is about breaking up, right before you shoot, you would benefit by flashing on the moments of the relationship that were magical, wonderful, giddy, safe, loving. So when your heart gets broken in the scene at hand, you'll be that much more devastated. Anytime you're dealing with loss, remember this: you can't know what you've lost until you know what you've had. The reason, in real life, that we feel pain over a loss - be it a death, or a break up, or what not - is because we remember the pleasure of it. We remember all the good times, and we mourn the loss of it. The same is true of a character. This serves you much better than focusing on the trouble in your character's relationship. Focusing on the horribly bad things in the relationship of the characters could cause you to anticipate the break up. When you anticipate an emotion, chances are you'll rarely feel it in the moment.

In the Jonathan/Jennifer scene we've been looking at, some helpful Flashes to do might be remembering moments of Grandpa's kindness or happy moments with Jennifer (like the birthday cake).

Now that you've reconnected to your character, think about your Prior Circumstances.

PRIOR CIRCUMSTANCES

The circumstances or events that lead up to the scene at hand.

If you have a fairly large role in the picture, one of the challenges commonly faced is keeping track of the character's emotional arc when shooting out of sequence. I would suggest that you create a timeline for the character, especially if you're dealing with a particularly complex script or journey. Almost every character will change emotionally as his or her circumstances change, either significantly or subtly. Otherwise, you have a relatively boring character, huh?

Ninety-nine percent of the time, you shoot out of sequence, because scheduling and budget prohibit doing otherwise. But if you have a personal timeline for the character, covering physical, emotional, geographical and other important biographical arcs, you'll always be able to pinpoint your place in the emotional journey for a particular scene.

In our Jonathan/Jennifer scene, the Prior Circumstances might be Jonathan arriving at the house after so many years, walking back in with all the memories of a time gone by, seeing Grandma again and various people from town gathered at the house, etc. Which leads you to your Prior Moments.

PRIOR MOMENTS

Moments before the scene begins.

The Prior Moments are the moments or minutes that lead up to the beginning of the scene. What bit of life is going on with the character in these specific moments? For example, but certainly not limited to: What are his/her thoughts? What is he/she expecting? Wishing? Hoping? Counting on?

In our Jonathan/Jennifer scene, it would be moments in the imagination right before Jonathan walks up to the sanctuary door. Which brings us to the Prior Instant.

PRIOR INSTANT

The instant before the scene begins. Specific character thoughts in the character's specific words. These are thoughts in the imagination - not spoken out loud.

When the camera first sees you, the audience should know exactly what you are feeling, thinking or experiencing without you even saying a word. You can achieve this with a Prior Instant. I think it's imperative to have one. In a Prior Instant, you are literally switching off a personal thought, and switching on a character thought. You can't think two things at the same time. The Prior Instant is comprised of the precise thoughts and exact words the character is thinking in this moment, as if you've spoken the thoughts out loud, yet they are silent. I call this exact character thought, in the character's own words, a "hard" inner monologue.

If you know exactly what your character is thinking, your mind and body will follow. A Prior Instant gets you out of the gate, so to speak, in exactly the way you need. Just make sure you are not anticipating what is about to happen in the scene; the actor knows what is about to take place, but the character does not. If the director gives you a note after a take, it may be necessary to change your Prior Instant slightly. Each Prior Instant will cause the scene to play slightly differently. In our scene with Jonathan and Jennifer, think of how differently the scene would begin using these two alternate Prior Instances:

If Jonathan is thinking in the moment:

> "Oh, please don't let Jennifer be in here. I don't know if I can bear to see her..."

OR

> "This is the last time I'll ever walk through this door...It's so wrong that Grandpa's not here."

Both of these work. But each one would produce different results. The first one is focused on Jennifer and the past relationship with her. Finding her sitting in the room would be somewhat uncomfortable. This Prior Instant could also account for the pause and hesitation in the beginning of the scene. There is a little bit of anticipation going on with this one, however - you half expect her to be there!

I would be more inclined to use something like the second Prior Instant. It is focused on the loss of Grandpa and doesn't anticipate finding Jennifer there. Again, this accounts for the hesitation at the top of the scene. You could have built into your Prior Circumstances and Prior Moments that you felt compelled to come to the house to let the family know you cared, but you were relieved to have actually missed Jennifer. You had opened the "sanctuary" door a bit ago, and Jennifer wasn't there. You went into the kitchen briefly to say goodbye to Grandma. As you were about to leave after paying your respects, you wanted to take one last look in that room. "This is the last time I'll ever walk through this door. It's so wrong that Grandpa's not here." Open the door, and Jennifer is there. To me this is a bit more powerful. It makes Jonathan a bit more vulnerable.

A Prior Instant is very personal. It is completely dependent on the character that you build. If the director had told you to suspect that Jennifer was going to be there, then you would opt for something like the first Prior Instant. If the director says nothing, then I would choose something like the second, which gives you a bit more surprise and removes the anticipation.

The simpler the Prior Instant or "character thought" is, the better. If one is working well, feel free to use a variation of it in the next take. If you use the same one over and over again, it *will* get stale after a few takes. So use the same meaning but change it slightly. An example would be, "I can almost still smell Grandpa's pipe...like he's still here."

An on-set example of this is probably best described in an actor's own words. So I'm going to relay to you exactly what the wonderfully talented Sarah Rafferty, who brings us the character of Donna in the long running series *Suits*, has to say about hard inner monologue:

> "...I want to mention one super quick life saver that you taught me. The hard inner monologue. After creating all the backstory, doing the Emotion with Detail work, having a moment before, in place before the cameras role, the hard inner monologue has saved me. That's what keeps me in the scene, keeps my attention off myself, which is the single worst place for it to go, prevents me from judging what just happened or dreading the moment to come.
>
> So, I just used the hard inner monologue on Friday. And I think this will make you laugh. And this is a massive spoiler, so I trust this story won't go wide for at least another six weeks. ;) As you know, Gabriel and I have been friends forever and have a very sibling like relationship. Our characters have been through seven seasons of fairly epic 'will they/won't they' slow burn. Sometimes that makes us laugh with the depth of the church laughs I shared with my sisters in the 80's. First scene up on Friday, Harvey walks into Donna's office, and she gets up, walks across the room and kisses him. No pressure. It's just been seven years of twitter hashtags about these two characters getting together. Twenty minutes before we shoot, I hear from the director and creator that the network wants many, many options of the type of kiss, because they don't know exactly what they want it to be – sexy, emotional, tender – a whole rainbow

of kiss options. So we're gonna do this many, many times, and it's totally on me as Donna, because Harvey doesn't see it coming. On top of that, I have a good ten feet of space to cover from where I'm sitting to where he is planted. Ten feet to start to laugh or get self-conscious or riddled with doubt, and awkwardness and shank the take. So instead, every time he walked in I spent the few seconds of potentially awkward time talking to myself as Donna. And every time it was a different hard inner monologue that was, you guessed it, sexy, tender, soulful...And that saved me. Even the take where I was directed to get to him faster, over shot my mark and banged my front tooth on his, I didn't crack up until they yelled cut, because I held on to that hard inner monologue with a death grip. And in the end I think the tooth bang take will be in the edit. Everyone knows a chipped tooth is super sexy. So it was a choice. A sexy, romantic, tender choice. That's my story and I'm sticking to it."

Sarah is as delightful in person as she is on screen!

All of these – Flashes, Prior Circumstances, Moments, Instants – are of course in your imagination. They'll serve you well. Kids so quickly go into their imaginations. As adults, we are sometimes reticent. I coached a young girl several years ago, and she keeps popping up in my head from time to time. She was genius at Emotion with Detail work. Loved it. It was pure play time for her. Right before she would shoot, she'd giggle and say, "Okay now, I'm putting on the shroud of ______. (She'd say the character's name and put a pretend blanket over her head.) Look! You can't see *me* anymore, because I'm *her*!" How magical is that? What a true and beautiful analogy. Put the shroud of the character over yourself.

"The perfection of acting lies in the imperfection of it all. Just like life."
~ Warner Loughlin

SHOOTING

Let's say you've just done the most brilliant take in the world! In reality, there's no such thing, but you can get pretty close. This is super important and sounds completely counter-intuitive: *Don't strive for the perfect take* (particularly on your coverage). Just be willing to go on the journey of the character. If you blow a line on your coverage, often you can back up a bit and repeat it again. At times, you'll feel you're not completely "there." Don't worry. Know that the editor can dip back into the master shot if need be. You'll usually have multiple takes of your coverage, so there are many options to choose from. It is no more your job to pass judgment on your own take than it is the director's job to stand in front of the camera saying your lines. I'm not saying don't seek to be brilliant. I'm saying don't beat yourself up over a take that is less than stellar in your opinion. Doing that only puts you "in your head." Just take the journey of the character. That is the most courageous thing to do. Like any human being who has to "go on," moment after moment, your character does too.

Even more important, don't try to repeat a take! The director may say, "Brilliant!" But if you try to repeat the brilliance, you will be watching yourself and judging yourself and going for a result rather than taking the emotional journey of the scene. Not what you want to do. There's a mantra I like to say after each take: *Breathe - Reset - Prior Instant*. It helps me go back to the emotion or thoughts that are present at the beginning of the scene so that I don't play the emotional end of the scene that I just experienced. I want to take the journey of the scene all over again.

Sometimes you'll feel like you are totally lost or like your mind is wandering during a scene. Some actors call that "going up." When this happens, and it will, rather than wasting time beating yourself up over it, try this: Pop your focus as quickly as you can to the other actor. Think a *character* thought related to the *other character* you're in the scene with. Have a character-related opinion about what you see. "How could she possibly afford that purse?" Or even, "Nice eyes." Think a *character thought about anything*, and you'll be back in the scene. You cannot be in two places at one time. So choose to be in the character's mind rather than in your own head beating yourself up. Seeking to have character-related thoughts at all times during your scene is hugely important. If you think it, camera reads it.

You've probably heard teachers or others say, "Throw all your homework away!" I'm not really sure what that even means. Why would you forget all the work you've done? I suppose it's a way of saying, "Don't let it get in the way." I would agree with that. With full-circle homework, you have the luxury of using that delicious knowledge of the character so that you can think character thoughts in the moment. You don't want to simply be an executioner of homework, watching to see if you've produced the desired outcome. Stay in your right brain, get lost in the moment, play with your imagination, and **seek to think character thoughts**.

You've also likely heard teachers say, "Give to the other actor!" This is going to sound counter-intuitive, **but I want you to *take*, rather than *give*.** Take in, drink in and really hear what the other character says to you. Allow yourself to feel. It is then that you inadvertently give to the other actor, because it is then that you are authentic. As human beings, we are reactionary creatures. We don't walk around only trying to be heard. We take in what is said to us, and we react. So seek to take, and you will thereby give.

In HBO's *Sharp Objects* from writer/creator Marti Noxon and based on the best-selling novel by Gillian Flynn, Amy Adams as Camille gives a riveting performance as a reporter who returns to her small town to cover the murders of two young girls. Camille, as we soon discover, deals with many personal demons. It's a deliciously complex character. Amy is a master at Emotion with Detail. She spent a good deal of time building her relationship with her mother, Adora, played by Patricia Clarkson. Watch those scenes and note how Amy allows the relationship to impact her. She is truly *taking* in the moment, not seeking to give. That allows the "homework" to show up inadvertently. Note how she is not chasing a result. The emotion springs out of her because of the beautiful groundwork she created before she stepped on set. It's one of the many reasons you can't take your eyes off her.

You'll want to remember to never chase a result. In other words, don't keep waiting for your homework to show up in the scene. Don't keep trying to build up to that emotional moment in the scene. If you look for that to happen, you are watching yourself; you are out of the moment at hand, and believe me, the emotion will leave you.

In the Oprah Winfrey produced series, *Greenleaf*, Broadway star and now television star Merle Dandridge plays Grace Greenleaf, the prodigal daughter who has returned to her family after twenty years. Here she recounts a moment in which she reminded herself of exactly that:

> "A cornerstone moment in the Greenleaf series was the Season 2 fight between Grace and Mac, our villain. It was a knock down, bloody, physical beast of a scene that took all day and left its marks (emotionally and physically) afterward. I have a rare and extraordinary gift in being surrounded by people who are unimaginably excellent at their craft. The way they show up for me is a wonderful lesson in being present for your fellow actors. It elevates the entire ship. With great trust and a loving friendship between Greg Alan Williams (the actor who plays Mac) and myself, he let the beast out on me. I didn't have to work hard to be present every take. What was difficult was the aftermath. I had an entire episode in 209 (The Bear) of different varying breakdowns ABOUT the fight.
>
> 1. The numb interrogation while sitting on the back of an ambulance watching the body being wheeled out.

2. Taking photos of the wounds in the hospital after the adrenaline wore off.
3. Coming face to face with my parents and the relief that my hard-nosed mother didn't blame me for killing her brother.
4. Recounting the events of the night to my teenage daughter.
5. Undressing in front of the mirror and seeing the wounds up close for the first time
6. Stepping into the shower to wash the blood off and feeling the sting of the physical and emotional cuts.

It goes on for six or seven more of these moments. But I'm gonna stop at the shower scene, because that's where I got stuck. In an episode of very personal breakdown moments (even one at the altar in the church), each one had to mean something different or it would become redundant. I'd already had a tremendously raw moment in the hospital gown being photographed in a clinical environment while the detectives watched and supervised. It felt demeaning and vulnerable. Undressing in front of the mirror was self-investigation and connection of the moments in the fight to these injuries. So, what was the shower about? I knew I had to cry over and over again...which is normally not a problem for me. I'd pocketed a wealth of memories from the fight that were terrifying and could elicit an emotional response. But by this time, Merle's personal walls and defenses started to go up. The trauma of the event wasn't enough. And trust me, I had a laundry list of scary moments that I thought would get me there. There was also the added pressure of being on the stages without a working shower, so someone had to hand pump the water into the shower (and I'm sure they were getting tired) as I tried to "get there" with my entire crew (whom I adore) watching me get wet in panties and pasties, plus we were going overtime with this last shot of the night. No pressure!

What did I do? I pulled it together and stopped trying to chase this moment. I was nervous about turning it into thousands of other rote shower breakdowns seen on TV. I was nervous about being naked. I was nervous about having SO MUCH nonverbal time on camera. My inner monologue had to be clear. So, I went back to the beginning: Core Knowledge. This catharsis wasn't just about the pain of the water hitting my wounds for the first time, it wasn't about the fight, it wasn't about fear of being convicted of murder. This was about the release of Grace's childhood trauma that she had been holding for more than twenty years: Mac having abused her as a kid, her silence making room for Mac to abuse her younger sister Faith, the accusations and disbelief thrown her way when Grace tried to blow the whistle on him, Faith's spiral and death and the fact that vindication had finally come decades too late. This was a mourning. She'd missed out on so much being ostracized by this unresolved conflict in her life..."

So Merle went back to basics and looked to her Core Knowledge and Base Human Emotion to give herself the fuel she needed to bring forth the emotion. Those thoughts of her childhood traumas that were held within and never released until now allowed for a riveting performance from Merle.

If you've done Emotion with Detail, your character will also behave without thinking of the behavior. It should be a knee jerk reaction. Literally the mallet (moment) hits the patella (you), and your behavior reflexively pops up. Like a real human being, for heaven's sake! You are at your best if you are naturally reacting as the character - without thinking. Above all, play with all the abandon that you possessed at five years old.

Being on set should be playtime, which means that all of your research and character work should be done before you set foot on the lot or location. Notice I say character work, for that is the most important thing you can bring to set (besides your good manners, great attitude, and lack of ego). Having the character deeply inside you allows you to mold, shape and change on a dime according to what your director says. It allows you to look at last minute, new pages (rewrites to the script) without freaking out! There's nothing you can't do if you have a firm grasp of your character.

If you play the lead in the picture, I would say you shouldn't have to memorize the entire script before you show up, but you should be extremely familiar with most of the lines. I like to memorize the next day's lines the night before. Sometimes it's good to spend a couple of hours on your off days getting the upcoming week's lines down. And always, always know your lines for the scenes you're shooting that day! Never, ever walk on set unprepared when it's time to shoot. Make sure that before you get to set, you've at least run them out loud, preferably with someone. If you've never said them out loud before, the sound of these words can be shocking coming out of your mouth for the first time.

If at all possible, take a look at the set before you shoot. If this is a place that your character is familiar with, make sure to take a few minutes to give objects on set an emotional reason to exist. For example, if your set is the character's living room, why did you choose this particular sofa or these chairs? Invent, in the moment, a super short and quick event, or Flash, concerning that sofa. Maybe you and your significant other saw it when you were window-shopping one Sunday after brunch. The two of you didn't have a lot of money but splurged and bought it anyway. You had to eat Ramen noodles for two weeks, but you were both glad you did it. What colors exist in the room? Invent a quick scenario. Maybe you deliberated for hours in the store, trying to choose the right paint. You brought home swatches and taped them to the walls and lived like that for weeks. What about placement of the furniture? Did you arrange it with your spouse? Build a quick memory of it. What does the room say about you? What paintings or photos hang on the walls? How are they significant to you? Did your grandmother give them to you? Were they in your childhood home? I'm talking about the character's grandmother and the character's childhood home, of course. The further you take this emotional grounding, the further ahead of the game you'll be.

On the set of *Wolverine*, Will. I. Am. was relatively new to acting at that time. Most of his scenes took place in his character's boxing gym office. The set was amazingly extensive – quite impressive. Because his character had spent many hours and years in this particular place, it was filled with hundreds of mementos, memorabilia, and objects that were his. The desk was covered with personal objects. We quickly went through as many objects and artifacts as time would permit and imbued each with personal character history. Even though we worked quickly, he found that it gave him a feeling of familiarity in the room. It was his.

In the feature *The Shallows,* Blake Lively gives a tour de force performance. As the story goes, her character, Nancy, is on a quest to find the secluded and highly secretive beach that her recently deceased mother spoke so fondly of. For the location, producers chose Lord Howe Island, a remote place off the coast of Sydney, Australia. The setting couldn't have been more stunning: a small cove with pristine white sand, ice blue water and mountains in the background, majestically jutting up from the sea. Rather than simply looking at those mountains and thinking "pretty," Blake infused them with great meaning. She noticed that they looked rather like a pregnant woman lying down. So she quickly added this to her Core Knowledge: Her mother first learned of her joyous pregnancy with Nancy at this beach. Blake further added a few Flashes: her mother telling her about being there, delighted that she was carrying a child; stories of times she spent on that beach in love with Nancy's father. In essence, Blake imbued this place with great meaning, giving it an emotional reason to exist. Go back and look at the beautiful moment when she first sees the beach. You can see it in her eyes. It's magical. Of course, Blake acted virtually alone in this film. Not to take away from any of the other actors, but 99.9% of the time, it was just Blake and her imagination. Look how powerful she was. A stunning performance, to say the least.

You may find that in the beginning, especially, nothing feels more unnatural than being on set. Notice how easy it is to execute the scene in your own living room or shower or in the car on the way to set, but once you're there, it suddenly feels much harder. Then when you're just about to shoot, you have noise and crew all around, talking and focusing on their own jobs. The First AD calls for "last looks." Wardrobe makes adjustments. You have last-minute touch-ups with your hair and make-up. The director may speak to you about the scene and may even give you new thoughts. How out of the character are you now? Simply breathe, reset focus, go to your Prior Moments, and then on "Rolling!" or "Action!" go to your Prior Instant.

You'll do a lot of waiting between takes, which is a great opportunity to put more time into your Emotion with Detail work. If you're new at this and find yourself standing around, watch the crew. There's so much to learn from them. You'll be much more comfortable on set once you understand what's going on, and every shoot will be more pleasant when you're on friendly terms with the crew. You'll find that they are some of the nicest, warmest people on the planet.

If camera and crew make you nervous just by their presence, here's a fun fix:

Acknowledge and Dismiss. *Acknowledge* the existence of the camera and crew, and *dismiss* them as being momentarily unimportant to your task at hand. Then from where you're standing on set, draw an invisible line in your imagination that blocks and separates you from camera and crew. Create an invisible bubble that starts at that line. Everything inside that bubble, where you are, is safe. That's your playground. Drop into the character and play! Avoid watching yourself to see if you're correct or landing the moments you want to nail. You've done your work. Now let yourself breathe and enjoy!

If nerves are an ongoing problem, my dear friend Dr. Peter Desberg has written many books on the subject. Pick up anything he writes. He's fascinatingly brilliant and very well-versed on the subject.

Learn to adjust. If a director is giving you result-oriented directions, such as "Be angrier here," or anything result-oriented, ask yourself, "Why would my character do that or feel that way? Why would he/she be angry here?" With the character work you've done, you'll be able to answer that for yourself. Let that be the fuel rather than trying to play a result. You'll run into many things on set that you'll have to adjust for. But time, experience and setting foot on set with a fully developed character will serve you well.

"Nobody ever had a rainbow baby, until he had the rain..."
~ Jim Croce

HITCHES IN THE GIDDYUP

We all face stumbling blocks, whether in this process or any other. There's no way to avoid them, so better to address each one as it comes up. I like to call these obstacles "Hitches in the Giddyup," because ... well ... I'm Southern, and that's what I call them. Remember, anytime you have a hitch (getting caught up), there's always a giddyup (forward movement) that follows.

Though all actors are gloriously different from one another, you may be delighted to learn that a lot of people share your questions. Below are a few that I've gotten from time to time. I hope they're helpful.

"Are Hows and Whys supposed to be taken from the character's point of view?"

No. In this stage, you should still be in the analytical phase, taking an objective viewpoint and assessing all information that you've been given. Like a detective, you'll be taking all the clues and will start assembling them to solve the puzzle that is the character.

"How do you know if you are creating Core Knowledge that is original rather than something you have seen or known?"

Don't feel as if everything you invent for the Core Knowledge has to be something that is completely foreign to you. It won't be. We all grew up, went to elementary and high school, etc. We've all had and lost love relationships. We all have something in common. It would be quite impossible to invent a Core Knowledge that you had absolutely no knowledge of or reference to, whether you've seen it on TV, known someone similar, or read about a similar life. Yes, your character's life history is unique, as all human beings are. But we all have similarities, too.

"Should I avoid the personal pronoun when doing Core Knowledge?"

At times, you'll find yourself saying "I," and other times you'll find yourself saying "he/she." It really doesn't matter at this point. The only place that it would matter is in the Emotion with Detail, when you are the character and the character is you.

"What if your Core Knowledge doesn't seem to line up with the director's/writer's idea of the character's backstory?"

If you've made your Base Human Emotion decision based on the Hows of Behavior, the emotional resonance of the character will be pretty spot on. Core Knowledge events, unless referred to in the script, will always vary from person to person. It's the emotional resonance, the emotional make-up of the character that counts. As long as the resulting emotional behavior is correct, your backstory or Core Knowledge is your secret to keep. But let's imagine that you find yourself in a circumstance where it's absolutely necessary to change something in that Core Knowledge. It's quite easy to do, even if you've already done Emotion with Detail on the event.

The amazing Emily Deschanel shares this about changing the Core Knowledge:

> "One of the things I love about working with Warner is that you can create a full inner life with personal character memories so you can essentially live the character rather than 'act.' Yet the best thing is that the work is flexible.
>
> When I first started work on the TV show 'Bones,' Warner and I developed a history for my character Brennan with child-

hood memories. Brennan lost her parents young, and we developed Emotion with Details related to her parents' deaths. A bit of time into the series, the writers wrote a back story for my character that contradicted what we had created, so we just went back and created new Core Knowledge with different Emotion with Details."

"How do you apply all of this to historical figures?"

It's lovely. If you do your research, you already have all the Core Knowledge work done for you. Discovering a Base Human Emotion will be of great help. Take your Core Knowledge events and live them through Emotion with Detail. But explore these events in depth, making sure the emotional component is there. Otherwise you're just living out facts. It's the difference between reading a list of historical facts and dates or being engrossed in an intriguing story with rich and vivid details that engage your imagination. Make the character's events live. Feel them.

"If I choose the same Base Human Emotion the majority of the time will my characters all be pretty similar?"

They may have similar emotional make-ups, but their Core Knowledge will be different, so it really doesn't matter. Sometimes we are cast in similar characters from role to role, so it's really fun to make them all different, even if their Base Human Emotions are a bit similar.

"Is it okay if I work better from more of a fear-based Base Human Emotion than a need-based one?"

Yes. It's a personal thing. You may relate more to fear-based characters. That's totally fine. Fear and need are so closely interrelated. Maybe the characters you're attracted to are indeed more fear-based. Or maybe that's just your perspective. It's totally fine.

"I can't remember what it was like to be little. I have no personal memories before the age of nine, so how am I supposed to discover the origins of a Base Human Emotion?"

Remember, you won't need to draw upon your own experiences as a child in order to create a child's world for the character. That's the beauty of your imagination. You may forget your own childhood events, but you *were* still a child once. A child's world is usually small and contained, with limited worldly experience. A child's coping skills are just being honed; he or she is usually very vulnerable to even the slightest suggestions. A child usually trusts until given a reason to mistrust. When we're small, the world impacts us. We are told what to eat, what not to eat, when to do it, what to wear, what time to sleep, what time to wake up, etc. A child is dependent on parents and elders for survival. It's only when we grow that we begin to realize that *we* can impact the world. Just as you can create a character different from you out of whole cloth, you can create that character's childhood without relying on your own.

"What if my Base Human Emotion is wrong, and I need to change it, but I've already done a bunch of work? Won't I have screwed up the character?"

On the contrary, if you've done a lot of work and discover a more appropriate Base Human Emotion for your character than the one you first selected, congratulations! You're getting to know this person so thoroughly that your information has become more specific. There is no wrong here, and the meaning of a single Base Human Emotion may vary from person to person. (Fear of Abandonment may mean one thing to you and something different to someone else.) Don't be afraid to make adjustments as you go along. Take care to do your analytical work thoroughly and meticulously, and you'll set yourself on the proper emotional track.

What you name your Base Human Emotion doesn't matter. How it makes you feel and how it resonates with you and the character is the only thing that matters. Who cares what you call it?

"I can't decide between two Base Human Emotions. They're both so right! What do I do?"

We call it the *Base* Human Emotion, because it lies at the foundation of the character and, as such, it is helpful if you choose only one.

All other emotions are filtered through this one. When two Base Human Emotions spring to mind for one character, ask yourself which one resonates more. If you sit still with it for a minute, the answer will come to you, and if you work with one and realize the other is more appropriate, then that's fine. Ask yourself which one of the two might have come first? Which one caused the other one to be? Often one of them that you chose could actually be a manifestation of behavior that sprang up from the Base Human Emotion. That's very common and can be useful to look at. For instance, "The Fear of Abandonment" we looked at in the grocery store example in the chapter "Base Human Emotion" could manifest itself into "The Need to be Seen" or "The Need to Please."

Or the two that you have chosen may actually be so similar that they amount to the same thing. Every emotion the character experiences - and he or she should experience many - will be altered by the Base Human Emotion. Enjoy feeling all this through the lens of the Base Human Emotion you've chosen for your character. Don't deliberate for an hour over which one is better. There is no "right" one. Choose with your gut instincts and move on.

"I just did a scene but didn't feel it had anything to do with the Base Human Emotion that I chose for the character."

The scene might not appear to be directly related to your Base Human Emotion, but know that the *emotion* in the scene will be influenced by your choice of the Base Human Emotion. In real life, you aren't tweaked or triggered by every interaction every day. Your character is like you in that respect: The Base Human Emotion won't be directly tweaked in every scene. Everything that happens to us within a day doesn't appear to be directly related to something that happened to us at five years old. But what happened at five years old somewhat determines how we approach life, how we view it, our perceptions of people and things. We all have "triggers," but they aren't played upon to a great extent every day and by everyone.

The whole idea of building a character has to do with creating nuance, texture, and layers within that person. In real life, when something happens to you, you usually react in a knee-jerk fashion. You react to something that someone says or does because of the person you have grown up to be. It's the same with a character. Build the character and simply let him or her live through you.

"How much do you plan or know you are going to do in the Emotion with Detail, and how much is imagined in the moment?"

Some actors follow the Core Knowledge guide that they've set up for the character exactly, step by step. This often happens when they have decided on very specific Core Knowledge Events. This is not wrong. Everyone is different. I like to let my Core Knowledge be an outline or guide. Then I'll start my Emotion with Detail event with a concept. For instance, I might say I want to investigate the concept of my character being ostracized at school. I may not know what that specific event will look like. I'll just put my character at her desk and see what happens. This kind of "wait and see what happens" sort of Emotion with Detail is usually easier once you've being doing the technique for a while.

"When do you scrap an Emotion with Detail, or do you?"

I think they're all valuable. Even if you don't get to an emotion within them, you're at least investigating the life of the character. Every Emotion with Detail won't be so emotionally charged, just as every event in our own lives isn't always emotionally charged. So it's all valid.

"Can I listen to music during Emotion with Detail?"

You can. Many actors find that helpful. But I wouldn't listen to a song that had a particular personal memory attached to it, because you'll be relating to an experience in your own life as opposed to an event in the character's life.

"What if you are empathically relating to a character during Emotion with Detail; should you pull yourself out?"

You actually want to be empathically relating to your character. Feel as much as you can. If you've experienced a similar event in your own life, it's okay as long as you're not recreating your specific life event and memory.

"Should I try to make Emotion with Details last longer than five minutes if I am striking an emotional chord?"

Striking an emotional chord is the whole idea. So if you've done that, you're done. Move on to the next one.

"Sometimes I have a hard time connecting the Emotion with Details with the other actor in the scene, since I am just meeting them for the first time. What do I do?"

This is why when doing Emotion with Detail, I never include a face. Some people can quite freely include a face, but it trips me up to do it. I create hands or hair or clothes or the smell of my mother's perfume, for instance. I create the essence of that person and not the actual face. During your scene, get lost in your suspension of disbelief. Perceive him/her to be the character you created in your Emotion with Details.

"I went through this whole Emotion with Detail about my parents being killed in a car crash, and I just didn't feel anything. It was as though I was just retelling something."

There are several ways to troubleshoot when you feel like the work isn't clicking. First, when your character is dealing with loss, remember that you must know what you've had before you can feel what it's like to lose it. In this case, build up the relationship with your parents. (The character's parents, obviously, not yours.) Bond with them. Do several Emotion with Details centered on the bonding of this relationship. Then raise the stakes on the event of the loss itself. In this case, try placing yourself in the car at the time of the accident. Maybe your parents are taking you to the concert that you really wanted to go to. Or you're in the car, because you were spending the weekend with your aunt, you acted up horribly, and they were forced to come get you. Now your character has a complicated web of feelings to navigate, because you've made the event emotionally significant.

Another reason you might not feel much is the normal tendency we all have to chase the emotion. We so badly want to feel that we pressure ourselves to do so, even when we're all alone doing an Emotion with Detail. But as I said before, anything you chase flies away. Chase a lover, a child, even a dog, and he will run. Chase a feather falling from the sky, and the air between your hands will push it away. Trust yourself. Avoid rushing through an Emotion with Detail just to get to a payoff. Keep being intentionally present and pushing forward, and you'll feel what you need to feel when it's right.

If you're having trouble living in the moment, practice taking note of visual details in the minutest form. Incorporate all you can of what you hear, touch, smell, see or taste. Imagine the experience as if it were occurring in the present; make sure you're not retelling it in the past tense. And redefine your own objective to stay in the moment for as long as possible rather than to get through it as quickly as you can.

Especially during particularly tragic Emotion with Details, we tend to try to avoid the pain and therefore merely visualize rather than letting go and living the experience. Allow yourself the luxury of feeling. Remember that you're just visiting the life of a character, the vibrations of a character, and that you will be able to debrief and release his or her pain again when you're through.

"I did Emotion with Detail for a character in a comedy, and it wasn't funny. What do I do?"

Multi-camera sit-coms are a whole different ball game. To my mind, doing *any* Emotion with Detail will drag sit-com down, so I like to stick with only the Givens, Hows, Whys, and Core Knowledge. And never to the degree and depth that I do in drama. Comedy is a face value medium that requires a different skill set and has specific "rules," if you will.

Your Emotion with Detail must align with the genre you're working in. For lighter fare drama, tailor your work to your medium and remember that this technique is like a toolbox: it's up to you to choose the appropriate tool for the right moment. If you're playing a deeply tragic and emotionally complex character in a drama, then by all means, craft your work to be particularly tragic. But if you're doing drama that isn't so terribly tragic, the events you experience need not be so heavy. You can create a full life that is not marred by abuse, rape, death and murder. The whole reason to do this work is so that the life of the character is informed, textured, and unique, so pay close attention to the tone of your work. When you're working in feature film comedy or television dramedy, tailor your exploration to be tonally consistent with the world of the film or show. Focus on building the important relationships. In a romantic comedy, for example, Emotion with Detail work is a great way to find the basis for the romantic dynamics.

"I see things, but I don't feel them. I don't have any trouble visualizing the details during Emotion with Detail work, but I'm just not fully there."

Get to know your own strengths. Analyze which moments in the work made you feel the most connected and which the least. If you do an Emotion with Detail and *do* find it effective, go back and ask yourself what worked. Did you incorporate many things that were visual, or did you incorporate many more auditory details? Did you connect most strongly to touching the things around you or to smells? Because we are all wired so differently, there may be a particular sense that you possess that is stronger than the others.

When doing Emotion with Detail work, make sure to give the objects in the space around you an emotional significance. Making objects just set dressing does you no good. Tie the things you see into the character's life and personality. You'll mine enormous emotional fuel that way. Slow down. Relish the moment. Don't be in a hurry to feel something. Like anything, it takes practice. There's a trademarked saying, "the slower you go, the faster you get there." There's a lot to be said for that.

"I was doing a scene where my character sees her best friend getting beaten. I had done some pretty effective Emotion with Detail work about being a kid and seeing my mom getting beaten. But when I did the scene, I didn't feel so much."

It's possible that although you used parallel events in your Emotion with Detail, the Base Human Emotion was being tweaked in different ways. The character will feel differently about her mother than she does about her best friend, and it may be the dissonance between the relationships that's making you feel disconnected. A child who relies on a parent for protection will have a whole host of feelings when that parent is beaten that might not be triggered in the same way by the assault on a friend during adulthood. Remember, it's about the way the situation affects *you,* the character. When it's a particularly upsetting time for a character, try focusing on Emotion with Detail work that tweaks the Base Human Emotion rather than just creating parallel scenarios.

"Do I have to live the entire life of the character in my Emotion with Detail?"

Heavens, no! It would take forever! Just hit the major life events. Stick with emotionally pertinent moments in the character's life. If time is a concern – say, before an audition – you'll just have to do less. You will still have gone further than most actors do.

"When I'm doing Emotion with Detail work and I voice other characters, it takes me out of the moment and throws me off. What do I do?"

Don't voice them if it takes you out of the moment; there's no need, so long as you can hear them in your imagination. Remember, this is a tool for building character, not a performance. Many actors feel they must voice the other characters, while many simply imagine what is being said. Either works. As always, if something doesn't work for you, change it. This is your work.

"I have trouble committing to choices during my Emotion with Detail work. I know that I'm not supposed to use my own childhood memories, but when I visualize an object that I've just made up, I can't seem to settle on the details. I'll see a rug, and the color and texture will change twenty times, and I feel anxious trying to make the right choice."

There is no right choice. Simply give the object an emotional reason to exist. This will help ground you in the moment. For example, the rug is not just a rug; it's the rug your beloved dog used to sleep on at the foot of your bed. Or perhaps it was handed down to you when your sister's room was redecorated; yours wasn't, and you resent it. When you give objects an emotional reason to exist, they become clearer in your mind. You have made them specific. Once you decide, move on. The whole idea is to give yourself a solid sense of place. The details are only important insofar as they help you explore the world of your character and ground you more deeply in the moment.

"I did amazing full-circle homework and had a great week on set. Then I was off for a week, and now I'm afraid I can't get the character back."

Have no fear. Simply review - in Flashes - your previous Emotion with Details. Or invent new Flashes for your character. You'll be right back in the character. If you've done your Emotion with Details succinctly, you won't forget them any more than you would forget your own life experiences.

"Why do I feel blocked in the audition room and not when I'm home?"

That's not uncommon. Sometimes in the audition room, we feel judged. Or we're too tied to an outcome and a result. In the "safety" of our own home, we allow ourselves the freedom to feel. I was in a sound booth once and saw a clever Post-It note taped to the window. It said, "Could we please have your best performance in the booth and not in the car on your way home?" Give yourself permission in the audition room to fully embrace the character, and let the outcome of the audition be the furthest thing from your mind. Walk into that audition room to *give something - never to get something.* Rather than having a personal thought when you begin your scene, make sure to use your Prior Instant. You can't think a personal thought and a character thought at the same time. A Prior Instant thought is much more useful to your journey of the scene than a thought such as, "Why did I wear this ridiculous shirt?!" Enjoy it. You get to BE this character for the next ten minutes! I also like to think of auditions as collaborative meetings as opposed to a try-out of sorts.

"So for a fifteen-page, multiple-scene audition, do you have to do the Hows of Behavior on all the scenes or just the first one?"

It's helpful to do it for all of your audition sides or scenes. Especially if the character is interacting with different people and in different situations. Does he/she behave differently in those situations? Much can be gleaned from that. Remember you do NOT have to break down the entire screenplay.

"My character has an accent that I didn't start to tackle until I got into the actual scene work, and now I feel like I can't connect."

It's important to use the character's particular accent from the get-go of your Emotion with Details. He/she didn't grow up and then start speaking with an accent in adulthood. Even if you feel you're not proficient at the accent, take a stab at it. You'll keep the character consistent, and your mind will come to associate the accent with that character every time you drop into him or her. Before you shoot, get a good dialect coach to help.

"The director told me he wants my character to have some sort of physical quirk to help show his vulnerability. He's left the choice up to me, but I don't know what to do."

Give physical quirks an emotional reason to exist. Where does the character's emotional vulnerability lie? Find the source. That will be the key to discovering what physical manifestations arise from it. Create an Emotion with Detail event that causes this quirk to pop up. For example, in our scene with Jonathan, we see that he fidgets. You could invent an Emotion with Detail exploring an incident when that first occurred. Could it be an event that tweaks his Base Human Emotion of "Fear of Not Being Enough," so that when that particular emotion pops up, his nervous energy comes out in the physical form of fidgeting?

"Should I do homework on both characters in a scene?"

Good question, but no! You don't want to do homework on the other character in the scene, because you want to react openly and honestly to what the other person brings to the table. In a relationship of any kind, whether it's a new friend you met an hour ago or a long-term intimacy, you are bringing *you and only you* to the situation. If the other character is someone you've known for a long period of time, you will, of course, have a history with them. When you've had a long-term relationship with someone, you know their stories, so to speak. You know things that happened to them in childhood – their likes, dislikes, their history. These things bond us to people. So from that aspect – yes, pay attention to what your character knows about that person. But you do not do Emotion with Detail on their life events unless you were present in the moment when such an event occurred. If that's the case, then you'd create the Emotion with Detail from your point of view. All you know about the other person's behavior is what's coming straight at you like a tennis ball.

When it comes to homework on your character, it is most important to know how he or she responds to the other characters in the scene and to look for patterns. Is there a type of person that seems to tweak your character's Base Human Emotion repeatedly? Or perhaps a certain behavior on the part of another character is always a trigger. Let the other actors be responsible for their own output, just like in real life!

"I'm shooting a scene in which my character is drunk. Wouldn't it help if I actually had a drink before the scene, just to get the feeling?"

This question comes up a lot, and the answer is a definitive *no.* Alcohol impairs your ability to react and to focus, even if you only consume a little bit. I certainly enjoy a nice single malt scotch or a perfect martini, but not at work. The idea that alcohol and drugs can take the edge off your nerves and therefore sharpen your abilities is a false one. Drugs and alcohol dull your senses, and as we've discussed at length in these pages, your senses must be at their sharpest to fuel the character you're building. Acting takes courage, but real courage doesn't wear off after an hour or two.

"I have to do a crying scene tomorrow and I'm terrified."

You'll be able to let go of that fear only by replacing it with something else. So instead of looking at it as a terrifying situation, let's look at it as actual fun. It's exhilarating to experience an emotion that is not caused by your own life events.

Focus on the task at hand: becoming this other being. Allow yourself to work rather than to fear something that hasn't even happened yet. Chances are you're less afraid of crying in the scene than you are of failing to cry, and when you're living as your character, you'll be amazed at how naturally the emotion comes.

Remember, you can't feel the loss of something if you never know what you had. Let's take a love relationship, for example. Your main work will be to bond with this lover. (I'm talking about the character, of course, not the other actor, please.) Build the relationship, first by growing into your character. Then, using Emotion with Detail, experience as much of the relationship as you can. Focus mainly on the good times: first meeting, first date, first kiss, first time making love, etc. Incorporate things you love to do together, what he or she knows about you that no one else does, what you know about him or her that no one else knows. Explore the particular and special bond you have together, and investigate the trust you share. Now dream of what the future may hold for the two of you together. Make it delicious.

Right before you shoot the scene, rip it all away. That will hurt. You'll cry. Don't rerun through this. There's no sense in repeatedly working up the loss of this other person (unless the character might have struggled with it for years and is now confessing or recalling for some reason). Recalling the loss repeatedly will desensitize you and weaken the effect of it over time. If you sit in the make-up chair or your trailer and keep experiencing the pain of this loss, I guarantee you won't feel it as deeply when you need to on set. It will have dissipated. So keep building the relationship until the moment you need to lose it. After each take, alter your Prior Instant slightly to keep each take fresh. On screen, it will be organic and beautiful. Unless, of course, you chase the emotion or demand it of yourself. In which case, you will NOT cry. So take the journey of the character, take the pressure off yourself and enjoy!

My hope for you…

…that embracing this craft will be a joyous journey for you. Know that this should be a sixty-year career, not a six-month one. I want you to look back when you're ninety-something and say, "Whew! What a ride!" If you are currently working with a teacher or collaborator who causes you pain and makes you feel "less than," or who makes you feel you are not an artist, please run. All teachers worth their salt will hold you above themselves, not the other way around. It cannot be about the teacher. It must be about you. And you are a force to be reckoned with; an artist who can create anything that you put your mind to. Along with normal "hitches in the giddyup," your life and art should be filled with tingling excitement, exuberance, passion and above all, excellence and extraordinary abundance.

I wish you great success in this journey and utter joy in embracing other lives.

A PEEK INTO AN ACTOR'S HOMEWORK

Below, you'll find a scene between a man and a woman. Let's pretend you've got an audition tomorrow, and this scene is all the material you've been given. Using the steps we've discussed, build your character, then drop him or her into the scene, and you'll have a sense of what sort of audition you'd be able to give. Start by choosing the part that's appropriate for you and reading the scene through once.

CURTIS AND CLAIRE

written by
Ellen Shanman

INT. LIVING ROOM – NIGHT

Claire, Curtis and Holly are siblings.

The remains of a party in a suburban living room. Plastic plates with smeared frosting are stacked on the coffee table. Half-filled cups of soda scattered here and there.

CLAIRE, tense, scrapes at a stain on her khaki pants. She exhales a huffy sigh and begins to gather wrapping paper and ribbon strewn about the floor.

CURTIS, Claire's brother, appears in the doorway and watches her, drinking whiskey. He wears a knit cap and an old concert t-shirt.

CLAIRE
(muttering)
Don't help, whatever you do.

CURTIS
You got it.

Claire gives him a dirty look as she shoves the trash into a garbage bag.

Curtis flops into an easy chair and shakes his glass, ice cubes tinkling. He sucks air through his teeth.

CURTIS
(sarcastic)
Great party.

CLAIRE
I was trying to make her feel welcome.

CURTIS
She doesn't need to feel welcome.
She needs to feel safe.

CLAIRE
(hushed)
These were not strangers! They're
her oldest friends.

CURTIS
Who she hasn't seen in a year.
(then)
She's not gonna be good in
groups. At least for a while.

CLAIRE
I thought she would like it.

CURTIS
You can't change where she's
been by hanging up streamers
and making a cake.

Claire opens her mouth to speak but thinks better of it. She keeps cleaning.

Pause. Curtis puts his glass on the table.

CURTIS
Are you gonna be able to
handle this?

CLAIRE
Oh, give me a break, Curtis.

Claire lifts the glass and wipes down the table with a rag. She replaces his drink on a coaster.

CURTIS
(gently)
We're not like you, Claire.

CLAIRE
Oh, are you two a team now?
I didn't realize her
nervous breakdown and your
penchant for snorting
your paychecks were the
same thing.

Beat.

CURTIS
I spent a lot of time on
myself—

CLAIRE
There's a surprise.

Claire stops. She takes a deep breath and turns back.

CLAIRE
I appreciate what you're
saying. I hear you.

Curtis looks amused. Claire gathers the trash and moves toward the kitchen.

CURTIS
I'm saying she can come
live with me.

CLAIRE
(in disbelief)
With you?

CURTIS
I can make room.

CLAIRE
(laughing, sarcastic)
Gee, no offense, but Holly
just got out of one asylum.
I'm not about to send her to
another one.

Curtis looks at her, shakes his head, gets up.

CURTIS
Must be a hell of a view from
up there, Claire.

Claire looks chagrined. Curtis drains his drink, puts the glass back down beside the coaster.

CURTIS
Tell her I'll come by tomorrow.

Curtis leaves. Claire stares daggers at his glass.

So there's your audition scene. You can take a lot of information away from the material right off the bat! Go through the steps, and see where they take you.

- Read the scene again. Establish the Givens.
- Line by line, start to come up with the Hows of Behavior for your character. Look for patterns of behavior to emerge.

- Fill in the Core Knowledge by answering the Whys.
- Based on the patterns that emerged and the Core Knowledge clues, determine your character's Base Human Emotion.
- Do some Emotion with Details, starting with the moment that defined your character's Base Human Emotion in childhood and working up incrementally to the point at which your character lives this scene.
- Now return to the scene and drop your fully formed character into it. You'll find it's a whole different experience than your first read.

The pages that follow contain an example of the process for Claire, completed by Hillary Tuck, amazing actress and teacher at Warner Loughlin Studios. You'll find her initial analytical work along with transcriptions of her Emotion with Details. You may choose to look at them to see how another actor approached this scene, or you may prefer to ignore them altogether. It's up to you! Just be sure not to look until after you've completed your own work. Have fun!

HILLARY TUCK IN THE ROLE OF CLAIRE:

GIVENS:

- She's getting a stain off her khakis. I had that she was tense but I crossed that out because it says that you can't prove that in a court of law.
- She's cleaning up.
- She puts a coaster under her brother's drink.
- Claire and Curtis are siblings.
- They have another sister, Holly. She was in an asylum. She had a nervous breakdown.
- She hasn't seen friends in one year (with a question mark next to it).
- Curtis doesn't live with Claire.
- He doesn't use a coaster.

- He also puts the drink back down beside the coaster.
- Coke habit? (Question mark because of the quote snorting paychecks.)
- He's drinking whisky.
- It's a suburban party at night.
- There's plastic plates and soda.

HOWS OF BEHAVIOR:

- When Claire cleans the mess → she seems to focus on one detail, physically releasing her frustration.
- When Curtis offers no help → she seems to passively criticize.
- When Curtis mimics her sarcastic tone → she seems to physically release her emotion.
- When Curtis is sarcastic → she defends herself.
- When Curtis refutes Claire and explains what is better → she seems to justify and defend herself.
- When Curtis 'educates' Claire - Curtis knows what's best → she seems to justify/defend herself/seek to prove that she's coming from a good place.
- When Curtis belittles her → she seems to hold back and channel emotions into cleaning.
- When Curtis challenges Claire's ability to handle Holly → she seems to be dismissive and keeps cleaning.
- When Curtis gently separates him and Holly from Claire → she seems to assert her dominance and attack him.
- When Curtis opens up and defends himself → she seems to cut him off with a dig, then stops herself, physically regroups and behaves diplomatically.
- When Curtis looks amused → she seems to ignore him by continuing to clean up.
- When Curtis clarifies/makes an offer → she seems to question him (face value).
- When Curtis defends his offer → she seems to attack Curtis and put him down.
- When Curtis calls her on her self-righteousness → she seems

to hold back her irritation.

- When Curtis defies her → she seems to stare daggers at his defiance.

WHYS:

- Issues with control.
- Doesn't feel free to express herself - painful past.
- Concerned with appearances.
- Past issues with Curtis.
- Have her intentions been misunderstood? Believes she's right.
- Gains control by fixing something.
- Seniority issues - she should know. She feels responsible. Parent figure?
- Seniority issues again. She's always cleaning up after him. He makes work for her?
- Seniority issues again. Can't confront real issues.
- Dominance issues.
- Issues of them separating from her. Feeling different/outsider.
- Tries to manage and control her emotions.
- Issues with: family, control, appearances, confrontation, Curtis's drinking, being heard, parent.

CORE KNOWLEDGE:

Note that Hillary did very loose Core Knowledge. Some of the Core Knowledge points are just thoughts - things that perhaps she'll explore and perhaps not. She's using it as a basic loose guideline and will rely more on the discoveries she makes with Emotion with Detail to determine the life's events.

- Dad leaves.
- First grade. I come home from school and have to take care of Curtis and Holly by myself while Mom works.
- Third Grade. Mom has a semi nervous breakdown. The stress

is too much. I clean and clean and clean – try to keep the house as neat as possible. Holly and Curtis are no help whatsoever.

- Sixth Grade. Explore that we're poor. What might I do with that? Hide the fact that we are? Pretend we're not? Am I ashamed? Curtis already has a bad reputation at school. This is not helping. I go to the principal's office often. In place of Mom. Explore the responsibility aspect.
- High school. Resentment starts to build. Other high school kids get to do fun things. I have to always go home and take care of Curtis and Holly. But they do need me. I do love them.
- Explore some instance where I have to give something up because of Holly or Curtis – could be an event I wanted to go to? Could be a material thing that was meaningful to me that I had to give up?
- Graduate and go to community college to be around Curtis and Holly.
- Curtis drops out of high school and leaves town. Gets into drugs. Works as a roadie.
- Holly flips out, and I have to commit her. She has no insurance, so I pay the bill?

BASE HUMAN EMOTION:

Hillary determined it to be: "Need to be Good Enough."

EMOTION WITH DETAIL:

Following is a transcript of her Emotion with Detail that informed the Base Human Emotion:

Um, I'm five years old. Curtis is three. Holly is two. I'm playing with them. And I'm hearing a fight. Okay. [PAUSES]

I feel my heart. I feel my stomach. I...see my sandals. I feel the sand between my fingers. I feel the board of the sandbox up against my back. I feel the heat of the sun on my hair. I feel the bow that my mommy put in my hair.

It's a pink bow and it's got my initials on it. She painted them on there. I can feel the paint on the ribbon. I feel the sand in my mouth. I see my brother. I see the dump truck in his little hands with the dump truck.

I hear him giggle as all of it poured out onto his feet. [LAUGHS] I see his pudgy hands. I see his striped shirt. I hear his voice. "You get me some water? I want water Claire. This dump truck [STAMMERS] it, it needs water for the dump truck. Okay?"

"Okay." I see Holly. I see her dress. Her yellow dress. I see her little fingers. I feel, I feel my feet walk up the stairs of the porch to get water. I hear the creak of the screen door. And I hear – I hear my daddy's voice. I hear his words.

I hear [CRIES] him call my mommy a bad name. A name that you're not supposed to say. A name that you get a spanking if you say it and Daddy said it. [CRIES] I hear, I hear my mom using her outside voice.

And I hear her telling him, telling him to get out and to never come back. And I feel – I feel scared. I feel scared because Daddy has the – he has the funny voice.

And I don't like it when he has that funny voice. And I'm scared because I don't want Mommy to tell him something like that because he might do it when he's got the funny voice. And I look back and I see, I see Curtis and I see Holly. And I'm happy that they don't hear. They're playing. I see them playing. [SNIFFS] I see Curtis's dump truck.

[SNIFFS] And I feel, I feel my hands on the cup. And I feel the sweat. And I feel the heat and then I – I feel scared when Daddy – I feel the whoosh of the door opening and daddy finds me there. And I see his overalls. And I – I see his big hands.

And I, I smell his stink. And I feel – And I feel his hands on my waist as he bends down and gets on one knee. And I see his eyes. [SNIFF] And I can smell, I smell his breath and he's got the funny voice and I'm – feel scared. And I hear his words. "Claire, you're nothing but trouble. You and those kids are nothing but trouble. I'm sick of it. Good luck." [CRIES] And I feel him take his hands away and I see him walking down the stairs and I don't want him to go.

I don't want him to go! [CRIES] I want my daddy. I don't want him to go. [CRIES] I don't want my daddy to go.

And I am – I'm just trouble. I feel like I'm trouble. I feel bad. I feel like I'm a bad girl. And I wanna tell him I'm sorry and that I can do it better. I can fix it. [CRIES]

And I feel my heart. And I feel my stomach. [SNIFFS] [BREATHES] And I breathe in Hillary. And I breathe out Claire. [BREATHES] [LAUGHS]

[END OF RECORDING]

Now look how quickly Hillary got to the emotion. Once she did, she didn't need to drag out the Emotion with Detail. She got there quickly, because she's a master at it. She's been doing it long enough that it's second nature to her now to go to those emotional places and then to snap right out of them (debrief) with a quick and efficient breath.

Following is a conversation we had about the character and what she might do next:

Hillary: If I was gonna take this to set, my triggers would be the feeling of his hands getting off of my waist and him starting to walk away. For sure. His voice. His voice when he called, when he called my mom a bitch. Um, just that sound...And in my mom's voice and that fear that that created. And the connection to Curtis, would be, um, (she's visualizing here) his, his hands in the sand. And just that feeling that – I didn't do a good job of talking about how that made me feel. That that just made me feel happy.

Warner: Yeah, you felt it. You just didn't say it out loud.

Hillary: I didn't say it.

Warner: [OVERLAP] Which is okay –

Hillary: [OVERLAP] I'm trying – when I'm trying – I know. But I was trying to have an eye on that of trying to say how I feel. Um, especially when you're doing it for other people.

Warner: But for yourself, you don't necessarily have to do that.

Hillary: I don't, no. I don't have to do it. But I will say I really do try, and even when I'm doing just for myself, I do try and check in with how it makes me feel. Because it sometimes then brings up – it brings up more. It goes deeper when I actually say it out loud.

Warner: [OVERLAP] When you voice it. Right.

Hillary: Yeah, when I voice it.

Hillary: Yeah. That made me feel happy – his hands. And I felt my connection to him, and I felt that he looked up to me – that he relied on me. Yeah. Those are the things that popped out that I would probably use on set for triggers. If I was flashing.

Warner: Where would you take your other Emotion with Details from here? Let's say you only have a few hours to prep for this role.

Hillary: Well, if I only have a few hours to prep for this role, I think I would definitely do an Emotion with Detail of life after Dad leaving and me taking care of Holly and Curtis. Setting up more of me being older and me taking care of them. I don't know if it's getting them out of trouble. Or, like, just packing their lunches. Or something. Just to feel how things used to be, because obviously, that's not how things are now. Of me, sort of, being in charge. And me fixing things. I would definitely do a time of connecting with Curtis. Maybe when we're in our teens. I don't know if it's, like, smoking weed together. Or sneaking out together. Or something that we did together that was a bonding experience.

Warner: Good. And Holly?

Hillary: I think I probably [PAUSES]. If I only had a few hours, honestly, I would focus more on Curtis. But I would definitely wanna do something with Holly. And it'd probably be something like the realization that something's off with Holly. That this child is not like the others.

And also maybe me defending her. So I don't know if it's Holly being made fun of at school. Something where I can combine those two.

Warner: Good, because combining Emotion with Details is really helpful when you're working on quick notice, so to speak. That's good.

Hillary: Yeah. So I probably would wanna combine the two and do something around me, defending something she did and at the same time realizing that her behavior's not quite normal. Because, as with anyone who you grow up with – you don't know that it's different. It feels like normal, because that's all you know. And then suddenly one day you're hit up with something like, oh, this isn't how all the other girls react or do.

Warner: Oh, that's brilliant. That's really good.

Hillary: Then I'd do – maybe one more grade school and then more teenage years. In college. And I would definitely do something...I don't know what the Emotion with Detail would be, but something along the lines of – there's something that happened, an instance where Curtis and Holly became buddies, and I was on the outs. Because it's always, you know, with the three, there's always a two and a one. And I think for a while it was a two and a one, but I was taking care of them so it didn't feel like a two and a one. And then, suddenly, they grew up, and it's a two and a one.

Warner: And don't you think that Claire might feel unappreciated for what she sacrificed?

Hillary: Yeah. So maybe do an Emotion with Detail of – I don't know if it has to do with college or it has to do with maybe she passed on a job that she was gonna take, because Holly was having a spell or going through one of her depressed stages or maybe tried to kill herself for the first time. Something along those lines. And so I gave up something to take care of her. And the reaction was, like, it was almost like expected of me. And there was no gratitude, and if anything, it was, "Get out of my face. You don't know." You know what I mean? So, yeah. That'd be a lot of Emotion with Detail.

Warner: You could do them quickly with Flashes. What about the idea of this thing where Claire is always cleaning around Curtis. Or she's got some kind of attitude toward the alcohol. Or something.

Hillary: [OVERLAP] Yes. She has – yes. She definitely has physical manifestations of how she's feeling. And there's, for whatever reason – I wonder where it comes from that she puts a cap on her emotions and it comes out physically. Right? To me, I think that has something to do with the fact that she always had to be in charge and take care of the two of them. It feels like they were allowed to be – me being controlled and steady allowed them to be [PAUSES] free.

Warner: Great. So there's an emotional reason for her to cap those feelings or to put that into a physical something. Right? Would you do that in a Flash, or would you do that with Emotion with Detail?

Hillary: I mean, I think for this, if I was doing an audition, I probably would do it in a Flash, because the physicality of this character is not going to come up that much in the audition. That's much more of a "once you have the job and book the role" sort of thing.

But if I book the role, I would definitely do lots of Emotion with Details. I think there was something that happened, it might've been, like, right after Daddy leaving, of that feeling of me wanting to fix. Of me going and straightening his office or cleaning the kitchen or if there was something like remembering him saying, "You kids are nothing but trouble." I would be trying to fix it in hopes that he's going to come home. And I feel like that physical manifestation of the cleaning...I feel like it's very close in time to the formation of the Base Human Emotion.

Warner: That's really excellent, because it does feel like it's a learned behavior in her.

Hillary: Way deep. Way early. It feels – I feel like whenever someone has some Obsessive-Compulsive behavior like that, it comes from that. It comes from their base – somewhere around their Base Human Emotion. So yeah. I would do – I'd probably do a couple integrating the physicality into her.

Warner: What else, just for the audition prep, would you want to include in that Emotion with Detail, since you only have X amount of time to do them?

Hillary: I'd definitely do a Flash of getting the call. Truthfully, I feel like I would probably choose that I committed her. Because I feel like that'll drive that wedge between us. I feel like I committed her, and I feel like she probably – if she's been there a year – I don't think she let me come visit her for the first six months. She's clearly come around. I think this asylum did help her.

Warner: And there's probably some guilt there. And you would probably make specific what that nervous breakdown looked like. And why you felt the need to commit her. Maybe do a Flash on that.

Hillary: Yeah, I would definitely do a Flash. I mean, for you to commit somebody just rationally and not trying to plan it out, but rationally, it would have to be some sort of attempted suicide or that she was walking down a highway babbling to herself and the cops found her. Something really cuckoo. Pretty much a break with reality. I don't know what mental illness she has. But she definitely has something. And then I would do something on coming home. Like, having not seen her for a couple of months...walking in the door. And, you know, there's [PAUSE] she's been going to the bathroom in diapers, maybe, and hasn't been able to throw it away. She's like saving her poop. Or she's saving her vomit. Or like, real – it's gotta be something to make me go – this is desperate. Because I think Claire truly feels she needs help.

But I think Holly did blame her for a while. And then I would have to do some sort of Flash on what the party was like. And how it didn't – whether it did or did not, I feel like it did not go the way that I wanted it to go. I think I would do a Flash of me getting ready for the party. And picking out the perfect plates and all the hours that I spent putting up the streamers. And all of the things that I did to show her I care as opposed to just telling her that I care. And it feels like that's kind of the difference between Holly and Curtis and me is that I care much more that things are in order, and that is how I show that I care, as opposed to just saying it.

And they care less – Curtis cares less about those things. I think I'd certainly do a Flash on what just happened. What brought me into the living room to clean up? It feels like everyone left in a rush, because she had a little bit of an outburst. It was too much for her. Like I failed.

Warner: Yeah. And so if your Base Human Emotion is what, again?

Hillary: Need to be good enough.

Warner: Need to be good enough. Then it's gonna go right to your

Base Human Emotion – tweak that Base Human Emotion, because –

Hillary: Because this party was not good enough. [LAUGHS]

Warner: Exactly. And it proved you didn't know what you were doing, therefore you were, yet again, not good enough. So you're walking in at the top of your scene with your Base Human Emotion being tweaked, right? Now let's say you had some extra time to do more Emotion with Detail for the audition. What would you do?

Hillary: Because there's a bit of contention in the scene, what would help me is to build the bonding. Let me do a bonding one of Curtis and me. Because that's who the scene is with. Again, assuming that we only have a short amount of time for the audition. Okay.

> [BREATHES] I feel my heart. I feel my stomach. I feel my bare feet curled up underneath my butt. I feel the chair against my back. I see the textbooks in front of me. I see the, the light. I feel the pencil in my hand. I taste the eraser in my mouth. I feel my eyes burning. I wanna go to bed. I'm so tired. But I need an A. I really, really want an A. I see the grass in front of me. I'm re-reading the same sentence.
>
> I feel how sore the back of my neck is. And I see headlights through the window. I hear a car door. [LAUGHS] I hear the window pulling up, creaking. And I see Curtis coming through.
>
> He doesn't know that I'm there. [LAUGHS] He's such an idiot. It's [LAUGHS] the dumbest fucking plan I've ever seen in my life. [LAUGHS] I see, I see his jean jacket that he always wears. I never wash his.
>
> As he tries to close the window. I see his face as he turns around. "Hi."
>
> "Fuck, you scared me. What are you doing?" I, I see him relax. I see him sit on the couch. "God, you sound like Mom."

"I'm just saying, it's 1:00 in the morning."

"So?"

"So? I'm saying you'll get in real trouble."

"Well, I didn't."

And I see his eyes. I feel a tightening in my chest. "Are you drunk?"

"No. I'm not drunk."

"Are you fucking drunk?"

"No, I'm not drunk...I am high, though." I feel, I feel mad that I can't stay mad at him. I feel mad that I can't stay mad at him as I see the half smoked joint he pulls out of his pocket.

"I saved some for you."

"Okay, I've got a chemistry test tomorrow."

"Jesus, Claire. You've got a 4.0. It doesn't get any better."

"No. But I wanna keep it." I see his face. I see the beard he's trying to grow. I see his blue eyes. I see his smirk. I, I feel safe. And I feel loved. "Fuck it."

"Really?!"

"Yeah. Hit me."

"Hit you?"

"Shut up."

"That sounds so awkward coming out of your mouth." I see him get the lighter. I, I'm watching him. I study how he's doing it, because I don't want to look like an idiot when I do it.

I see him suck in the smoke and hold it. He nods his head as if 'got it?' Yes. Got it, yes. I feel the joint in my fingers. I feel the smoke in my lungs burning. [COUGHS]

I, I see him laughing. [LAUGHS] I'm so mad at him for laughing. And I'm really happy. I feel safe. I feel not alone.

And she ended there.

Hillary: Got a little shortened. But, yeah. I felt I had already gotten where I wanted to get even before I smoked the joint.

Warner: Good job. Basically, for an audition in which you have very little prep time, you covered the bases on this one. Formation of the Base Human Emotion; Flashes mixed with Emotion with Details of Holly and, more particularly, Curtis, since you're interacting with him in the scene. Also very smart to do a bonding one with him so that the frustration or heartache or annoyance or whatever with Curtis in the scene becomes particularly disturbing to you. Good job, Hillary.

WARNER LOUGHLIN TECHNIQUE GUIDE

1. Read the scene. Establish the Givens.

THE GIVENS:

- From an objective distance, write down only what is explicit in the scene – just the facts. Who? What? When? Where?
- Make no assumptions based on these facts, even if you have immediate associations.
- Avoid the "Why?" for now. That comes later.
- Make note of any unusual or particular facts or circumstances in the scene. (i.e. There's a baggie of coke on the floor. Or, she's in a Chanel suit, etc.)
- Leave all emotion out for now.

2. Line by line, start to come up with the Hows of Behavior for your character. Look for patterns of behavior to emerge.

THE HOWS OF BEHAVIOR:

- We don't know how a character feels, because we haven't investigated his/her life on first reading of a scene. But the writer has given us character-indicative behavior to work with. Taking one scene, or several if given the entire screenplay, write down, working line by line, how the character is behaving but NOT how the character is feeling.
- Make note of what stimulus the behavior is in response to. (i.e. When her boyfriend talks about her ex...she seems to deflect with humor; when the conversation gets too intimate... he seems to change the subject; when asked about the past... he seems to be curt, etc.)
- Write every behavior down. Actions are also behaviors.
- Remember that silence is a choice, and the choice to be silent is a behavior too.
- When a behavior in the scene occurs more than once, make sure to write it down again. You are looking for *patterns* of behavior, and those patterns will be your most important discovery at this stage of the process.
- Read the "HOWS of Behavior" out loud, even if you're by yourself, to help reinforce the information in your brain.
- Complete ALL Hows of Behavior in the scene before moving on to the Whys in the Core Knowledge.

3. Fill in the Core Knowledge by answering the Whys.

CORE KNOWLEDGE:

- This is the history of the character. Make only "jogger" notes on this (quick notes to jog your memory).
- Experiment with either Intuitive or Linear Core Knowledge work.
- Intuitive work takes clues from the script dialogue, actions,

events, etc., couples it with the patterns of behavior and expands upon that to come up with events that may have occurred in the life.

- In the Linear approach, take a look back at the Hows of Behavior. For each of your Hows, ask WHY? (i.e. *He seems to be confused about how to behave when Jennifer lets him off the hook.* Is he awkward? Unsure of himself? Has he always been unsure of himself? What big picture, overall issues are indicated by this behavior?)
- As you answer your Whys with emotional reasons and explanations, begin to create events in the character's history that might have led to these emotions. You have now given the event an emotional reason to exist.
- Note the milestones in the character's life until you've developed a basic timeline that brings him to the current moment.
- For broad or general revelations, make notes in your "Notes and Ideas" section. Keep it all brief and loose, not too detailed, and feel free to make changes as you discover new information.

4. Based on the patterns that emerged and the Core Knowledge clues, determine your character's Base Human Emotion.

BASE HUMAN EMOTION:

- The Base Human Emotion is the overwhelming, overriding emotion (caused by an event in the character's early life) that causes him or her to interpret and perceive the world in a specific and unique way.
- The BHE is formed in childhood and reinforced over the course of the character's life.
- Read aloud the Hows of Behavior. Look for patterns to emerge.
- Consult your Core Knowledge for help.
- Assign a BHE in terms of a "FEAR" or a "NEED."
- When in doubt, ask which one might have occurred first.

- The "Need for Power or Control" and the "Need for Love" are too broad and vague.

5. Invent Emotion with Detail experiences, starting with the moment that defined your character's Base Human Emotion in childhood and working up incrementally to the point at which your character lives this scene.

EMOTION WITH DETAIL:

- Start out at age three, four, five, six, or seven.
- Speaking out loud, create and live the emotionally pertinent event that created the BHE. Remember, you may have to set up this moment. (For example: You can't feel loss until you know what you've had.)
- As you speak the experience out loud, refer to the character as "I."
- Speak the inner monologue out loud as well as actual conversation.
- Live the event as if it's in the present rather than narrating it in the past.
- Experience rather than watching, and relate in a way that feels natural to you.
- Let your imagination flow freely.
- Create and hold in your mind the character's surroundings. Start out small, perhaps with an object. Justify why your character is holding it or using it. Or begin in the child's bedroom, for instance, and expand from there.
- Give details an emotional reason to exist.
- Incorporate as many of the senses as you can – what you see, touch, taste, smell, feel.
- Do not force the emotion to come.
- Let one Emotion with Detail inform the next one; allow the domino effect.
- Move forward in the life to live as many moments as you can.
- Build in necessary relationships and events.

- Go slowly and create as much detail as possible, loading the character with emotional fuel.

6. Now return to the scene and drop your fully formed character into it. You'll find it's a whole different experience than your first read.

It really is that easy. Don't over complicate it.

Here's some space for you to start working through the process on your own.

WARNER LOUGHLIN TECHNIQUE HOMEWORK GUIDE

GIVENS:

(Just the cold hard facts given. No assumptions.
Who. What. When. Where.)

HOWS OF BEHAVIOR:

Stimulus	Response
When...	*He/she seems to...*

WHYS:

Complete the Hows of Behavior, and ask why a behavior might occur. What overall big picture issues might account for this behavior? (For example does the character have issues with intimacy? Trouble with authority? Parental neglect? Or any number of other issues the character may have dealt with in the past.)

NOTES AND IDEAS:

CORE KNOWLEDGE

Adulthood

21 years +

High School Graduation

High School

Middle School

Elementary School

First Grade

Ages three, four, five ...

BASE HUMAN EMOTION

EMOTION WITH DETAIL

(Use your Core Knowledge to guide you through.
Let your Emotion with Details lie in the imagination and not on the page.)

WORDS FROM YOUR FELLOW ACTORS

Amy Adams

Emotion with Detail is just a beautiful thing and it's really taught me to love acting. It really has.

I was able to find my voice, and to find tears and to find levels, because I was able to have a safe place to go, that I could come back from. With your technique, in character prep, when I visit a character's life, her past and create an event good or tragic – that belongs to her. I don't take ownership of that pain with me. I don't take it on as my own.

So when I return from their life at the end of the day or the end of the scene, I am in a healthy place as opposed to feeling as though I have gone through something horrible myself.

So this allows me not to be scared to go there, which allows me freedom as an actress to do anything, because I don't own it. It belongs to my character.

Ryan Reynolds

I came to see Warner for help with a character that required extremely authentic vulnerability. The first thing I noticed was her coffee tasted like pavement. The second thing was that tools she provided previewed a glimpse of infinite possibilities. Her method is easy, and most importantly, it is effective. She's truly one of a kind with much to teach, and I'm happy she's a part of my life. If you happen upon her studio, B.Y.O.C.

Zooey Deschanel

I have been training with Warner since I was nineteen. She is the best of the best and has helped me to do some of my most favorite performances. I love her versatility and ability to adapt to any style. She's truly a gift!

Emma Roberts

I love going to work with Warner! Nobody makes me feel more comfortable, confident, and inspired!

Sosie Bacon

Before I started working with Warner on the technique, I felt like acting was just something that I could somedays do, and some days not do. It was only through doing deep Emotion with Detail on each of the characters I got, that I could act everyday how I wanted to, because I ended up knowing the character inside and out. The thoughts are no longer my own, but the character's, so I don't have to work as hard during the scenes. Now being on set and being the character is fun and never feels pushed. I love the technique and it has helped me immensely.

Malcolm Jamal-Warner

Warner's approach to creating and developing a character is the perfect blueprint for those who are willing to do the work. She takes the guesswork out of the process and makes it imaginative as well as fun.

Josh Close

Through Warner and her technique, I have rediscovered my great love for acting. Her imaginative approach and Emotion with Detail has helped break through past barriers once limiting the depth of exploration.

Shiri Appleby

When I'm not on set shooting, I make it a priority to be in Warner's class. Her room is a safe space to question, explore and try out new things with someone who's guiding you every step of the way. To me, that's all it's about. Having a partner on this wild ride, and Warner is that.

Merle Dandridge

Warner is a true artist, teacher, encourager and friend. She gave me the tools to confidently use my skills from Broadway and apply them to a fun and exciting television career. Learn her technique; you will find success and creative fulfillment.

George Lopez

Without Warner Loughlin, my career would have taken a hard left. She kept me on the path to success. Simply put...Sabes Que! The Greatest!!

Majandra Delfino

After exhaustive and pointless acting classes that felt more geared at making actors audience members for posturing, self-congratulatory teachers with quasi-god complexes, there is absolutely nothing more refreshing and no one out there that compares to Warner Loughlin. She will give you the very tools and insight (and then some) that an actor needs to understand a character, serve the story, all while building a strong life-long foundation in the craft – all without clutter, confusion or ego. Warner makes your abilities and their results her number one priority, and that is what you leave with every time without fail. Her approach is truly second to none and will carry you through every job and every audition with a deep understanding of the process and what we're actually really here to do.

Ashley Williams

I called Warner years ago when I was the star of a sitcom on NBC. The show had been wildly publicized as the next Will & Grace and was put on just after Friends on Thursday nights. I had never had any comedy training, was scared out of my mind, and was tanking well-written jokes and not understanding why. "Tell me what's going on, baby," she said when I called her, and from that moment until even today, I have felt like she was holding my hand. Warner's innate talent for understanding comedy, combined with her genuine warmth and enthusiasm, has allowed me – someone not innately funny at ALL – to relax when handed comedy material. My career is now fun, safe, and feels like playtime. Warner's technique has allowed me to approach comedy with confidence, ease and...well...HUMOR!

Amanda Schull

Warner's technique allows me the ability to completely immerse into the being of my character without sacrificing myself or my sanity. The Warner Loughlin Studio is the safest and most nurturing of places. Within those walls, I have flown and I have fallen and I have never been judged.

Sarah Rafferty

Not that I ever experience audition dread, but if, say, hypothetically, I did, Warner would banish it. Warner restores your joy in acting and trust me, Warner is a game changer. I personally would never dream of going to an audition or going on stage or film without being "Warnerized." She is a true uplifter, she'll uplift your acting and your spirit at once. Double whammy. Doesn't get any better than that.

Nikki DeLoach

As soon as I walked through Warner's door, I knew I had found what I was looking for as an actor and as a human being. Her technique is unlike anything I have ever known. It is joyously playful with unlimited possibilities. It allows you to create a life instead of reenacting a character. It is magical, great fun, and I want to work like this for the rest of my career. It breathes into every aspect of your life, giving you greater sensibility than you could possibly imagine. Besides learning her technique, which will become one of the greatest gifts you will ever be given, you get to feel safe, supported, and loved just by walking through the door into her studio. Warner reminds all of us of just how fortunate we are to do what we do – and how much fun it is! Her life-force is truly contagious. To Warner, you are not just a student. She takes you into her life and creates a special place for you in her heart. With a heart that big, there's enough space for everyone. I cannot wait to learn more, play more, and act more. It puts a big smile on my face to know that I am finally becoming the actor that I always knew I could be.

Valerie Cruz

The very first thing I noticed about Warner was her positive energy. She walked into the room, and you literally felt good. All of sudden you felt like "ok maybe this isn't going to be all serious thespian stuff – maybe this is going to be fun. Maybe." It is important to mention this, because at the base of her whole technique is the placement of one's attitude. Leading up to working with Warner, I had a history of studying with people whose technique was to tear you down. This is not uncommon for most actors. In fact, I've met very few actors on my journey that take a compliment with a smile and a thank you without some auxiliary comment of how it could be better. You then associate harsh critique with learning; [you perceive] someone tearing you down as beneficial. For me the more brutal the better, and if I felt I wasn't getting enough abuse, of course, that meant I could no longer grow at that particular venue. Meeting Warner changed this belief system for me completely. And after joining her class I really began to soar. Not just because I eventually started to book work, but because I was enjoying the process again. I realized I could be both happy and an actor.

Carter McIntyre

The Warner Loughlin Technique has especially helped me in my ability to develop characters, in the sense that, after using the technique, I feel a certainty about the character and their point of view. Before I found Warner and her technique, there were times I would feel I was "reaching" for a character or guessing about "how would he react here?" With Warner, I KNOW how the character would react, because I have a deep emotional as well as intellectual understanding of the character. I can know with certainty why this particular person sees the world in his unique way.

Kimberly Williams-Paisley

Warner's loving and supportive attitude is sometimes all I need to get me ready for a project. However, the technique she's developed is so much more than that. It arms me with essential tools to get where I want to be in a role, on any given day or scene, no matter what else may be going on, on the set or in my life that day. The technique is very useful, specific and adaptable. I love Warner and her method!

Terryn Westbrook

Warner's technique has allowed me to find genuine emotion and depth in a character without having to go into my own life and personal history. While there is validity in using your own personal feelings in acting, which is how I was taught before studying with Warner, her technique feels safer to my soul and even more authentic than the stuff from my real life, because instead of putting onto a character something that's happened in my life and trying to tailor it to the character (i.e. using memories of a boyfriend that left me heartbroken years ago to trigger emotions about my fictitious child's death in the scene), I am creating a pure homemade past that is specific to this character and how she would feel based on her life leading up to this scene. (Using the scene at hand as a guide to finding out what exactly that life would be.)

And just because you aren't using your own memories for the character, it doesn't take YOU away from it because you are making this character come to life, and only you will play her this way. You are totally unique in your look, your voice, your manner of speaking and your physicality, and your perception of the character is what will ultimately tell the story. I like to imagine that the new life I create for a character is "poured" through the vessel of me, and what emerges is a new character that has her own fullness and depth but through my eyes.

Ryan Rottman

Working with Warner has been such an enlightening experience for me. She's opened a whole new window on how I approach and look at characters and scenes. I leave every class better than when I went in, with such a positive attitude. I've booked so much more since working with her! Every teacher there has such a gift.

AJ Langer

Two things Warner has provided that I had never experienced before are: a healthy, empowering approach to developing full and rich characters; a creative space full of practical support and talented professionals. Egos checked at the door, freedom awaits. Warner Loughlin and her studio are essential to my life as well as my career. If you are in this for the long run, and you would like to stay sane and enjoy the ride, meet Warner Loughlin.

Rachel Boston

Warner Loughlin is a bright light and beautiful heart in the city of Los Angeles. She is a blessing to the arts, and I am so thankful for her!

Rachel Cannon

The genius of Warner's technique is that there are no boundaries to who you can become. And you don't have to emotionally drudge up your past, you just create memories from the character's past...that way, you can clear it out of your system when you're done instead of dragging that around with you day after day, reopening painful emotional wounds – that's just unhealthy. Warner creates a safe place for you to play, and the possibilities are endless. She's absolute magic.

Darren LeGallo

Warner is the brightest light in this city. There is such a good vibe here. There's no room for ego – it's just about the work.

Marla Sokoloff

Warner's technique has completely changed my approach as an actress. Her contagious energy gives me the confidence to take on any material. I wouldn't even think of walking onto a set without consulting her genius.

Sharon Gardner

Warner's technique creates a reliably solid foundation for a character layered with surprise, specificity, and the patterns of a lifetime. I feel confident that I can adjust to any directorial change in a rehearsal room or on a set, because I know I am breathing and behaving in a fully developed character. It is the most powerful tool I have encountered and seems to be the missing link between my Stanislavsky-based training, Michael Chekhov technique, Grotowski and Viewpoints work, as it allows the body to develop and hold emotional memory. The body has its own reactions, pre-consciousness, and when traveling through an Emotion with Detail exercise, I create and respond to the stimuli of lived experience – it is remarkable to find a year later that the exercises I have done for a character can still upset or delight me if I choose to flash on them. I have always had powerful dreams, and this technique feels like directing myself in a waking dream. The power of imagination and belief are channeled into craft.

Amber Valetta

Warner has given me a simple and insightful approach on creating interesting characters. Working with her has elevated my performances. I love her!!!

Daisy McCrackin

Using the Warner Loughlin Technique is the only way for me to achieve depth of emotion and authentic emotion in a scene – to be able to play moment to moment as the character deep in the circumstance. I can trust Emotion with Detail to work every time, with any scene. My successful auditions are the ones where I did the most or the deepest Emotion with Detail.

ACKNOWLEDGEMENTS

Much gratitude to Ellen Shanman, Jeff Marlowe, Angus McQueen and Henry Martin for your exceptional guidance, insights, wildly inspiring creativity and generally holding my hand throughout.

A particular shout out to Dr. Peter Desberg, talented clinical psychologist and one who I am particularly honored to call friend, for his guidance, thoughts and contributions - not to just this book but to life over the years.

To Wes McGee, Hillary Tuck and Matt Godbey, thank you for putting your private work out there for us to see!

And to the glorious, completely gifted and crazily talented teachers of Warner Loughlin Studios: Kimberly Bigsby, Erin Cardillo, Jen Dede, Nikki DeLoach, Elena Evangelo, Wendy Haines, Eric Hunnicut, Megan McNulty, Aimee Parker, Jackie Seiden, Chelsea Taylor, Joe Towne, Hillary Tuck, Stephen Van Dorn, thank you for guiding so many actors through this technique. And to Erin Taylor who makes our world go 'round.

To you wonderful actors who contributed here, I am humbled and grateful to be a part of your lives and a collaborator in your work. Thank you, Amy Adams, Ryan Reynolds, Blake Lively, Merle Dandridge, Rachael Taylor, Emily Deschanel, Shiri Appleby, Malcolm

Jamal-Warner, Sarah Rafferty, Mary Jo Deschanel, Zooey Deschanel, Emma Roberts, Kyra Sedgwick, Sosie Bacon, and Ryan Rottman for sharing your work in these pages. And to the actors not mentioned by name here, thank you for using this technique and giving your powerful work to the world.

To the amazing team at JKS Communications in Nashville, including Julie Schoerke, Marissa DeCuir, Kendall Hinote, Sara Wigal, Max López, Sydney Mathieu, Benjamin Prosser, and Karyn and Ralph Henley. To Glen Edelstein for conceiving the book cover.

To my wonderfully patient husband, constant source of encouragement and love. Without you I would not have had the time, resources and ability to do it.

Much love to my beautiful son, Jon Kyle Hansen, whose help was invaluable and whose very existence makes me happy. I am constantly amazed at your talent as a director, writer, and all things creative. You are a blessing to me.

ABOUT THE AUTHOR

For over 20 years Warner Loughlin has been a teacher and coach to Oscar, Emmy, Golden Globe, Tony and Grammy winners and nominees. Known for her warmth and intuitive approach, her technique shatters the myth that an actor's past emotional traumas must be the fuel or foundation for their work. Warner's technique is imaginative, practical and psychologically deep, giving actors a safe and effective way to access emotion and create extremely nuanced and unique performances. Warner studied Contemporary Literature and Shakespeare at Oxford University and received her Bachelor of Arts degree from the University of North Carolina at Chapel Hill. She now lives in Los Angeles, CA with her family. You can visit her at www.warnerloughlin.com.

PRAISE FOR WARNER LOUGHLIN

"Before I started working with Warner on the technique, I felt like acting was just something that I could some days do, and some days not do. It was only through doing deep 'emotion with detail' that I could act everyday how I wanted to. Now being on set and being the character is fun and never feels pushed. I love the technique and it has helped me immensely."—Sosie Bacon

"The Warner Loughlin Technique has become part of my creative process. Warner worked with us on Disney's Frozen and helped us create truthful characters. I've never felt so comfortable animating a character before and I think the sophistication in the performance in the film speaks for itself."
—Lino DiSalvo, Head of Animation for Disney's Frozen

". . . an in-depth exploration of the transformative acting methods of Warner Loughlin, one of the era's beloved and experienced acting coaches... a groundbreaking acting technique that helpfully debunks the notion that actors must be tortured to be successful. Its helpful guidance will help actors to unlock their creativity in a way that is safe for their hearts and minds." —Foreword Reviews

"I was able to find my voice, because I was able to have a safe place to go, that I could come back from. When I visit a character's past and create an event good or tragic - that belongs to her. I don't take ownership of that pain with me. So this allows me freedom as an actress to do anything, because I don't own it. It belongs to my character."—Amy Adams

"I've been working with Warner Loughlin for years. Not only has she helped me become a better actor, but she's also helped me truly enjoy this work in ways I never imagined."—Ryan Reynolds

"I met Warner over 10 years ago. She has coached me through comedy, drama, and even life! She has not only given me tools to be better at my job, but tools to be 100% confident through the process."—Emma Roberts

"Working with Warner was a revelation. I doubted that I could ever work without 'observing' and judging every moment. I will be forever grateful [to Warner] for helping me get back to the joy of living in the spontaneous truth of every scene."—Kyra Sedgwick

CPSIA information can be obtained
at www.ICGtesting.com
Printed in the USA
LVHW040347220723
752879LV00001B/107

9 780999 527009